The Trial of Mangal Pandey, State Papers presents the official records of the trial that culminated in the death sentence of Mangal Pandey, hailed by some as the one who initiated India's First War of Independence in 1857, and dismissed by others as a disgruntled sepoy who under the influence of bhang defied the writ of the British.

The trial records throw fresh light on Mangal Pandey's role in the First War of Independence in 1857, leaving the responsibility of discerning an accident from a deliberate act of rebellion solely with the reader.

Leela Sarup, née Gujadhur, was born in Calcutta, India. Initially educated in Mauritius, she returned to India to complete her studies. With her keen interest in History, Leela Sarup has compiled the Colonial Emigrants Acts (1837-1932) On Indentured Labour, and is now in the process of completing various writing projects amongst which is Narratives of the Sepoy Mutiny of India.

THE TRIAL
OF
MANGAL PANDEY

THE TRIAL OF MANGAL PANDEY

State Papers

Presented by
Leela Sarup

NIYOGI
BOOKS

Published by
NIYOGI BOOKS
D-78, Okhla Industrial Area, Phase-I
New Delhi-110 020, INDIA
Tel: 91-11-26816301, 49327000
Fax: 91-11-26810483, 26813830
Email: niyogibooks@gmail.com
Website: www.niyogibooksindia.com

Illustrator: Nuruddin Amarjee

ISBN: 978-81-89738-23-5

Year of Publication: 2007
First Reprint: 2008
Second Reprint: 2016

Printed at Niyogi Offset Pvt. Ltd., New Delhi, India

This book is dedicated

to

my mother

Bharti Gujadhur Sharma

who enthralled me with stories of

India's movement for Independence

including her

10 days in jail

when she was 13 years of age!

'I miss you Mother!'

Contents

Acknowledgements

Words do not suffice to express my gratitude to Akhilesh Mithal who gave me access to his exhaustive records on the First War of Independence. Without him, this book would not have been possible.

My warmest thanks to:

My staff Arup Dutta, S. Sil, Ajita Banerjee and Kamal Banerjee for their patience in typing and retyping this entire book!

Nuruddin Amarjee, who particularly sat with me for the illustrations and then counter-checked the records at the British Council and the internet to ascertain that these illustrations were as accurate as possible. I thank him also for the almost life-size painting of Mangal Pandey—replicating even the *chandan* on Mangal's forehead!

Babwi for reproductions of the illustrations and cover of the book!

My nephew Aloke Vanshylla for the last-minute rush jobs of typing the inside flap, and delivering the CDs on time.

Bikash and Tultul Niyogi, my publishers, without whom this book would not have seen the light of day.

Itihaas: A Glimpse of 1857

About 150 years and almost six generations have passed since the great upheaval of 1857-58 when Indians rose against their alien rulers en masse—only to lose after the most bitter fighting, a war that has been called 'The First War of Independence'.

We offer a glimpse into 1857 by reproducing in its entirety the official British or 'authorized' text of the trial of the first sepoy to rise in revolt. This primary source has been overlooked and not studied in the depth it deserves so far.

'Mungul Pandy'—Sepoy No. 1446, 5th Company, 34th Regiment, Native Infantry of the Bengal Army, with an impeccable service record of over seven years, was aged 26 years two months and nine days when hanged at 5.30 a.m. on the 8th April 1857— the first person to lose his life during the uprising.

What makes 'Mungul Pandy' and his trial and execution special?

Mangal was not the first Indian to suffer grave injustice at British hands. That place of honour goes to Maharaja Nand Kumar, hanged on 5th August 1775, for daring to accuse the then Governor General, Warren Hastings, of corruption:

> The crime for which Nuncomar (Nand Kumar) was made to suffer, was not a capital offence by the laws of Hindostan. It was affirmed that this atrocious condemnation and execution were upon an *ex post facto* law, as the statute which created the Supreme Court and its powers was not published till 1774, and the date of the supposed forgery was 1770....that the evidence was not sufficient to warrant condemnation. (Wilson 1858).

Was Mangal arraigned, tried and hanged with an unseemly haste so that death from his self-inflicted wounds did not cheat the hangman? Was Mangal already dead when hanged?

We reproduce evidence to enable readers to judge for themselves.

Major General J.B. Hearsey, C.B. commanding the Presidency Division, in his report to Col. R.J.H Birch C.B. Secretary to the Government of India in the Military Department states:

"As we approached the mutineer we quickened our pace. My son, Captain Hearsey, called to me, 'Father, he is taking aim at you, look out sharp.' I replied— 'If I fall, John, rush upon him, and put him to death.' Immediately after the mutineer, Mangal Pandey, fired his musket, the whistle of the bullet was heard by the guard, for all but three bent down apparently to avoid being struck by it. The mutineer suddenly altered his mind; seeing there was no chance of escape (for a body of officers had either joined or were coming up, armed and close to the left rear of the guard). He turned his musket muzzle towards his own chest hurriedly, touching the trigger with his toe. The muzzle must have swerved for the bullet made a deep graze ripping up the muscles of the chest, shoulder and neck, and he fell prostrate."

Further, when a guard called out—"He has shot himself," a Sikh sepoy took out Mangal Pandey's *tulwar* (native sword) soaked in blood from under him, for as he fell he partly covered his sword with his body. His regimental jacket and clothes were burning. Major General Hearsey bid the *jemadar* and the sepoy to put the fire out, which they did. He wrote, "I then (thinking that the mutineer was dying for he was shivering and convulsed) directed Brigadier Grant (who had come upon foot to form a court of inquest from the officers assembled there)."

A medical practitioner (Dr. Hutchinson) being present, it was soon ascertained that the wound was severe, and the man was conveyed to the hospital of the 34th Native Infantry, for medical treatment.

The Court of Inquiry could not proceed as the two Britishers wounded as well as their assailant were too ill to face questioning.

Mangal was examined on the 4th April. The Indian attendant administering to his needs in his sick bed was ordered out in order to make sure that only the British version would be recorded.

The next report recorded is that of the doctors:

"Sepoy Mungul Pandy has not improved in health since he came under my charge; he has been gradually becoming weaker, and is now much debilitated. The wound also presents an unhealthy appearance.

I still, however, consider him fit to be removed to the mess house of the 34th Regiment, Native Infantry."

Camp Barrackpore

The 6th April 1857 (sd) T. B. Reid, Asst-Surgeon, 53rd Regiment

Another medical certification follows—"I, James Allen, F.R.C.S. Asst. Surgeon, 34th Regiment, Native Infantry, do hereby certify that Mungul Pandy, sepoy

No.1446, 5th Company, 34th Regiment, Native Infantry, is in a fit state to undergo trial this day."

The British records hide as much as they reveal and have to be treated as the evidence led by one interested party. The contention of General Hearsey that Mangal shot himself as he could not escape appears tainted. It is much more likely that Mangal came out half in uniform and wearing a dhoti in order to make a demonstration against the British army for trying to make the soldiers 'bite the bullet'. He tried to rouse his fellows but failed. If there had been the desired response, matters would have been quite different. Mangal had come prepared for this eventuality and used the loaded musket on himself. The subsequent behaviour of Mangal gives credibility to this interpretation.

Although accused of a capital offence, Mangal Pandey, remains silent throughout the trial. He does not offer a single comment on the evidence led against him or cross-examine any of the witnesses despite the knowledge that his life is at stake.

It would appear that his failed attempt at self-destruction wounded him so severely as to leave him practically dead—the slightest physical effort was a Herculean task, well nigh impossible.

The Court of Inquiry examined Mangal in his sickbed as early as the 4th April for an offence committed on Sunday, the 29th March 1857 although all the dates intervening were working days. Could it be that the hopes for improvement in his health finally had to be abandoned and he became so weak suddenly as to be at death's door?

Mangal admitted that he had been under the influence of 'bhaang', which he had started taking only recently, under the stress of the suspicion that his employers were trying to trick him and his colleagues into losing their caste, leaving no other alternative than conversion to Christianity, the faith of the masters.

He denied the existence of a conspiracy and said that it had not been his intention to cause harm to anyone else and that he loaded his musket only expecting to die from it. But, was the denial forced?

It should be noted that Mangal's fellow soldiers when asked as to why they did not restrain him pointed out that he was under the influence of intoxicants and armed to boot. It was best to leave him alone until the effect wore off. If the British had understood the situation as the Indians obviously did and Mangal left alone to work off his intoxication, he would have offered no violence. The violence occurred because he was attacked by the panic-stricken, arrogant and hectoring British officers. All he did was in order to defend himself. His agility, skill and strength saved him from injury.

In the event, he injured the British without suffering a single graze although they outnumbered him two to one. The only sepoy to intervene, Shaikh Pultoo, approached Mangal from behind and secured him by the waist so that the injured British officers got the opportunity to escape. Mangal could have killed either with the bullet or the sword. The fact that he did not shows that he was not out to kill.

But, this version of truth from Mangal's fellow soldiers repudiates any suggestion that an uprising was brewing or that Mangal ever got wounded in the scuffle. It undermines his revolutonary posture to that of a man acting under the inpulse of *bhang*. The reality emerges from the letters of soldiers with the cartridges and the fact that Mangal got mortally wounded.

It would appear that the British acted in haste and under the shame of having lost face. Rattled by the incident and worried inordinately by the fact that not a single sepoy had come out in support of the European officers who attacked Mangal, they hastened to put him to trial and hang him.

As the accuser, the prosecutor and the judge were all British, Mangal Pandey, was condemned to death by hanging and executed.

The sentence was intended to set an example for the likes of Mangal as delay could have seen him cheat the gallows by dying of his self-inflicted, most severe and festering wounds.

Mangal Pandey's army unit, the 34th Regiment, Native Infantry, was disbanded soon thereafter. But, by calling all sepoys who rebelled in 1857-58 'Pandies' the British Tommies have immortalized Mangal Pandey's name.

1857-58 has been happy hunting ground for the British to create major national myths of supreme bravery for themselves and heap on Indian heads lowered by defeat all weaknesses. As the embodiment of British heroism, the ruins of the Lucknow Residency became the only site in the Empire 'on which the sun never set'. The Union Jack was not taken down here at sunset to be re-hoisted at dawn—it flew all 24 hours here unlike at other places where the uprising occurred—till the midnight of 14-15August 1947 when India won freedom.

The double-dealing, treachery, cowardice and cruelty of Indians was commemorated in nearby Cawnpore (now Kanpur) where a marble encased well, surmounted by the sculpture of an angel, honoured English women and children alleged to have been murdered and thrown into it. This monument to Indian cruelty, financed from a fine imposed on the citizens of the guilty city (Kanpur) was forbidden ground for Indians until Independence.

Emperor Bahadur Shah II or 'Zafar' whose ancestor Farrukhsiyar granted the East India Company the permit to trade and have factories in India was, after the fall of Delhi in September 1857, lured into surrender by promises of a dignified and honourable peace. He had the alternative of accompanying

General Bakht Khan, the commander-in-chief of the rebel forces in the revolt to East India and continuing to support the struggle by allying with Begum Hazarat Mahal, the queen of Awadh, in Lucknow.

Immediately after General Bakht Khan and the army supporting his cause was sent away and Zafar's person secured, his two sons and a grandson were murdered in cold blood and in public, to strike terror in the hearts of the survivors.

Kangaroo court trials sentenced Princes, Rajas and Nawabs to disgraceful death by hanging while the 82-year old Emperor himself was exiled to Burma to be subjected to daily humiliation and be buried in an unmarked grave lined with quicklime to ensure quick dissolution of the corpse.

The place chosen by Bahadur Shah Zafar as his final resting place lies vacant alongside the ruins of the Zafar Mahal palace in Mehrauli. Not one lamp has ever been lit to honour his memory. His immortal verses bemoaning his exile continue to echo in the ruins as if to mock at liberated India and remind its inhabitants of the debt they owe to the martyrs of 1857.

For generations to come, Indians were haunted by nightmares of massacre, arson, looting, desecration of holy places and humiliation at the hands of vengeful victors. Daily reminders were provided by gutted palaces and city centres of Delhi and Lucknow, the rubble strewn in residential areas, fragrant Mughal gardens, noble mosques, elegant aqueducts, sturdy bridges and hoary monuments—by the vengeful victors delighting in the destructive powers of gunpowder.

The British wanted abject surrender and to make sure that Indians would never dare to raise their heads again.

The 1,00,000 ill-paid overworked and inhumanly treated sepoys who rebelled, their supporters from all walks of life—from peasants to princes along with the civilians who came in the path of the vengeful British carrying fire and sword from Peshawar in the north-west to Arrah in the east, have almost disappeared without trace from the pages of history.

No prisoners were taken. Wherever apprehended, the sepoys and those suspected to be their adherents were brutally massacred—blown from the cannon or strung from the tallest trees in village and town squares and along the highways of the country to shock and awe onlookers and passers-by and serve as a deterrent.

Even a whiff of suspicion of a person or his relatives having participated in the rebellion invited sanguine punishment including loss of property and persecution besides exclusion from any office or profit or avenue of trade for himself and his descendents.

With four generations forced to treat the Indian version of 1857 as taboo, the British design of ensuring the erasure and obliteration of the uprising from the memory of ordinary people has succeeded to a great extent. The trauma of the event was, however, too great to be totally forgotten. Some recollections, howsoever hazy, of the 1857 Uprising survive.

Indians have, long after Independence and very slowly, started studying 1857. The jigsaw is being assembled—pieces are being retrieved and put in their proper places and soon we shall have a balanced history of the movement, the occurrences and the underlying motivations. A sustained effort to document and analyse the scraps and shreds that remain of the Indian evidence will help establish the enormity of the outrage inflicted upon a defeated and disarmed people.

The unabridged records that appear in this volume from January 1857 onwards should help the reader understand the background of the events that led Mangal Pandey to act as he did. The only change made has been in laying out the text in smaller and more reader-friendly paragraphs in place of the very long paragraphs, running into several pages in some cases – of the text as originally presented.

It is to be hoped that other characters of 1857-58 such as Nana Saheb Dhondho Pant Peshwa, Begum Hazarat Mahal, Tantya Tope, Bakht Khan, Kunwar Singh of Arrah and Ahmad Shah of Nilibar in the Punjab (now in Pakistan), will receive similar attention.

Akhilesh Mithal
New Delhi, March 2007

The Indian Uprising

Events that led to the trial of Mangal Pandey have been chronicled by George W. Forrest, Director of Records of the Government of India, from 1890 to 1893. These records were subsequently published under three volumes by the Military Department Press in 1893. These three volumes contain selections of letters, despatches, State papers amongst others.

The first volume introduces incidents in Barrackpore, Berhampore, Meerut and Delhi. The second volume covers events in Lucknow and Cawnpore, while the third volume deals with the Defence of Alumbagh and capture of Lucknow.

The first volume pertaining to the trial of Mangal Pandey begins with a background of despatches from Major General J.B. Hearsey. As early as January 1857, he is reporting to the Headquarters that the *khalasis* and workmen employed in the arsenal at Dum Dum, to manufacture the new cartridges for the new Enfield rifles that were to replace the muskets, were under the impression that the grease used for the cartridges is made of pig and cow fat—materials that were anathema to both Muslims and Hindus. Major General Hearsey suggested that the workmen themselves may be allowed to purchase the materials from the market that may be considered safe so as to restore their belief that their religion and caste were not in jeopardy.

As narrated in the despatches, great efforts were made by the British officers to explain and demonstrate to the sepoys that the grease used was not made out of pig and cow fats.

Apparently, the story of cow and pig fat being used for the new cartridges started with a *khalasi* working at the Dum Dum magazine. He asked a 2nd Regiment Native (Grenadier) Infantry to supply him with a glass of water from his *lota*. The Native Grenadier, who was of an upper caste, refused, stating he was not aware of the caste the *khalasi* belonged to. The *khalasi* immediately rejoined, "You will soon lose your caste, as ere long you will have to bite cartridges covered with the fat of pigs and cows." From the despatch of Lieutenant and Brevet Captain J.A. Wright posted at Dum Dum, it appears that this rumour had already spread all over India.

Major W.A.J. Mayhew, Deputy Adjutant of the army, in his despatch dated the 27 January 1857, explained that the lubricant made out of coconut oil and beeswax was unfit to grease the cartridges. He explained that the grease being used was made out of tallow (though he does not explain which animal fat was used) but he stressed the point that if oil and wax were used, the cartridges needed to be used immediately as in course of time, this mixture would dry up if the cartridges were stored for long periods.

To further the despatch of Major Mayhew, Major General J.B. Hearsey reported the seriousness of the situation in his despatch of the 28th January, 1857, that a bungalow occupied by the sergeant at Raneegunge was burnt down besides the electric telegraph bungalow as well as two unoccupied ones, within a span of two weeks in January 1857. An Ensign, F.E.A. Chamier of the 34th Regiment, removed a lighted arrow from his thatched roof. Major General Hearsey reports that these were reactions to rumours that the British were keen to convert the Hindus and Muslims to Christianity. By now there was widespread discontent —socially amongst the common people on another sensitive issue of widows remarriage.

Commanding Officers of all the regiments were asked to parade their men and ask for the reasons of discontentment. These Officers went to great lengths to assure their sepoys that it was not the intention of the British to convert the Indians to Christianity.

By this date, Major General Hearsey had received a letter from Headquarters permitting ghee or other materials to be used for greasing the Enfield Rifles; he endorsed copies of this letter to the Commanding Officers of all the regiments, besides Lieutenant Colonel C.S. Reid, Commanding Officer at Dum Dum.

Major General Hearsey was disgruntled that a letter from an officer commanding H.M.'s 53rd Regiment at Fort William to his counterpart at Dum Dum that a mutiny had broken out at Barrackpore was not endorsed to him. He was himself posted at Barrackpore. Neither was any such letter sent to the superiors at Dum Dum. Such rumours caused by their own officers were detrimental to the sepoy, he felt.

By the 7th February 1857, in another despatch, Major General Hearsey wrote that all attempts to remove the suspicion in the minds of the native sepoys seemed to have failed as this belief was too deep-rooted. Major General Hearsey suggested that it would be unwise to continue the efforts and instead the Government should consider using the same methods used in the preparation on the paper of the muskets for the Enfields.

A special Court of Enquiry was set up at Barrackpore on the 6th February 1857 for the purpose of investigating into the problems regarding the discontentment of the native soldiers. Several despatches were placed on the table of the court.

The witnesses queried regarding these matters were:

1) Byjonath Pandy, Sepoy, 5th Company, 2nd Regiment, Native (Grenadier) Infantry.
2) Chand Khan, Sepoy, 7th Company, 2nd Regiment, Native (Grenadier) Infantry.
3) Khoda Buksh, Subadar, 9th Company, 2nd Regiment, Native (Grenadier) Infantry.
4) Buddun Singh, Jemadar, 6th Company, 2nd Regiment, Native (Grenadier) Infantry.
5) Gunness Singh, Jemadar, 10th Company, 2nd Regiment, Native (Grenadier) Infantry.
6) Golaub Khan, Jemadar, 2nd Company, 2nd Regiment, Native (Grenadier) Infantry.
7) Ram Singh, Jemadar, 9th Company, 2nd Regiment, Native (Grenadier) Infantry.
8) Wuzear Khan, Jemadar, 7th Company, 2nd Regiment, Native (Grenadier) Infantry.
9) Ajoodiah Singh, Havildar-Major, 8th Company, 2nd Regiment, Native (Grenadier) Infantry.

Barring two, all the seven witnesses were suspicious of the fat used in the greased paper. Thereafter, several British officers attested in this Special Court of Enquiry that they had assembled their sepoys at several stations to explain and demonstrate the paper of the new cartridges. They all were unanimous in their reports submitted to the Court that there was general dissatisfaction. The Court directed all the officers to take the evidence of senior and high-caste Hindu native commissioned and non-commissioned officers as well as subadars, jemadars or havildars of the Muslim faith. The Court also directed that these officers display in detail the making of the cartridge—the advantage of a thinner paper, the powder, etc., so that the suspicions are removed from the minds of all the sepoys.

On the 8th February 1857, Major General Hearsey acknowledged that the Headquarters would give separate allowance to purchase a grease that would not be objectionable to the sepoys. Major General Hearsey directed Brigadier Grant to make all the Commanding Officers of regiments display and explain to their respective battalions on parade and show the paper with the cartridges to all native officers and men. Instead of being satisfied, the glazed paper increased the suspicions of the men!

Lieutenant A.S. Allen in his statement dated the 8th February 1857, reported that a sepoy belonging to the 34th Regiment came to his bungalow at night and informed him that four sepoys of different regiments were apprehensive that they, the sepoys, would be forced to give up their caste and be made Christians. Therefore, these four men were inviting the sepoys to react by plundering and burning the bungalows at Barrackpore, then proceed to Calcutta and attempt to seize Fort William or failing that, to take over the Treasury. This native sepoy informed Allen that some men were to clandestinely assemble at about 9 p.m. under a tree close to the station magazine. Allen was also informed of the rumour of the arrival of a European Regiment from Dinapore with artillery, brought down to assist the Government to carry out their plans to convert the sepoys. Allen took the matter to his immediate superior, then to the next officer and all three proceeded to Hearsey's residence who ordered them to check the spot where the meeting was to take place. No one was found at the place, as they reached too late.

Between the 8th to 10th February 1857, it was felt that there was a rebellious mood at Barrackpore. Hence on the 10th February, a deposition of Jemadar Durriow was recorded to the effect that about 309 sepoys of different regiments had met at the parade ground on the 5th February 1857, after the eight o'clock roll call; they had their faces and heads tied up with cloth and they were discussing the possibility of killing all Europeans, plundering the station and going where they liked. This plan could not be carried out due to inadequate preparations.

Based on the above information, Major General Hearsey questioned one sepoy Ramsahai Lallah, 8th Company, 34th Regiment. Lallah was the informant of Allen and insisted that a meeting did take place as informed but Allen reached the place too late.

On the 11th February 1857, Major General Hearsey wrote to The Secretary to the Government of India in the Military Division that at Barrackpore the situation was such that it felt like sitting on a mine ready to explode. In this despatch, Hearsey wrote a more detailed version of the *khalasi* at DumDum asking for water from the *lota* of a Brahmin.

Several despatches over the next two months were exchanged about the new cartridge, attitudes of the sepoys, rumours, discontentment.

Another Court of Inquiry was held at Berhampore on the 27th February 1857, regarding refusals of the sepoys of the 19th Regiment, Native Infantry to use the cartridges; in all, 25 witnesses were examined.

It transpired that the corps had mutinied at Berhampore—as they had turned out in a disorderly manner at the parade ground at 11 a.m., broken their bells-of-arms, seized their muskets, belts and pouches and refused to obey the orders of Colonel Mitchell. Order for their disbandment was passed just the way the 34th Regiment, Native Infantry at Meerut was disbanded. The regiment to be disbanded was to reach Barrackpore on the 31st March, in the morning, so that the disbandment was to be carried out in front of all the other regiments stationed at Barrackpore, as a warning.

This warning could not be carried out as on Sunday, the 29th March 1857, Mangal Pandey entered the scene.

Leela Gujadhur Sarup
Kolkata, 2007

Mangal Pandey (1831-1857)

A *khalasi* working at the magazine at Dum Dum asked a high-caste Havildar for water from his *lota.* The Havildar refused, saying he was not aware of his caste. The *khalasi* retorted, "You will soon lose your caste as you will have to bite cartridges smeared with the fat of pigs and cows".

The *pandit* and *maulvi* get involved in spreading discontentment.

29th March 1857: Mangal Pandey walked up and down the parade ground, brandishing his musket and *talwar* (sword), exhorting his fellow sepoys to join him to oust the British.

Sgt. Maj. J.T. Hewson, mounted on his horse advanced towards Mangal, who shot the horse.

Hewson and Baugh charged at Mangal.

Mangal engaged both the officers with his *talwar* in self-defence, while two sepoys came forward to help.

Mangal fought Hewson and Baugh single-handedly.

Mangal turned his *talwar* on Baugh. A soldier joined him.

Sheikh Pultoo, Havildar, 34th Regiment, Native Infantry, came forward to restrain Mangal and managed to hold him.

Mangal Pandey turned his musket on himself. His chest, neck, cheek and ear were grazed

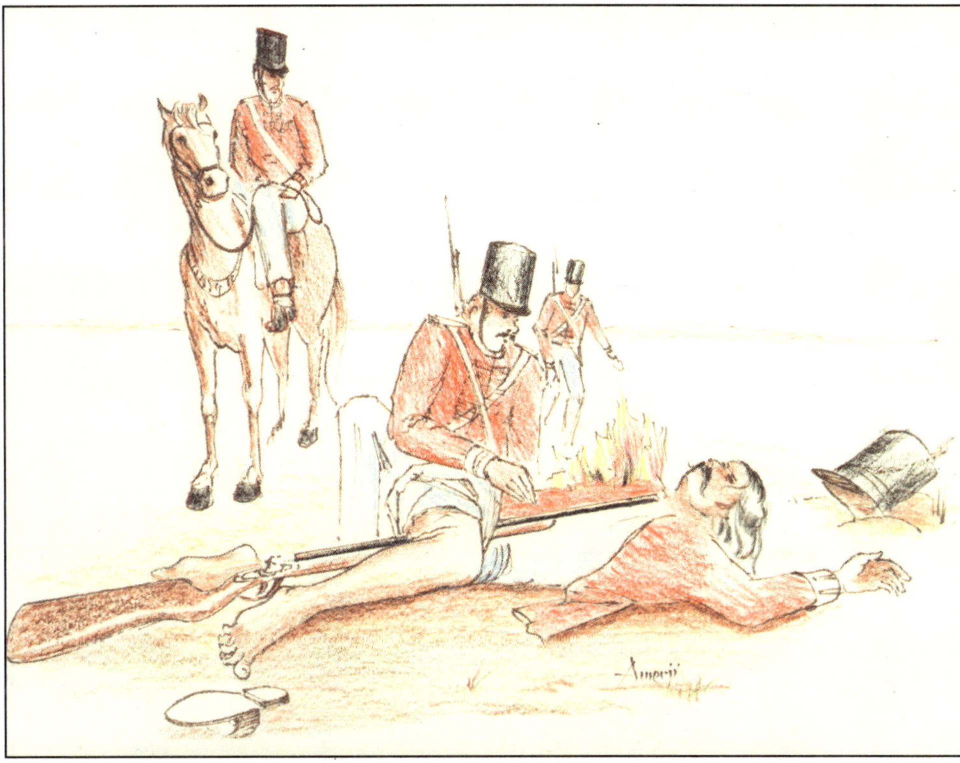

After shooting himself, Mangal Pandey's clothes caught fire. A sepoy puts out the fire.

The Kangaroo court in session.

On Wednesday 8th April 1857. 5:30 a.m. Mangal Pandey, Sepoy No. 1446, 5th Company, 34th Regiment, Native Infantry, 26 years, 2 months and nine days with a service of 7 years, 2 months and nine days was hanged.

SELECTIONS

FROM THE

STATE PAPERS

INDIAN MUTINY

1857-1858

The Indian Mutiny

BARRACKPORE AND BERHAMPORE

From Major General J. B. HEARSEY, C.B., *Commanding the Presidency Division, to Major* W.A.J. MAYHEW, *Deputy Adjutant-General of the Army—No. 24, dated Headquarters, Presidency Division, Barrackpore, 24th January, 1857.*

I have the honour to forward herewith, for immediate submission to the Government of India through its Military Secretary, the accompanying letter in original from the Officer Commanding at Dum Dum, dated the 23rd instant,

1. **Letter dated 23rd January 1857, from the Officer Commanding Depot of Musketry, to the Station Staff Officer at Dum Dum.**
2. **Letter, dated 22nd January, 1857, from the Officer Commanding Rifle Instruction Depot to the Adjutant of that Depot.**

together with two others as marginally noted reporting that an unpleasant portion of the men attached to the depot for instruction in rifle practice, caused by the belief that the grease used in the preparation of the ball cartridges received from the Arsenal in Fort William consists of a mixture of the fat of cows and pigs.

2. This foolish report must have been invented and circulated by some evil disposed persons, possibly the *khalasi* or other workmen employed in that arsenal, and, though no doubt totally groundless, still it will be now most difficult to eradicate this impression from the minds of the native soldiers, who are always suspiciously disposed when any change of this sort affecting themselves is introduced.

3. I would accordingly beg leave to recommend, for the consideration and orders of Government that the Officer Commanding the Rifle Depot may be authorised to adopt the necessary measures in view to obtaining from the bazar whatever ingredients may be required for the preparation of the bullet patch, which the sepoys themselves may be allowed to make up.

4. This appears to me to be the only remedy, though it will doubtless be attended with much additional trouble and inconvenience.

From Lieutenant-Colonel C. S. REID, *Commanding at Dum Dum, to Major* A. H. ROSS, *Assistant Adjutant-General, Presidency Division—No.12, dated Dum Dum, 23rd January, 1857.*

I have the honour to forward, for submission to the Major-General Commanding the Presidency Division, a letter, in original with annexure, from Major J. Bontein, Commanding the Depots of Musketry at this station, and to request the favour of his orders on the subject therein contained as early as convenient.

From Brevet-Major J. BONTEIN, *Commanding Depot of Musketry to the Station Staff Officer at Dum Dum—dated Dum Dum, 23rd January, 1857.*

I have received the accompanying report from Brevet-Captain J. A. Wright, one of the officers attached to the depot of musketry under my command.

2. A rumour of this nature had attracted my attention for some days previously, but I was willing to believe it a mere idle prejudice which would not assume any form of consequence. Brevet-Captain Wright's statement, however, and my subsequent enquiry, has convinced me that the case is of sufficient importance to require a reference to higher authority.

3. I last evening paraded all the native portion of the depot, and called for any complaints that the men might wish to prefer. At least two-thirds of the detachment immediately stepped to the front, including all the native commissioned officers. In a manner perfectly respectful they very distinctly stated their objection to the present method of preparing cartridges for the new rifled musket. The mixture employed for greasing cartridges was opposed to their religious feeling, and as a remedy they begged to suggest the employment of wax and oil in such proportions as, in their opinion would answer the purpose required.

4. I have felt it my duty to bring this circumstances to the knowledge of the officer commanding the station, and I would further request that my report may be forwarded through the appointed channel for the consideration of His Excellency the Commander-in-Chief.

From Lieutenant and Brevet-Captain J. A. WRIGHT, *Commanding the Rifle Instruction Depot, to the Adjutant of the Rifle Instruction Depot—dated Dum Dum, 22nd January, 1857.*

I have the honour to report, for the information of Major Bontein, Commanding the Depot, that there appears to be a very unpleasant feeling existing among the native soldiers who are here for instruction, regarding the grease used in preparing the cartridges, some evil disposed persons having spread a report that it consists of a mixture of the fat of pig and cows.

2. The belief in this report has been strengthened by the behaviour of a *khalasi* attached to the magazine, who, I am told, asked a sepoy of the 2nd Regiment, Native (Grenadier) Infantry, to supply him with water from his lota; the sepoy refused, observing he was not aware of what caste the man was. The khalasi immediately rejoined—"You will soon lose your caste, ere long you will have to bite cartridges covered with the fat of pigs and cows",—or words to that effect.

3. Some of the depot men, in conversing with me on the subject last night, said that the report has spread throughout India, and when they go to their homes their friends will refuse to eat with them. I assured them (believing it to be the case) that the grease used is composed of mutton fat and wax; to which they replied—"It may be so, but our friends will not believe it; let us obtain the ingredients from the bazar and make it up ourselves; we shall then know what is used, and be able to assure our fellow soldiers and others that there is nothing in it prohibited by our caste."

In conclusion, I most respectfully beg to represent that by adopting the measure suggested by the men, the possibility of any misunderstanding regarding the religious prejudices of the natives in general will be prevented.

Demi-official from Colonel A. ABBOTT, C.B., *Inspector-General of Ordnance and Magazines, to Major* W. A. J. MAYHEW, *Deputy Adjutant-General of the Army—dated 27th January, 1857.*

I hear that an objection has been made by the sepoys to use the cartridges made for Enfield rifles agreeably to the instructions sent from home, because, one end of each cartridge (that which contains the ball) is greasy.

It is absolutely necessary that grease should be used, and the composition used for patches is said to be unfit for cartridges. It was of cocoanut oil and bees wax. The present grease is tallow. I think that a committee had better decide what grease shall be employed. In the meantime *practice* cartridges may be issued to sepoys without grease, and the men may *see* that grease of unobjectionable quality is applied.

The wax and oil would, I dare say, answer well enough if used immediately, though it dries up if the cartridges are kept long in store.

From Major General J. B. HEARSEY, C.B., *Commanding the Presidency Division, to Major* W.A. J. MAYHEW, *Deputy Adjutant-General of the Army—dated Barrackpoe, 28th January, 1857.*

I beg leave to report, for the information of Government, that an ill-felling is said to subsist in the minds of the sepoys of the regiments at Barrackpore. A report has been spread by some designing persons, most likely Brahmins or agents of the religious Hindu party in Calcutta, (I believe it is called the *Dhurma Subha*), that they (the sepoys) are to be forced to embrace the Christian faith.

On this report was grafted, as an overt act to cause them to lose caste, the distributing amongst them of ball cartridges for the new Enfield rifle that had the paper forming them greased with the fat of cows and pigs.

2. I should not have allowed these idle and groundless rumours to have had any weight on my mind, knowing that the latter circumstances (regarding the cartridges) would be remedied as soon as reported to higher authority, and trusting to the well-known repugnance of all officers with native regiments to act or do anything that could be constructed into a wish or desire to interfere with the religious prejudices of the men under their command.

3. But the circumstances of a sergeant's bungalow being burnt down at Raneegunge, supposed to have been caused by an incendiary, [a wing of the 2nd Regiment, Native (Grenadier) Infantry, from the station being now there], and also three incendiary fires having occurred at this station within the last four days; one, the electric telegraph bungalow, and since then two bungalows that were occupied; the second occurring only last night; as also Ensign F.E.A. Chamier, 34th Regiment, Native Infantry, having taken a lighted arrow from the thatch of his own bungalow; has confirmed in my mind that this incendiarism is caused by ill- affected men, who wish thus to make known or spread a spirit of discontent, and induce the sepoys to believe they are all labouring under some grievance, which they have not the manliness to make known to their officers.

4. Perhaps those Hindus who are opposed to the marriage of widows in Calcutta are using underhand means to thwart Government in abolishing the restraints lately removed by law for the marriages of widows, and conceive if they can make a party of the ignorant classes in the ranks of the army believe their religion or religious prejudices are eventually to be abolished by *force,* and by *force,* they are all to made Christians, and thus by shaking their faith in Government lose the confidence of their officers by inducing sepoys to commit offences (such as incendiarism) so difficult to put a stop to or prove, they will gain their object.

5. Brigadier Grant directed commanding officers of regiments at this station the day before yesterday to parade their corps, and ask them if they had any grievance to complain of. Three of the officers have reported their men to be perfectly satisfied and Colonel S. G. Wheler, Commanding the 34th Regiment, Native Infantry, assured them the rumour so industriously circulated was false, and the native officers and men said they were satisfied that it was so, but one native officer respectfully asked if any orders had been received regarding the Enfield rifle cartridges. This he could not answer, as the letter permitting the *ghee* or other material to be used for that purpose by the men only arrived this morning. I have, however, directed its contents to be made known to every regiment in the cantonment, and a copy to be sent to Lieutenant-Colonel C. S. Reid, Commanding at Dum Dum, for Major Bontein's information.

6. It is my purpose, should this uneasy feeling not abate, to parade the brigade, and myself explain the absurdity of the notion that any, the most distant, intention to interfere with their religion is contemplated by Government.

7. I am sorry to add that I this morning heard that the Officer Commanding Her Majesty's 53rd Regiment in Fort William wrote to the officer in command of the wing of that rergiment at Dum-Dum to warn a company to be ready to turn out at any moment, and had distributed to the men of the company ten rounds of balled ammunition, informing that officer that a mutiny had broken out at Barrackpore amongst the sepoys !!! No copy of this letter or note was sent to Lieutenant-Colonel C.S. Reid, Commanding at Dum-Dum, nor to Brigadier Grant, or to myself. I need not enlarge on the great impropriety of such a proceeding, as if it becomes known to the sepoys, it will undoubtedly create an ill-feeling amongst them.

From Major General J. B. HEARSEY, C.B., *Commanding the Presidency Division, to Major* A. SANDERS *Deputy Quarter-master-General of the Army—No.43, dated Headquarters, Presidency Division, Barrackpore, 5th February, 1857.*

I beg that you will do me the honor to submit, for the consideration and orders of Government, my strong recommendation that the wing of the 2nd Native Infantry (Grenadiers) now at Raneegunge may be relieved by a similar detachment of the 63rd Regiment from Soorie, to enable the former to return to Barackpore.

2. I am induced to make this proposal for the following reasons:-

1st— The wing of the 2nd Regiment, Native (Grenadier) Infantry, at this station is more than usually short of European officers, having only attached to it one captain and three subalterns, two of the latter being very young and inexperienced lads.

2nd— By re-uniting both wings, therefore, the corps will be rendered more efficient, though even then the number of senior officers present will be much too few.

3. The headquarters wing has been for the last nine months on detached duty in the district, during which period both officers and men have been receiving a higher rate of pay (full *batta*), which is, in my opinion a distinction not altogether desirable to draw between the wings of the same regiment longer than is absolutely unavoidable.

4. Had the wing at Barrackpore been more efficient in point of officers than it is, I might have felt disposed to suggest that it should relieve the other at Raneegunge, but under existing circumstances this measure would not be at all expedient.

5. I further desire that the 2nd Regiment Native (Grenadier) Infantry should be brought together, that I may have an opportunity of inspecting that corps, for from the circumstance of the bungalows being set fire to at Raneegunge and also in this cantonment simultaneously, I have a strong suspicion that an ill feeling exists in that regiment, which by having it together under my own eye I may be able to remove.

6. I am therefore of decided opinion that the detachment for Raneegungee should be furnished by the 63rd Regiment, Native Infantry, and the Government may probably consider that a smaller force than a complete wing is now sufficient for the duties of that outpost. Perhaps a couple of companies, or 200 men, would answer every military purpose, in consideration of the present easy communication by railway between Raneegunge and Barrackpore.

From Major General J. B. HEARSEY, C.B., *Commanding the Presidency Division, to Major* W. A. J. MAYHEW, *Deputy Adjutant-General of the Army—No. 44, dated Headquarters, Presidency Division, Barrackpore, 7th February, 1857.*

With refernce to my official letter to your address, No. 24, dated the 24th ultimo, I have now the honour to forward for submission to the Government, the Proceedings of a Special Court of Inquiry which has been assembled at Barrackpore for the purpose of ascertaining from the evidence of a selected portion of the 2nd Regiment, Native (Grenadier) Infantry, the cause of their continued objection to the paper of which the new rifle cartridges are composed.

2. A perusal of the several statements and opinions recorded in these proceedings clearly establishes in my judgment that a most unreasonable and unfounded suspicion has unfortunately taken possession of the minds of all the native officers and sepoys at this station, that grease or fat is used in the composition of this cartridge paper; and this foolish idea is now so rooted in them, that it would, I am of opinion, be both idle and unwise even to attempt its removal.

3. I would accordingly beg leave to recommend, for the consideration of Government, the expediency (if practicable) of ordering this rifle to be made up of the same description of paper which has been hitherto employed in the magazines for the preparation of the common musket cartridge, by which means this groundless suspicion and objection could be at once disposed of.

PROCEEDINGS of a Special Court of Inquiry assembled at Barrackpore on Friday, the 6th of February 1857, at 11a.m. at the Mess of the 34th Regiment, Native Infantry, by order of Brigadier C. GRANT, C.B., *Commanding at Barrackpore, for the purpose of investigating such matter as may be laid before it by the Officiating Brigade-Major.*

PRESIDENT

Brevet-Colonel S.G. WHELER, 34th Regiment, Native Infantry.

MEMBERS

Major H.W. MATTHEWS, 43rd Regiment, Native Infantry.
Captain G.N. GREENE, 70th Regiment, Native Infantry.

INTERPRETER

Lieutenant A. F. CORBETT, 43rd Regiment, Native Infantry.
The Court met at the time appointed by station orders.

Letter No. 29, dated 5th February, 1857, from the Officiating Brigade-Major, addressed to the President of the Court, is read and appended to the Proceedings, marked "A".

Letter No. 89, dated 4th February, 1857, from Captain N.C. Boswell, commanding the Left Wing, 2nd Regiment, Native (Grenadier) Infantry, addressed to the Major of Brigade, is read and appended to the Proceedings, marked "B".

Demi-official note from the Brigadier Commanding at Barrackpore, of no date, addressed to the President, Court of Inquiry, is read and appended to the Proceedings and marked "C".

Captain N. C. Boswell, Commanding the Left Wing, 2nd Regiment, Native (Grenadier) Infantry, is desired to call in his evidence.

1st Witness

Byjonath Pandey, sepoy, 5th Company, 2nd Regiment, Native (Grenadier) Infantry, appears in Court, and having had explained to him the provisions of para 7, section 22 of the Military Regulations, voluntarily states as follows:-

Question: Were you on parade on the evening of the 4th instant, when the new cartridges, &c, were shown to the men of the regiment?

Answer: I was.

Question: Did you make any objection to the materials of which those cartridges were composed?

Answer: I felt some suspicion in regard to the paper, if it might not affect my caste.

Question: What reason have you to suppose that there is anything in the paper which would injure your caste?

Answer: Because it is a new description of paper with which the cartridges are made up, and which I have not seen before.

Question: Have you ever seen or heard from any one that the paper is composed of anything which is objectionable to your caste?

Answer: I had a report that there was some fat in the paper; it was a bazar report.

Question: Are these the cartridges and paper which you examined on the parade?—(the paper and cartridges being shown to the witness).

Answer: Yes.

Question: The Court from a careful examination of the papers of which the cartridges are made up are unable to detect anything beyond the appearance of ordinary paper. Examine the paper again carefully in the light, and endeavour to explain to the Court what you see objectionable in it.

Answer: My suspicion of the paper proceeds from its being stiff and like cloth in the mode of tearing it; it seems to us different from the old paper in use amongst us.

The witness withdraws.

2nd Witness

Chand Khan, sepoy, 7th Company, 2nd Regiment, Native (Grenadier) Infantry, appcars in Court, and having had explained to him the provisions of Para 7 section 22 of the Military Regulations, voluntarily states as follows:-

Question: Do you object to the paper of which the new cartridges are made, now lying before the Court ; and if so, on what grounds?

Answer: I have no objection to the bullet or powder, it is only the paper which I have doubts about, which appears to be tough; and in burning it, it smells as if there was grease in it.

Question: Were you present when a piece of the paper was burnt, and when?

Answer: On the evening of the 4th instant a piece of the cartridge paper was dipped in water and afterwards burnt; when burning it made a fizzing noise and smelt as if there was grease in it.

Question: Who were present when this burning of the paper took place?

Answer: Two or three were present; I do not recollect what their names are. A piece of the cartridge paper is burnt in Court by the witness.

Question: Are you still of opinion that there is any smell of grease in it?

Answer: No, there is not.

Question: Have you now any objection to use these cartridges with paper of that description ?

Answer: I object to this paper being used, as every one is dissatisfied with it on account of its being glazed, shinning like wax-cloth.

The witness withdraws.

3rd Witness

Subadar Khoda Buksh, 9th Company, 2nd Regiment, Native (Grenadier) Infantry, is called into Court, and the provisions of para 7, section 22 of the Military Regulations, explained to him:

Question: Do you object to anything in the new cartridge, which lies before the Court?

Answer: I have no objection to the cartridge myself, but I know there is a general report in the cantonment that the paper is made up with fat.

Question: Do you know where the report comes from?

Answer: I do not know.

Question: Examine the paper not shown to you, and see if you can detect any grease in it, or anything objectionable in it.

Answer: There is nothing that I can see objectionable in it.

Question: If you carried a musket, would you then have any objection to load the musket with the cartridge?

Answer: I would use it if there was no grease in it.

The witness withdraws.

4th Witness

Jemadar Buddun Singh, 6th Company, 2nd Regiment, Native (Grenadier) Infantry, called into Court, and the Provisions of para 7, section 22 of the Military Regulations, explained to him:

Question: Have you any objection to the new cartridge which lies before the Court?

Answer: Nothing; except the paper, which I have some suspicion about, as I have never seen anything of the kind before, and the general report is that there is grease in it.

The witness withdraws.

5th Witness

Jemadar Gunness Singh, 10th Company, 2nd Regiment, Native (Grenadier) Infantry, being called into Court, and the Provisions of para 7, section 22 of the Military Regulations, explained to him:

Question: Have you any objection to the cartridge which lies on the table?

Answer: I have no objection to the cartridge myself, but there is a report amongst the men that there is grease in it.

Question: How did this report get abroad ?

Answer: I do not know.

Question: What, in your opinion, would be the best plan to un-deceive the minds of the men on this point?

Answer: I know no other way than to substitute other paper in its place.

The witness withdraws.

6th Witness

Jemadar Golaub Khan, 2nd Company, 2nd Regiment, Native (Grenadier) Infantry, is called into Court, and the provisions of para 7, section 22 of the Military Regulations, explained to him:

Question: Have you any objection to the use of the cartridges now lying before you?

Answer: I have objection to the paper, as there is a report got about that there is grease in it.

Question: Can you prove yourself that there is grease in it, or have you taken any measures to do so?

Answer: There is grease in it I feel assured, as it differs from the paper which has heretofore been always used for cartridges.

The witness withdraws.

7th Witness

Jemadar Ram Singh, 9th Company, 2nd Regiment, Native (Grenadier) Infantry, is called into Court, and the provisions of Para 7, and section 22 of the Military Regulations, explained to him:

Question: Have you any objection to the use of the cartridges now lying before you?

Answer: A report got about, which I think came from the magazine *khalasis* in Calcutta, that there was some grease in the paper; on this account I have some suspicion about it.

Question: How can this suspicion be removed from your mind?

Answer: I cannot remove it.

The witness withdraws.

8th Witness

Jemadar Wuzeer Khan, 7th Company, 2nd Regiment, Native (Grenadier) Infantry, called into Court and the provisions of section 22., para 7 of the Military Regulations, explained to him:

Question: Have you any objection to the use of the cartridges lying upon the table?

Answer: I have no objection to it; it appears to be new.

Question: Would you have any objection to use it in the way the old cartridges are used?

Answer: I should have some objection in consequence of the suspicion which exists generally in the cantonment.

The witness withdraws.

9th Witness

Havildar-Major Ajoodiah Singh, 8th Company, 2nd Regiment Native (Grenadier) Infantry, called into Court and the provisions of section 22, para 7 of the Military Regulations, explained to him:

Question: Have you any objection to the use of the cartridges lying on the table?

Answer: I have suspicions about the paper on account of the bazar report that there is grease in it.

Question: Have you taken any measures to prove whether this report is true?

Answer: I have tried it in oil and also in water, and where it was wet with the oil it would not dissolve; after this trial I thought there was no grease in it.

Question: By the experiment, in your opinion, there was no grease in the paper; would you object to bite off the end of the cartridge?

Answer: I could not do it, as the other men would object to it.

The witness withdraws.

10th Witness

Havildar Bheekun Khan, 10th Company, 2nd Regiment, Native (Grenadier) Infantry, called into Court, and the provisions of section 22, para 7 of the Military Regulations, explained to him:

Question: Have you any objection to the use of the cartridges lying on the table?

Answer: I suspect that there is cow and pig grease in them from a bazar report.

Question: If you had any doubt, why did you not ascertain the point from your officer?

Answer: I could not report it to the officer, it being merely a bazar report.

Question: When the paper and cartridge were shown you upon parade, had you any reason to suppose that there was any grease mixed with the paper?

Answer: I have heard that it smells of grease when it is burnt.

The witness withdraws.

The Court closes its proceedings and adjourns *sine die.*

A

From Captain S. RICHARDS, *Officiating Major of Brigade to Brevet-Colonel* S. G. WHELER, *Commanding the 34th Regiment, Native Infantry, President, Court of Inquiry—No.29, dated Barrackpore, 5th February, 1857.*

I am directed by the Brigadier Commanding to request you will have the goodness to instruct the Court, of which you are nominated President in this day's station orders, thoroughly to investigate the subject of the objection to the paper forming a part of the new rifle cartridges, reported in the accompanying letter, No. 89, dated 4th February 1857, from Captain N.C. Boswell, Commanding the Left Wing, 2nd Regiment, Native (Grenadier) Infantry, to the Officiating Major of Brigade.

B

From Captain N.C. BOSWELL, *Commanding Left Wing, 2nd Regiment, Native (Grenadier) Infantry to Brigadier* C. GRANT, C.B., *Commanding at Barrackpore, No. 89 , dated Barrackpore, 4th February, 1857.*

I have the honour to report that, in obedience to instructions contained in a note of yesterday's date from the Brigadier Commanding the Station to the address of officers commanding regiments at the station, I yesterday afternoon, at a parade of the wing under my command, had fully explained to the men of the wing that the cartridges for the new rifles were to be made up exactly like the five produced on parade, and of the same paper as that sent with the cartridges, and that the sepoys would dip the cartridges themselves in wax and oil before using them.

I took the cartridges into the ranks and showed them to the men (having one broken open); and upon my asking several of the men here and there in the ranks if they could see anything objectionable in them, their reply, made in the most civil but soldier like manner, was "that the paper was not the same as that used for the old cartridges, and that they thought there was something in it".

I deem it my duty to report this circumstance for the information of the Brigadier Commanding, as I imagine there will be no difficulty in substituting the old cartridge paper for that made use of in the construction of the new cartridges.

C

Demi-official from Brigadier C. GRANT C.B., *Commanding at Barrackpore, to Brevet–Colonel* S. G. WHELER, *Commanding the 34th Regiment, Native Infantry, President, Court of Inquiry.*

On the Court of Inquiry to-day, besides the evidence of what occurred on parade from Captain N. C. BOSWELL and the men (sepoys) who objected to the cartridge paper, it is desirable to have the evidence of all the senior and highest caste native commissioned and non-commissioned officers, Hindus; as also all the subadars, jemadars, or havildars of the Mahomedan religion, and direct them to examine the paper of which the Enfield rifle cartridge is made, the powder and the bullet. To explain to them that the cartridge is different from the musket, the paper being thinner but more tough, so that the cartridge may contain the quantity required to throw the bullet to the utmost range without being of too long a form; for if it was made of the old thick paper, without it was made very long, it could not contain the powder required, the bore of the Enfield rifle being so much smaller; that the material of the paper is the same, but it is more carefully made; the powder a little stronger perhaps, and the bullet made of lead to the shape that will go most true to the mark aimed at from long distances.

The new Enfield musket is much lighter and therefore less fatiguing for a sepoy to carry on a long march; in fact, a very superior weapon to the old musket; and that all European and the Turkish Mohamedan Army are gradually being armed with it.

Let each native officer be asked separately if he can point out anything in the paper, powder or bullet that can in any way militate with the caste of the men.

Have the answers and opinions of each native officer carefully inserted in the Proceedings of the Inquiry.

Lieutenant J. Hearsey, A.D.C., has kindly come forward to attend the inquiry with his Enfield rifle, he having passed the Enfield School of Practice, and explain anything that may be required.

From Major General J. B. HEARSEY, C.B., *Commanding the Presidency Division, to Major* W.A.J. MAYHEW, *Deputy Adjutant-General of the Army—dated Headquarters, Presidency Division, Barrackpore, 8th February, 1857.*

I have the honour to report, for the information of Government and of the Commander-in-Chief, the following circumstances which have taken place at this station.

2. On receiving the orders of the government that an allowance would be authorised for the purchase and preparation of a grease such as the sepoys could have no objection to, for applying to the cartridges of the Enfield rifle, and having been supplied by Colonel Abbott, Inspector-General of Ordnance and Magazines, with some cartridges made up at the arsenal, also the paper in sheets, I directed Brigadier Grant to make known to commanding officers of regiments my desire that the order of the Government should be distinctly explained by them to their respective battalions on parade, and that the paper sent by Colonel Abbott with the cartridges should be shown to all the native officers and men.

3. This was accordingly done, and I confess I was surprised to learn that the paper (which has a somewhat glazed appearance) excited their suspicion that it had been prepared with grease as one of the materials, and Captain Boswell, who command the wing of the 2nd Regiment, Native (Grenadier) Infantry, at this station, sent me a report that such was the impression on the minds of his men.

4. Colonel S. G. Wheler, Commanding the 34th Regiment, Native Infantry, also waited upon me, and stated that the same objection had been raised by the men of his corps.

5. I lost no time in ordering Brigadier Grant to assemble a Special Court of Inquiry to investigate this matter, and the native commissioned and non-commissioned officers of the wing of the 2nd Regiment, Native (Grenadier) Infantry, were to be directed to attend and to state freely and plainly any objection they had or could possibly have to the use of this new ammunition.

6. The Court accordingly met, and was attended by my son, Lieutenant John Hearsey, a College passed officer, who is now residing with me, and has been instructed in the Musketry School at Hythe when lately in England on sick furlough. Lieutenant Hearsey took with him to the Court one of these Enfield rifles and materials for making up the cartridges, to show to the native officers. This was done; the rifle was much admired but they still objected to the glazed paper, frankly stating their suspicion that it contained grease, and they would prefer to have the cartridges made up of the old paper which had been so long served out them. In short, their suspicions are fairly roused on the subject of cow and pig fat, and it will be quite impossible to allay them, unfounded though they be.

7. The Proceedings of the Court of Inquiry were yesterday transmitted to you, for the purpose of being laid before Government and His Excellency the Commander-in-Chief.

8. On Friday night, the 6th instant, between the hours of eight and nine o' clock, Brigadier Grant, Colonel Wheler and Lieutenant Allen of the 34th Regiment, Native Infantry, waited upon me at my quarters, and the two first named informed me that Lieutenant Allen had startling matter to communicate. This will be found in the written statement of that officer hereto appended. A descriptive roll of the sepoy who gave the information in question is likewise attached to this letter.

9. I immediately directed the Brigadier to order Lieutenant Allen and Lieutenant Harris, Adjutant of the 70th Regiment, Native Infantry, an intelligent young officer, to mount their horses and ride in the direction of the spot indicated where these delegates were to meet, and to bring me intelligence if they saw them assembled, or any men returning from that direction. I also instructed the Brigadier to lose not a moment in having the roll of every company called in its battalion lines, and all men absent to be reported to him. Brigadier Grant's official report on this subject is hereto annexed, from which it will be seen that all were present in their

respective lines, save a few whose absence was satisfactorily accounted for. It is likewise shown by this report that the two officers returned from their mission without having seen any party assembled or proceeding to their lines from the spot indicated.

10. There can be little doubt but that a bad spirit prevails amongst the sepoys, particularly in the 2nd Regiment, Native (Grenadier) Infantry. The simultaneous fires at Barrackpore and Raneegunge (certainly by incendiarism) afford strong and reasonable ground for such a suspicion; though I am happy to add that none have occurred for several nights past, which may be perhaps attributed to there being strong picquets posted in the officers' lines from which patrols are constantly sent to watch and apprehend any suspicious persons who may be moving about.

11. I have also directed that a register shall be taken of all bazar people and camp followers, in order that the bad characters may be summarily ejected from the cantonments, and I have further offered a reward of one thousand rupees to be paid to any person who may come forward and produce such evidence as will convict the incendiary or incendiaries of the telegraph and other bungalows.

12. Deeming it to be my duty to keep the Government fully informed of all that may be occurring at this station, I have thought it proper to enter into these details.

13. I, moreover, consider it necessary to add my conviction that the sepoys are tampered with by the designing villains when on duty in Fort William and Calcutta, it having been frequently noticed by old military residents at this station that after frequent absences on such detached duty, many of them return to their lines with strange ideas and unsettled minds. I therefore think that if it could be possibly managed to have all the duties in that garrison and in Calcutta exclusively taken by the European regiment and the native militia, especially in Calcutta, the arrangement would be highly desirable.

14. It is my intention to have the brigade paraded to-morrow, and myself explain the absurdity of the notion that the Government entertains the most distant intention of interfering with their religion or caste.

STATEMENT made by Lieutenant A. S. ALLEN, *34th Regiment Native Infantry, and countersigned by Lieutenant-Colonel* S. G. WHELER, *Commanding the 34th Regiment, Native Infantry, dated Barrackpore, 8th February, 1857.*

On Friday, the 6th instant, about 7 a.m., as I was sitting in the verandah of my bungalow, a sepoy belonging to the company of which I have charge, came up to where I was, and said he wished to speak to me privately on some family matters; at the same time requesting that I should tell my servant, who was standing close by, to go away as he did not wish him to hear what he was about to say. I accordingly directed my servant to withdraw, and then enquired of the sepoy what it was that he had to communicate.

He began by saying that he had become cognisant of a plot amongst the men of the different regiments, four in number, at this station, that they were apprehensive of being forced to give up their caste and be made Christians; and that consequently they were determined to rise up against their officers, and commence by either plundering or burning down the bungalows at Barrackpore; they next proposed to proceed to Calcutta and attempt to seize Fort William or failing that, to take possession of the Treasury.

Delegates from the different regiments were to assemble the same evening about eight or nine o'clock at a large tree close to the station magazine, and concert what their future proceedings should be; that an artilleryman had informed them of the approaching arrival of a European regiment from Dinapore, as also that artillery were being brought down to assist in carrying out the measures of the Government, and consequently unless immediate action was arranged on the part of the sepoys, it would shortly be too late for their doing anything, and therefore some decided line of conduct must at once be settled.

The sepoy, my informant, on my expressing doubts as to the probability of his story, begged that I would go myself to the place of meeting indicated by him, when I could satisfy myself by personal observation of the correctness of his statement. But he entreated that I would not mention his name to any one, as if his comrades suspected his being a spy on their conduct he was apprehensive of their using violence towards him or at all events that he would be unable to find out anything hereafter with regard to their intentions and proceedings.

He further stated that the burning down of the electric telegraph office was part of a concerted plan to prevent the Government receiving speedy information of what was going on. Also, that the men of other regiments were to be informed of what was being done here, and that they were to be called upon to co-operate with their comrades, the affair being one which concerned them all equally. He also said that it was proposed to seize the magazine here, and obtain possession of the arms and ammunition kept there. On hearing all this I directed the sepoy to return to his lines, and if he could hear anything additional on the subject, he was to come to me again and communicate what more he knew.

As the information appeared of sufficient importance to be laid before the authorities, I proceeded to the quarters of Colonel Wheler, commanding my regiment, and stated to him what I had heard. Colonel Wheler and myself then went to Brigadier Grant's house, and I repeated the substance of what I knew to him. The Brigadier considered it necessary to lay the matter before the Major General Commanding the Division, and we accordingly went to Major-General J. B. Hearsey about nine o' clock the same night, and I again told all the above facts.

I was then directed to ride round by the place where the meeting of the sepoys was to have taken place, and to observe whether anybody was there. I accordingly did so but saw no one in the neighbourhood of the magazine except the sentries, who challenged as usual. On my return from this mission, I met Brigadier Grant near the gate of my own compound, when I told him of the result of my observations, and that I had seen nothing suspicious. When I arrived at my own house it was about 10 p.m.

Descriptive long roll of a sepoy belonging to No. 8 Company, 34th Regiment, Native Infantry.

Regtl. No	Rank and name	Caste	Present age	Height		Village	Pergunnah	District	Date of enlistment	Remaks
			Years.	Ft.	Inch.					"Scinde"
1097	Sepoy Ram Sahai Lalla	Kait	30	5	7 3/4	Kundahar	Nagaon	Lucknow	26th February 1844	A steady, well-behaved man: reads, writes, and speaks English, and has kept the books and written for the company for six months past. He has also acted as Pay Havildar of the company satisfactorily during two months past, is kote sepoy. (sd) A.S. ALLEN, *Lt.* *In charge of company.* WUZEERABAD, *The, 1st November 1852.*

(sd.)
BARRACKPORE
The 8th Februay, 1857

(sd.)
S.G. WHELER, *Lt. Col.,*
Comdg. 34th Regiment, Nat. Infy.

(sd.)
A. STEWART ALLEN, *Lt.*
In temporary charge of No. 8 Co.,
34th Regt. Native Infy.

From Brigadier C. GRANT, C.B., *Commanding at Barrackpore, to Major A. H. ROSS, Assistant Adjutant-General, Presidency Division—dated Barrackpore, 8 February, 1857.*

I have the honor to report, for the information of Major General J.B. Hearsey, Commanding the Presidency Division that agreeably to instructions, on the night of the 6th instant, Lieutenant Allen, 34th Regiment, Native Infantry, and Lieutenant Harris, Adjutant, 70th Regiment, Native Infantry proceeded to the tree near the magazine of this station, and did not find any persons in the vicinity. also to report that the roll was called in every regiment at the same time during the night of Friday, and all the men reported to be present in their lines.

From Major-General J. B. HEARSEY C.B., *Commanding the Presidency Division, to Major W. A. J. MAYHEW, Deputy Adjutant-General of the Army—NO.47-D. dated Headquarters, Presidency Division, Barrackpore, 11th February, 1857.*

I have the honour to enclose for the information of Government, a voluntary deposition made yesterday before Brigadier Grant, Colonel Wheler and Captain Drury, of the 34th Regiment, Native Infantry.

2. This mutinous spirit would seem to have taken deep root among the sepoys here.

3. On the afternoon of the 9th instant I assembled the whole of the troops now present at the station, and addressed them on the parade, pointing out the absurdity of the dread of their religious prejudices being interfered with and other matters concerning the introduction of the new rifle greased cartridges and paper, with good effect. I think from what I have since heard I do not consider it advisable to seize and confine the sepoys named by the jemadar until I can obtain further evidence, because his sole deposition will not convict.

4. I am of the opinion that as the force here consists of Native infantry only, without Europeans or either of the two other arms, artillery or cavalry, to fall back upon in case of a serious outbreak, this is sound policy.

DEPOSITION of Jemadar DURRIOW, *8th Company, 34th Regiment, Native Infantry, taken at Barrackpore on the 10th day of February 1857 in presence of Brigadier* C. GRANT, C.B., *Commanding at Barrackpore, Colonel* S.G. WHELER, *Commanding 34th Regiment, Native Infantry, Captain* C. C. DRURY, *8th Company, 34th Regiment, Native Infantry, Lieutenant* B. H. BAUGH, *Adjutant, 34th Regiment, Native Infantry. INTERPRETER – Lieutenant* A. F. CORBETT, *43rd Regiment, Native Infantry.*

Jemadar Durriow, 8th Company, 34th Regiment, Native Infantry, having been solemnly affirmed states as follows:-

On the night of the 5th instant (February 1857), soon after eight o' clock roll-call, two or three men (sepoys) came to me and made me accompany them to the parade ground, where I found a great crowd assembled, composed, to the best of my belief, of the men of the different regiments at this station; they had their heads tied up with cloths, leaving only a small part of the face exposed; they asked me to join them, and I asked them what I was to join them in; they replied that they were willing to die for their religion, and that if they could make an arrangement that evening, the next night (6th February 1857) they would plunder the station and kill all the Europeans, and then go where they liked.

I told them they had better go to their lines and explained to them that if they did anything of this kind, they would not get such good masters in future. I went away after this, and the crowd dispersed.

Question: How many men do you suppose were assembled?

Answer: About three hundred.

Question: Did you recognise anybody in the crowd?

Answer: The two men who took me away were sepoys, by name Kassee Persaud Doobie, No.8 Company and Mohun Sookul, No.7 Company, 34th Regiment, Native Infantry.

Question: Were there any non-commissioned officers or commissioned Native officers in the crowd?

Answer: I cannot say; they all had their heads so tied up that I could not recognise any.

Question: How long were you with the crowd before they dispersed?

Answer: About a quarter to half -an-hour.

Question: What arrangements were made with regard to killing the Europeans and plunder of the station?

Answer: Nothing further than that if they could settle anything that night, then the affair was to come off on the ensuing night, the 6th February 1857.

Question: Did you recognise the voices of any of the speakers in the crowd?

Answer: I think I recognised that of Mookta Persaud Pandy, drill-havildar, 34th Regiment, Native Infantry.

Question: What prevented the proposed assembly taking place on the night of the 6th February 1857?

Answer: I do not know.

Question: Has any similar meeting taken place since the 5th instant or do you know if any such is contemplated by the men?

Answer: There has been none since nor do I know if any meeting is contemplated.

Question: You say you recognised the voice of the drill-havildar, 34th Regiment, Native Infantry. Can you state anything that he said?

Answer: No, I cannot.

Question: Are you aware if any particular regiment takes the lead in these disturbances?

Answer: No, I think they are all equally implicated.

Question: Do you know how the late fires in the station originated and whether they were the work of sepoys or others?

Answer: I do not know; I was only relieved from the fort duty* on the 3rd February.

The foregoing deposition was taken in presence of us, this 10th day of February 1857.

(sd.) C. GRANT, *Brigadier, Commanding at Barrackpore.*

(sd.) S. G. WHELER, *Lieutenant-Colonel, Commanding 34th Regiment, Native Infantry.*

(sd.) C. C. DRURY, *Captain, in charge of No.8 Company, 34th Regiment, Native Infantry.*

(sd.) B.H. BAUGH, *Lieutenant, Adjutant, 34th Regiment, Native Infantry.*

(sd.) A. F.CORBET, *Lieutenant, 43rd Regiment, Native (Light) Infantry—Interpreter.*

From Major General J. B. HEARSY C.B., *Commanding the Presidency Division, to Colonel* R. J. H. BIRCH, C.B., *Secretary to the Government of India, in the Military Department, dated,11th February, 1857.*

I have this moment received the enclosed statement of Sepoy Ramsahai Lalla, 8th Company, 34th Regiment, Native Infantry, from Brigadier Grant. It gives but little more information than his first statement, which no doubt has been laid before Government.

I have every reason to believe all is now quiet, but I must try and get such evidence as will convict the leaders of this intended outbreak, if I possibly can.

EXAMINATION of Sepoy RAMSAHAI LALLA, *8th Company, 34th Regiment, Native Infantry.*

Question: Are you aware that a meeting of the sepoys of the different regiments at this station was held on Thursday, the 5th instant?

Answer: Yes, there was, but I only heard of the assembly next day, and cannot state with certainty what took place there. I only know that a second meeting was arranged for the following night, Friday, at which I heard that the sepoys intended taking an oath and arranging what their future proceedings were to be. I understood the delegates or representatives from each of the four regiments at Barrackpore were to attend on this occasion. This is all I know on the subject of the first meeting, but I considered it my duty to go to the officer in charge of my company, and whom I know well, having been in the habit of writing for him for several years, and whom I believe to have confidence in me.

I waited till evening on Friday before I gave the information, as I was anxious to be quite certain that this second meeting was to take place, and having ascertained that it actually was to be at the time appointed I then proceeded to the quarters of Lieutenant Allen, the officer in question, and imparted the information to him, at the same time begging that if he doubted me, he would go himself to the appointed place, between eight and nine o' clock, when he would be sure to perceive some assembly or meeting going on.

I returned to the lines of my regiment, and shortly afterwards, at eight o'clock, roll-call was held as usual, when all were present, but on their names having been answered, and between eight and nine o'clock, the men began to proceed to the place of assembly. This I saw with my own eyes and forthwith returned to Lieutenant Allen's quarters, to tell of it, and suggest his proceeding to the place indicated at once. Lieutenant Allen was not in his house, but returned in a short time, when I mentioned these circumstances to him, and I then went back again to the lines.

Shortly afterwards the roll was called, when all were found present in their lines. I am convinced that the reason of there being no assembly that night was owing to a suspicion having gone abroad amongst the men of the different regiments that their intentions had been discovered, and that consequently it would be both unadvisable and dangerous for them to meet together that night. But if Lieutenant Allen had been able to go to the parade ground, near the magazine, about nine o'clock, he must have seen some sepoys about the place, either going or returning.

I do not think that the calling of the roll about 10 p. m. had any effect in preventing their assembly, as their intention was abandoned for that night on their becoming aware that news of the affair had got abroad and come to the knowledge of the authorities. The various orderlies or sepoys of the different guards about cantonments could easily have sent information to the different lines that something was going on connected with their intended proceedings.

The foregoing statement has been written down by me from the sepoy's own mouth, and on being read over to him, he declares that it was not in his power to give any more information on the subject of these meetings, nor could he mention the names of any of those concerned; at least if he did he would not reveal them, saying, and truly, that though he had his suspicions, it would be impossible for him to bring direct proof, as all concerned would combine together against him, and a single man's evidence would be worthless in such a case. I have no doubt of the correctness generally of this sepoy's revelations, as I have always found him a respectable and well-behaved man, and one whose word may be relied on, as far as my knowledge of him goes.

BARRACKPORE — (sd.) A. S. ALLEN, *Lieutenant*

The 11th February 1857 — *34th Regiment Native Infantry*

From Major General J. B. HEARSEY C.B., *Commanding the Presidency Division, to Colonel* R. J. H. BIRCH, C.B., *Secretary to the Government of India, in the Military Department—dated Barrackpore 11th February 1857.*

We have at Barrackpore been dwelling upon a mine ready for explosion. I have been watching the feeling of the sepoys here for some time; their minds have been misled by some designing scoundrels who have managed to make them believe that their religious prejudices, their caste, is to be interfered with by Government. "That they are to be FORCED to turn Christians".

2. Any reasonable person would doubt, after the experience we have had, that such an absurd notion could possess them, but nevertheless it is a fact, and it will take time to disposess their minds of this stupid idea.

3. I was told that a circumstance occurred at Dum Dum, where the School of practice for the Enfield rifle is assembled, which I may say gave credence amongst them to this supposition.

4. A sepoy from one of the regiments here was walking to his chowka to prepare his food, with his lota, full off water. He was met by a low-caste *khalasi* (it is said one of the magazine or arsenal men). This *khalasi* asked him to let him drink from the lota. The sepoy, a Brahmin, refused saying— "I have scoured my lota; you will defile it by your touch". The *khalasi* rejoined—"You think much of your caste, but wait a little, the *saheb-logue* will make you bite cartridges soaked in cow and pork fat, and then where will your caste be?"

The sepoy made this speech known amongst his comrades at Dum Dum; the report was not long in traveling to this station; the men brooded over it for some time at Dum Dum and though it seems to have been known to the officer there, it was treated as a silly and foolish notion, until Major Bontein perceived it had taken hold of their minds as a fact, when he reported it to me. I lost no time in writing to Calcutta, making known what had occurred, and suggesting a small allowance might be granted to the officer at Dum Dum to purchase wax and ghee or cocoanut oil by the hands of one of the high-caste men, and direct him to grease the bullet portion of the cartridge before the men when they were served out for practice.

5. This I had every reason to believe would practically convince the men of the falsity of the *khalasi's* speech, and that every care would be taken that their caste would not be interfered with. It seems to have had all the effect desired at the school of practice at Dum Dum, and as no cartridges were to be served out or practice was to take place here, I could not dream, that it would become a cause of trouble or dissatisfaction at this place.

6. Colonel Abbott sent me a parcel of cartridges and paper; and as the burning of the telegraph bungalow and several officers' thatched houses

had occurred at this station—certainly by incendiaries, for Sonthal arrows with lighted matches attached to them had been taken out of the thatch—I ordered officers commanding corps to parade their men, and explain to them that no grease would be used in the cartridges but what would be applied by one of themselves when they were required to use the new Enfield rifle.

The paper sent by Colonel Abbott was not the same kind of which the common cartridge is made, and had a glazed or shinning appearance; this excited suspicion in their minds, and such was reported to me by Captain N. C. Boswell, Commanding a wing of the 2nd Regiment, Native (Grenadier) Infantry; and Colonel S. G. Wheler, Commanding the 34th Regiment, Native Infantry, also waited upon me and made known that this shining appearance was deemed by the Native officers and men to be caused by the objectionable fat or grease mixed with the paper in the process of making it.

7. I had a Court of Inquiry assembled, before which the native commissioned and non-commissioned officers of the wing of the 2nd Regiment, Native (Grenadier) Infantry, were examined as to their opinion and feeling on this point; the proceedings have been sent to Government. Amidst all this business the alarm in Fort William took place, and the company of Europeans was hurried from Dum Dum without any report being made to me. I had succeeded in putting a stop in the incendiarism here by posting strong picquets, and sending patrols constantly through the lines of thatched bungalows, and by issuing an order that all houses burnt were not to be rebuilt with thatched roofs, and that all thatched verandahs or "lean-tos" affixed to *pucca* houses were to be removed, for the last attempt at incendiarism was the firing of one of these thatched verandahs.

The fires occurring at Raneegunge about the same period fixed suspicion strongly on the men of the 2nd Regiment Native (Grenadier) Infantry as Sonthal arrows had been used in igniting the bungalows, and that regiment had been employed in the Santhal District. I reported the objection the Native officers and men had raised to the glazed paper to Government, and as I deemed it folly to fight with such shadows, recommended it should be changed to the old cartridge paper; to this I have received no answer. On the 6th instant, a Kait sepoy, who can read and understand English, waited in the evening on Lieutenant A. S. Allen of the 34th Regiment, Native Infantry, and informed him that a meeting was to take place amongst the disaffected men of the different regiments between eight and nine at night to discuss what should be done to prevent their religious prejudices or tenets from being abused by the Government and *Saheb-logue*.

This was immediately made known to me, as I have reported, and I took measures to find out if it was true. I learnt nothing. The native officers of the different regiments must have known it, yet they reported it not to their European officers. The day before yesterday a jemadar of the 34th Regiment, Native Infantry, sent one of my orderlies (or a sepoy) to me to ask my permission to wait upon me. I replied—"By all means; but the rules of the service required that he should have the consent of his immediate commanding officer". The jemadar asked for the permission he desired the next day. When questioned by Colonel Wheler and Lieutenant Bunbury, he stated he wished to communicate all he knew on the subject of evil disposition now prevailing amongst the sepoys. This was made known to the Brigadier Grant, who instantly waited upon me to report the circumstance. I directed a Court to be formed, and that the jemadar's (by name Durriow) statement should be taken on solemn affirmation, which was done, and I forwarded it yesterday to Government.

8. I must mention that I had the whole brigade paraded on Monday afternoon, the 9th and myself energetically and explicitly explained in a loud voice to the whole of the men the folly of the idea that possessed them that the Government or that their officers wished to interfere with their caste or religious prejudices; and impressed upon them the absurdity of their for one moment believing that they were *to be forced* to become Christians. I told them the English were Christians of *" The Book"* i.e. "Protestants", that we admitted no proselytes but those who being adults could read and fully understand the percepts laid down therein; that if they came and threw themselves down at our feet imploring to be made *"The Book"* Christians it could not be done, they could not be baptised until they had examined in the tenets of *"The Book"* and proved themselves fully conversant in them, and then they must of their own good-will and accord desire to become Christians of *"The Book"* ere they could be made so. I asked them if they perfectly understood what I said especially the2nd Regiment, Native (Grenadier) Infantry; they nodded assent. I then dismissed the brigade.

9. I have since heard from the officers commanding regiments that their Native officers and men appeared quite *"khoosh"* (pleased) and seemed to be relived from a heaviness of mind that had possessed them.

10. I cannot but with great caution put any man into confinement, unless I can get full proof of his being one of or a leader at a mutinous meeting, and this is yet wanting.

11. May I state my opinion in regard to the policy of having five or six regiments of native infantry assembled in brigade here, without any European corps of infantry or artillery or cavalry at a *point d' appui,* in case of a mutiny

occurring? You will perceive in all this business the native officers were of no use. *In fact, they are afraid of their men,* and dare not act. All they do is to hold themselves aloof, and expect by so doing will escape censure as not actively implicated. This has always occurred on such occasions, and will continue to the end of our sovereignty in India. Well might Sir Charles Metcalfe say—that he expected to awake some fine morning, and find India had been lost to the English Crown.

12. I had written thus far intending to send this letter to Major-General Low, but having just received a note from Major Mayhew, Deputy Adjutant-General, that Government wished me to communicate direct, I have altered it to this address of Colonel Birch, Military Secretary to Government. I have kept no copy of it.

13. The only circumstances that led to a suspicion of an ill-feeling here was the incendiarism, and I reported it. I could not, nor can I yet fix it, on the sepoys. I can only, as others do, suspect.

From Colonel R.J.H. BIRCH, C.B., *Secretary to the Government of India, in the Military Department, to Major* W.A.J. MAYHEW, *Deputy Adjutant-General of the Army— No. 388 dated Fort William dated 11th February 1857.*

I am directed to acknowledge the receipt of your letter No. 165, of yesterday's date, forwarding a communication from the Major-General Commanding the Presidency Division, bringing to notice a spirit of disaffection prevailing among the native troops at Barrackpore, and in reply to acquaint you that Government are of opinion that Major-General J.B. Hearsey should be requested to keep on the alert to detect meetings among the sepoys, and that he should instruct the officers of the several regiments to go into the lines of their corps and converse with the men, and make use of their best native officers for the purpose of convincing the sepoys that their apprehensions are groundless.

2. The native officers of the several regiments should be reminded by their commanding officers of paras 16 to 21, of G.G.O. No. 132, of the 23rd January 1856, which hold the native officers responsible to Government for the conduct of the men.

Herewith sent for ready perusal

3. The delay which has occurred in submitting to Government a report of the Proceedings at Barrackpore the Governor-General in Council considers most reprehensible; and His Lordship in Council desires that it may be

ascertained where it lies, in order that notice may be taken of it at once. Apparently this delay has not been in your office. It was only on the afternoon of the 10th that Government was informed of what occurred on the 6th instant, and General Hearsey's report is dated the 8th.

4. The Major-General was to have addressed the regiment at Barrackpore on parade on Monday morning, the 9th, and up to this hour nothing is known to Government of the result.

From Major-General J. B. HEARSY C.B., *Commanding the Presidency Division, to Colonel* R.J.H. BIRCH, C.B., *Secretary to the Government of India, in the Military Department, dated Barrackpore—12th February 1857.*

I had this morning the honour to receive from the Deputy Adjutant-General of the Army a copy of your letter to that officer's address, No. 388 of yesterday's date, and in reply to the first and second paragraphs beg to acquaint you for the information of Government, that the directions contained therein have been this forenoon, at my own quarters, by myself carefully communicated to the Brigadier and the several officers commanding regiments at this station, for their particular guidance. I may, however, observe that the measures adverted to had already been carefully adopted by them.

2. As regards the third paragraph of your letter, allow me to remark that if any undue delay has occurred in your receipt of my letter dated the 8th instant, such cannot be attributed to any want of attention of myself or the Divisional staff officer, since the letter alluded to was written and despatched to the post office at this station on the day I obtained Lieutenant Allen's written statement. Unfortunately that officer got one day's leave of absence from his commanding officer to visit Calcutta on duty connected with a deceased officer's estate, without my knowledge, so that one day was lost.

3. Not having any mounted orderlies or express camels, I have no other public means of communicating with Calcutta but by the post office, which leaves this station at 3 p.m., a most inconvenient hour. Government may rest assured of my being constantly on the alert to prevent any unauthorised or mutinous assemblages of the sepoys; and further, that I shall not hesitate to seize and confine every man against whom I can procure sufficient proof of being an adviser or leader in these most discreditable proceedings.

4. I have this moment heard from Major H. W. Matthews, Commanding the 43rd Regiment, Native Infantry, that one of his native doctors has informed him of a conversation he accidentally overhead. I enclose this statement in original. If the *kossid* mentioned could be intercepted en route to Dinapore, it might lead to a discovery of the originators of this foolish conspiracy.

5. I have taken no copy of this letter to save delay.

STATEMENT sent to Major H.W. MATTHEWS *Commanding the 43rd Regiment, Native Infantry—dated 12th February 1857.*

Ramjan Khan, Native Doctor, states as follows:- "I overhead a sepoy of the 2nd Regiment, Native (Grenadier) Infantry, mention at the hospital to someone that a *kossid* had been sent to the *Ung-ka-pultan** at Berhampore and to the regiments at Dinapore, informing them that ten or twelve of us have raised a disturbance, and we want you to support us."

Ramjan said he did not remember the date that he heard the above, but it was some days ago. I told him to try and find out the sepoy's name and company whose conversation he had overhead.

Telegram from Colonel R. J. H. BIRCH. C.B., *Secretary to the Government of India, in the Military Department, to the Major-General* G. W. A. LLOYD, *Commanding the Dinapore Division—No 469-56, dated Fort William, 13th February 1857.*

It is understood that a *kossid* has been sent to the Native regiments at Dinapore with a letter from some men of the 2nd Grenadier Regiment, requesting the men at Dinapore to support them in raising a disturbance. Measures should be taken without delay to trace this letter, and if possible, to secure the *kossid.*

From Major General J. B. HEARSEY C.B., *Commanding the Presidency Division, to Colonel* R. J. H. BIRCH, C.B., *Secretary to the Government of India, in the Military Department, dated Headquarters,. Presidency Division, Barrackpore, 13th February 1857.*

In continuation of my letter of yesterday's date, I have now the honour to transmit, for the information of the Government, reports in original from the four officers commanding native corps at this station regarding the present feeling of their men, and other matters connected with this subject, which is I think satisfactory.

2. To prevent delay I have considered it advisable to address you direct, and to send the packet by my son, Captain Hearsey, as the post office arrangements would seem to be defective.

* The 19th Bengal Infantry

From Colonel J. D. KENNEDY, *Commanding the 70th Regiment, Native Infantry, to Captain* S. RICHARDS, *Officiating Major of Brigade, Barrackpore—No.26, dated Barrackpore, 12th February 1857.*

With reference to an extract of a letter from Government, read this morning to commanding officers of regiments by the Major-General Commanding the Presidency Division, in presence of the Brigadier Commanding, I have the honour to report, for the information of Brigadier C. Grant, that some time during the past month I was in the lines of my regiment conversing quietly with the native officers upon the apparent disaffection that seemed to exist in this station amongst some of the men; and that again on the 3rd instant, I proceeded to the lines, taking with me the five new cartridges and the sheets of paper I had that forenoon received from the Brigadier. That I explained to my native commissioned or non-commissioned officers and sepoys that there was nothing in the least objectionable to their religion or caste in either the one or the other, distributing at the same time the cartridges and paper amongst them, that they might themselves closely examine them. This they did, when one and all told me they were perfectly satisfied with them, and also with my explanation and assurance that no greased cartridges would be served out to them by Government.

2. I further beg to add that the men of my regiment thoroughly understood and were perfectly satisfied after hearing the address made to the troops the other evening by Major-General J. B. Hearsey, Commanding the Division. The words of the report made to me were that the men were quiet *"Khoosh"*.

From Captain N. C. BOSWELL, *Commanding the left wing, 2nd Regiment, Native (Grenadier) Infantry to Major* A. H. Ross, *Assistant Adjutant-General, Presidency Division—No. 94, dated Barrackpore, 12th February 1857.*

I have the honour in accordance with the instructions communicated to me, this day by the Major-General Commanding the Division, to report for his information that I am decidedly of opinion that the address made by him to the men of the wing under my command at parade on the evening of the 9th instant had a most beneficial effect on the minds of the men.

2. Any apprehension which might have existed amongst them appeared to be done away with, and they expressed to the Major-General himself, when questioned by him, that they fully understood his address.

3. The men of the wing under my command continue to behave in the most orderly, quiet, and soldierlike manner.

From Lieutenant Colonel S.G. WHELER, *Commanding the 34th Regiment, Native Infantry, to Major* A. H. ROSS, *Assistant Adjutant-General, Presidency Division—dated Barrackpore,12th Februrary 1857.*

In accordance with the wishes of the Major-General Commanding the Division, expressed by him at the meeting of the commanding officers this day assembled at his quarters, I have the honour to state, for his information, that on the 26th January last I spoke to the native officers and men on parade, denying the false reports that were spreading about the station to the effect that we intended to make them all Christians by force; and which I reported as having done to the Brigadier commanding the station the next day in a demi-official note. Since which I have spoken to the subadar-major and native officers separately, warning them of the responsibility which rests upon them, and the consequences they will draw upon themselves if they conceal from their officers any meetings or assemblies of men which they hear are likely to take place at, or near, or at a distance from their lines, or any matter whatever which they know is likely to prove injurious to their officers or the service at large.

From Major H.W. MATTHEWS *Commanding the 43rd Regiment, Native (Light) Infantry, to Major* A. H. ROSS, *Assistant Adjutant-General, Presidency Division—No. 23, dated Barrackpore, 12th February 1857.*

Having this morning heard Major-General J.B. Hearsey, Commanding the Presidency Division, read part of a letter he had received from the Deputy Adjutant-General of the Army, I have the honour to report that I have already in person explained to the native commissioned officers and others under my command that it is their duty to bring to my notice every occurrence affecting the discipline and credit of the corps. I beg further to state that I have been and am endeavouring to ascertain the cause of the excitement prevailing amongst the troops and to find out the leaders of the disaffected. I have to add that I believe the speech lately made to the troops by the Major-General had a good effect; and it was reported to me that the men of my regiment returned to their lines well pleased and satisfied.

From Major General J. B. HEARSEY C.B., *Commanding the Presidency Division, to Colonel* C. CHESTER, *Adjutant-General of the Army, Meerut—dated Headquarters, Presidency Division, Barrackpore, 13th February 1857.*

Referring to my official communication to your address, No. 3 of the 25th ultimo, I have now the honour to transmit, for the information of His Excellency the Commander-in-Chief, copies of several letters which I have since addressed to the Deputy Adjutant-General and Deputy Quartermaster General of the Army for direct submission to the Government of India, having reference to the same subject—namely, an uneasy and groundless apprehension in the minds of the sepoys of the regiments at Barrackpore that their religion and caste were to be interfered with by Government.

2. In explanation of this correspondence being unaccompanied by various documents connected therewith, I would beg to state, for His Excellency's information, that to save time, which was of much importance, copies of these papers were not taken.

3. This omission can be, however, remedied hereafter by the Deputy Adjutant-General being authorised to obtain copies from the Military Secretary's Office, if the Commander-in-Chief is of opinion that this measure is desirable.

4. I am happy to be able to add that all unpleasant excitement in the minds of the Native troops at Barrackpore on this subject has now quite subsided, never again to revive I confidently hope.

MEMORANDUM from Colonel K. YOUNG, *Judge Advocate General of the Army, to Colonel* C. CHESTER, *Adjutant-General of the Army—No. 182, dated Meerut, 24th February 1857.*

(Report upon papers relating to disaffection among the native troops at Barrackpore.)

A spirit of disaffection has been found to exist amongst the native troops at Barrackpore, arising apparently from an idea that has got abroad amongst them that fat of cows and pigs enters into the composition of the paper with which the cartridges for the new rifles are made up; and is also supposed that the sepoys are under the impression, misled by some designing enemies of the British Government, that it is intended to force them to embrace the Christian religion.

A Court of Inquiry was held to investigate the subject of the objection to the cartridge paper, and the proceedings clearly show that the men have got the absurd idea into their heads, on account of the glazed appearance of the paper, that grease of some kind is used in preparing it. In the first instance it seems that the objection was understood to apply merely to the composition used in greasing the cartridges, but the enquiry has shown that the objection goes also to the paper.

2. On the evening of the day on which the Court of Inquiry sat (the 6th February), a sepoy of the 34th Regiment, Native Infantry, came to the officer of his company, Lieutenant Allen, and told him of a plot amongst the sepoys, who were apprehensive of being forced to give up their caste and be made Christians, to plunder Barrackpore and attempt to seize Fort William or the Treasury. A meeting of delegates from different regiments was, Lieutenant Allen's informant said, to take place the same night and at his suggestion, Lieutenant Allen, having reported the matter to the senior authorities, proceeded with their sanction in the direction indicated, but saw no appearance of any meeting, and the roll having been called in every regiment at the same time all the men were reported to be present in their lines.

   The sepoy who gave the information to Lieutenant Allen, when subsequently questioned on the subject, stated that he knew that a meeting had taken place on the 5th February, though he was not present at it himself, and he understood that it was then arranged that another meeting should be held on the following night (the 6th); and he adds that after he returned to the lines from Lieutenant Allen's he actually saw the men leaving their lines and proceeding to the place of assembly, but he supposes that a suspicion must have got abroad that their intentions were discovered, inducing them consequently to abandon the projected meeting. The sepoy informant (Ramsahai Lalla) appears to bear a very good character, and there seems no reason to doubt his story, except that he has probably very much exaggerated matters. He has not named any individuals who were present at the meeting of the 5th.

   But on the 10th February, a Native officer of the 34th Regiment, Native Infantry, Jemadar Durriow, came forward of his own accord and stated that he was involuntarily present at the meeting on the 5th February, two or three men (sepoys) having come to him after the eight o'clock roll-call and made him accompany them to the parade ground where he found a great crowd, composed to the best of his belief of the men of the different regiments at the station, to the number of about three hundred, who had their heads tied up with cloths, leaving only a small part of the face exposed.

   The jemadar says that the question of killing the Europeans and plundering the station was discussed, but he reasoned with the mutineers, and at length on his going away they dispersed. The jemadar mentions the names of two sepoys who took him away, and he thinks he recognised the voice of the drill-havildar of the 34th Regiment, Native Infantry. The above is apparently all the principal information that has been hitherto obtainable regarding these mutinous proceedings at Barrackpore, and I am requested to state what course I consider best to be pursued towards the parties implicated in the night meetings, and to report as to the possibility or otherwise of substantiating charges against any of them.

3. The only individuals against whom charges could be framed are the two sepoys who took away the jemadar to the meeting on the 5th, and their conviction would be dependent upon his evidence, corroborated as it would be in some measure by the testimony of the sepoy who gave Lieutenant Allen notice of the intended meeting on the 6th. I do not think that the trial of these men would be desirable. The best course, it appears to me, would be to take no active steps at present in the matter, but for Major-General J. B. Hearsey to quietly proceed in his enquiries, when, if further information is eventually procurable, fixing the guilt of assisting at these mutinous meetings on the men named or on others, to place them on their trial or to summarily discharge them, as circumstances may render most expedient.

From Major-General J.B. HEARSEY, C.B., *Commanding the Presidency Division, to Colonel* R.J.H. BIRCH, C.B., *Secretary to the Government of India, in the Military Department—No. 96, dated Headquarters, Presidency Division, Barrackpore, 5th March, 1857.*

In forwarding for the orders of Government the enclosed letter, dated the 2nd instant, received yesterday evening from the Officer Commanding the Depot of Musketry at Dum Dum, I beg distinctly to state my opinion that the new mode of loading the Enfield rifle (as proposed by Major Bontein) should be adopted, and taught not only at this but at the two other depots.

2. This new mode of loading may be considered as a part of the intended drill for a new weapon about to be introduced into the service, and not as a concession extorted by discontented men. I am the more convinced that this would be proper, since I have myself already carefully explained to the whole of the Native troops at Barrackpore, at a general parade, that neither the Government nor its officers ever have or ever will interfere with their caste prejudices, or permit others to meddle with such.

3. By introducing this new mode of drill,—namely, breaking the cartridge with the hand instead of by biting it,—all discontent or uneasy feeling in regard to their caste prejudices on that account will be or ought to be

effectually removed. We shall thus be keeping our word with the sepoys, and at the same time introducing a better plan of loading with reference to their religious scruples.

4. I propose, therefore, with the sanction of the Right Hon'ble the Governor-General of India in Council to empower Major Bontein to adopt this alteration in the rifle exercise.

5. I beg to add that a copy of this and of Major Bontein's letter will be sent to Army Headquarters, for the information of His Excellency the Commander-in-Chief.

From Brevet-Major J. BONTEIN, *Commanding Depot of Musketry, to Major* A. H. ROSS, *Assistant Adjutant-General, Presidency Division, Barrackpore—dated Dum Dum, 2nd March 1857.*

I am sorry that it should be my duty to report, for the information of Major-General Hearsey, Commanding the Division, an unwillingness on the part of some of the sepoys (Hindus belonging to the Dum Dum School of Musketry) to bite the cartridge according to the established regulation for loading the rifle musket.

2. This unwillingness has not manifested itself in any decided form, for the course of instruction has not yet arrived at that period when the cartridge is brought into practice; however, as the feeling of objection has been expressed in my presence, I feel it my duty to bring the circumstance to notice.

3. During the past week the European and native officers belonging to this depot have been learning the process of cartridge-making, which forms a portion of the course of instruction at the Hythe School of Musketry. The native officers performed this duty with perfect readiness; accordingly I ordered No. 2 section, composed of sepoys belonging to the 2nd Regiment, Native (Grenadier) Infantry, and 7th Regiment, Native Infantry, to attend the lecture room for similar instruction.

A sepoy of the name of Peturn Singh of the 2nd Regiment, Native (Grenadier) Infantry, stated his objections to the process. I immediately called upon him in the presence of the other men to explain his reason; he was quiet and respectful in his manner. He said that individually he had no objection; but that on rejoining, the men of his regiment would consider that he had forfeited caste if he put the cartridge to his mouth. I replied that he had not *then* been required to bite the cartridge. I gave him the option to obey my orders and take his place amongst the other men at cartridge-making or I should not allow him to join his section at instruction, and should punish him for disobedience. My order was of course immediately attended to, and thus to the extent of cartridge-making no difficulty exists.

4. This sudden and very unexpected participation in a feeling which I had heard existed elsewhere has induced me to make further enquiry, and in venturing to offer the following suggestion, I trust that I may not be suspected of inclining to favor a groundless caprice, or yielding in the smallest degree to an unwarrantable spirit of opposition on the part of the Native soldier. Amongst the men of this depot there never has been the least tendency to insubordination; my orders have on every occasion been implicitly obeyed, and even in the instance now brought to the notice of the Major-General there was not a symptom of disrespect nor unsoldierlike remonstrance.

5. The question with which I now venture to trouble Major General J. B. Hearsey, and further to solicit a reference to His Excellency the Commander-in-Chief, is whether the existing regulation for loading the firelock or rifle musket may not, with increase of efficiency and advantage to the service, be slightly modified.

6. Permit me to quote the regulation as it now stands—The firelock being at the word *"Prepare to load"* placed on the ground six inches in front of the body, and held at the full extent of the left arm, the recruit receives the order *"Load"*, upon which the regulation says –

   "1st–Bring the cartridge to the mouth, holding it between the fore-finger and thumb with the ball in the hand, and bite off the top; elbow close to the body."

7. The above regulation is at present in force; but I would submit that the practice of biting the cartridge is a mere remnant of the platoon exercise introduced in the days of the flint and steel firelock, when the musket being brought to the right side with the left hand, for the purpose of priming, it was almost impossible to use the cartridge without the aid of the teeth. However, as the system was of long standing, and no objection could be pointed out to the materials employed, beyond an absurd dislike to the new quality of cartridge paper, I very naturally enquired why they should not adhere to the old established practice. If I may trust the statement of the native officers belonging to this depot, it would appear that, notwithstanding the existence of the rule, it has been always more or less evaded throughout the service. The form of biting the cartridge has been duly observed, but the practice has been to tear it immediately afterwards with the left hand.

8. The truth of this statement will doubtless be disputed by most commandants and adjutants of regiments. I give the information as it has reached me; and with every deference to my superiors in rank, I would respectfully observe that it is quite as probable as it is practicable.

9. Having thus entered upon the present state of feeling with regard to biting the cartridge, and having ventured to point out the peculiar character of the existing regulation, I beg permission to bring to the notice of Major-General J. B. Hearsey a plan whereby all difficulty may be accommodated, and the same end attained in a manner more military and (under certain physical difficulties) more effectual.

10. I would suggest that at the third motion of the order *"Prepare to load"*, the left hand, instead of holding the musket at the full extent of the arm, should, after placing it on the ground in front of the body, slip up and seize the rifle at the brass band or tip to the stock. It will then be in a position to meet the right hand, which conveys the cartridge from the pouch, to tear off the cartridge paper in place of using the teeth, and (at the fourth motion of the word *"load,"* when the right hand seizes the head of the ramrod) to return to the centre part of the stock ready to throw up the firelock into the *capping position* at the sixth command of the platoon exercise.

11. The above suggestion I offer with every deference to the judgment of superior experience. I do not in the least intend to consult the caprice of the native soldier. My motive is an *increase of efficiency,* and I venture to believe that if Major-General J. B. Hearsey will be pleased to forward my letter with his recommendation to His Excellency the Commander-in-Chief, the plan proposed will be found to contain all that is desirable in the process of loading either the Enfield rifle or common firelock.

12. In conclusion, to return to the state of feeling upon this question at the Dum Dum School of Musketry, I beg that I may be favoured with such instructions as the Major-General may deem best suited to the occasion.

13. I do not anticipate any positive refusal to bite the cartridge in the first instance; but I am prepared to find that the Hindu sepoys will as above described go through the *form* only, adopting at the same time their old practice.

14. I can either tacitly overlook this pending the decision of authority, or I am prepared to obey the orders of the Major-General and enforce the due observance of the regulation. In the latter case I may possibly have prisoners for disobedience of orders.

From Major-General, J. B. HEARSEY, C.B., *Commanding the Presidency Division, to Colonel* C. CHESTER, *Adjutant-General of the Army—No. 11, dated Headquarters, Presidency Division, Barrackpore, 6th March 1857.*

I beg that you will do me the honor to submit to His Excellency the Commander-in-Chief the accompanying copies of letters as per margin, which I yesterday forwarded to Colonel Birch, for the information and orders of the Right Hon'ble the Governor-General of India in Council.

1. **Letter No. 96, dated 5th March 1857, from the Major-General Commanding the Division, to the Secretary to the Government of India in the Military Department.**
2. **Letter, dated 2nd March 1857, from Major J. Bontein, Commanding Musketry Depot at Dum Dum, to the Assistant Adjutant-General, Presidency Division.**

Demi-official from Lieutenant-Colonel W. ST. L. MITCHELL, *commanding the 19th Regiment, Native Infantry, Berhampore, to Major* A. H. ROSS, *Assistant Adjutant-General, Barrackpore—dated Berhampore, 16th February 1857.*

I received your letter of the 13th February 1857 yesterday; by the same post I received a letter from Colonel Birch, Military Secretary to Government, dated Council Chamber, Fort William, 13th February 1857, informing me that a *'kossid'* had been sent to my regiment from some men in the 2nd Regiment, Native (Grenadier) Infantry, at Barrackpore, requesting the men of my regiment to support them in raising a disturbance.

This morning early I went to the lines of my regiment and made private enquires of the sergeant-major, the subadar-major and the drill-havildar, each separately, and they declared positively in the presence of my adjutant that no *kossid'* had arrived in the lines; if any kossid had arrived and tried to create a bad feeling towards Government in the minds of the men of my regiment, they would certainly have heard of it and reported the circumstance to me. At eleven o'clock this day I assembled all the Native commissioned and non-commissioned officers (pay and color havildars) of my regiment at the mess-house, and mentioned them as to what reports they had heard regarding the Enfield rifle and ammunition about to be served out to the Bengal Army: the subadar-major replied that the report was that the cartridges about to be served out to the army were made up with cows' and pigs' fat, so that when the sepoys bit off the end of the cartridges they would lose caste.

I asked all present if they believed such a report they said they did not believe that Government would serve out anything with cows and pigs fat to Hindu and Mussulman soldiers, as both were contrary to their religious prejudices. There has not been the slightest appearance of uneasiness in the minds of the men of the 19th Regiment, Native Infantry. About a fortnight ago a Brahmin pay-havildar, a man of good character, and in whom I have great confidence, said to me—"What is this story everybody is talking about that Government intends making the native army use cows' and pigs' fat with the ammunition for their new rifles?"

I asked him if he believed there was any truth in the report; he replied he could not believe it. I assured him he might set his mind at rest on the subject, for if the men of the regiment had any doubts on the subject, I would apply to the Major-General Commanding the Division to allow the pay-havildars of companies to provide any grease that was required for their companies, so that the men of the regiment might see what grease they used and how it was prepared. This conversation was circulated through the regiment, and nothing more was thought of it.

If any *'kossid'* was sent from Barrackpore, whatever message he may have brought has had no effect upon the men of my regiment.

I have desired the native commissioned and non-commissioned officers of my regiment to report to me without delay any rumours connected with the army that may reach the regiment from any quarter. At the close of this meeting I had paras 6, 7, 8, and 9 of section 9 of the Standing Orders for the Native Infantry read and explained to all present.

I have now been nearly sixteen months in command of the 19th Regiment, Native Infantry, and I consider the men as a body are quiet, orderly and obedient, and some of the native officers very superior to the generality of native officers; I mean they are well educated men for their rank in life.

If anything occurs here to make me change my opinion I will immediately report the same to you for the information of the Major-General Commanding the Division.

From Major-General J. B. HEARSEY, C.B., *Commanding the Presidency Division, to Colonel* R.J.H. BIRCH, C.B., *Secretary to the Government of India, in the Military Department, Fort William—dated Barrackpore, 21st February 1857.*

I deem it my duty to forward the accompanying letters to be laid before the Governor-General of India in Council, being very desirous that every matter connected with the ill-feeling or discontent of the sepoys of the Barrackpore brigade should be laid before Government.

It is evident to me that having failed in the first attempt, a second is being or is about to be made on the men to induce them to misbehave.

Who the authors are I can only suspect, but my suspicion leads to the followers of the King of Oudh.

From Major-General J.B. HEARSEY, C.B., *Commanding the Presidency Division, to Major* W.A.J. MAYHEW, *Deputy Adjutant-General of the Army, Calcutta—No. 85, dated Barrackpore, 1st March 1857.*

I have the honor to forward, for submission to Government, the enclosed demi-official letter from Lieutenant-Colonel Mitchell, Commanding the 19th Regiment, Native Infantry, dated the 27th ultimo, reporting the mutinous conduct of that battalion on the night of the 26th idem, and the measures which he consequently adopted for the restoration of order and discipline.

2. I have directed Lieutenant-Colonel Mitchell by this day's *dâk* to exert his utmost endeavours to discover the ringleaders of this disgraceful outbreak, and particularly whether the party of the 34th Regiment, Native Infantry, alluded to were the originators of such.

3. I have despatched a copy of Lieutenant-Colonel Mitchell's letter to Army Headquarters for the information of His Excellency the Commander-in-Chief.

Demi-official from Lieutenant-Colonel W. St. L. MITCHELL, *Commanding the 19th Regiment Native Infantry, to Major* A. H. ROSS, *Assistant Adjutant-General, Barrackpore—dated Berhampore, 27th February 1857.*

On the 25th a detachment of European invalids, under the command of Lieutenant Ferris, Her Majesty's 29th Regiment, arrived at this station bringing with them a guard of one havildar, one naick, and twelve sepoys of the 34th Regiment, Native Infantry, which was relieved the same day by a guard of the same strength from my regiment. The havildar's party of the 34th Regiment, Native Infantry are encamped on the left of our lines, about a hundred yards. Yesterday I ordered a parade for this morning for exercise, each man to be served with fifteen rounds of blank ammunition. It is the custom in this regiment to serve out the copper caps to the men in the afternoon and the blank cartridges in the morning; the men refused the caps saying there was a doubt how the cartridges were prepared; this information was given to me by my adjutant between seven and eight o'clock.

I went down with him to the lines, and called up all the native commissioned officers in front of the quarter-guard and explained to them that the cartridges about to be served out in the morning were cartridges made up by the 7th Regiment Native Infantry upwards of a year ago, and that they had better tell the men of their companies, that those who refused to obey the orders of their officers were liable to the severest punishment. The native officers said they would speak to the men of their companies, and they had no doubt everything would pass off quietly. I ordered a general parade in the morning of all the troops in the station. Between ten and eleven o'clock at night, as I was about to sleep, I heard the sound of drums and a shout from the direction of the lines.

I dressed immediately, went over to my adjutant's quarters, and directed him to assemble all the officers at my quarters quietly. I then went to Captain Alexander and directed him to bring his cavalry as soon as possible into cantonments, and to be ready at some distance on the right of our lines. I then went to the artillery lines and got the detachment of artillery, guns, and ammunition, ready for immediate action. I must explain that by the time I got to the adjutant's quarters the drill-havildar of the regiment was making his way to the adjutant's quarters. I asked what the disturbance was in the lines; he said the regiment had broken open the bells-of-arms and had forcibly taken possession of their arms and ammunition, and that they had loaded their muskets. As soon as I got the cavalry and artillery ready, I marched down with the officers of the regiment to the lines. I found the men in undress formed in line and shouting. Some voices among them called out—"Do not come on, the men will fire."

I loaded the two guns with grape, dismounted some of the troopers, and marched down on the men (leaving the guns within range behind). I called a bugler, sounded the officers' call, on which the native officers and a number of men surrounded us, and I asked them the meaning of all this disturbance. The native officers made all kinds of excuses, begging that I would not be violent with the men. I then addressed the men and asked them what they had to complain of. I told them that I had explained to the native officers some days ago that if grease was required to be used for the new cartridges I would apply to the Major-General Commanding the Division to allow the pay-havildars of companies to make up what was required for their companies; the men said they were never told so by the native officers.

I told the officers they must immediately call upon their men to lay down their arms; the native officers told me the men would not do so in the presence of the guns and cavalry, but if I would withdraw them they would go off quietly to their lines. This was about three o'clock in the morning. I ordered a parade at sunrise, and retired, sending the cavalry to their lines and guns to the magazine. This morning at sunrise I went to the parade; the regiment turned out as usual.

I inspected the arms and examined the pouches; several of the men had not their ten rounds of ammunition in pouch, some had nine rounds and a bullet with the mark of the screw in it, as if a charge had been drawn.

The parade this morning was quiet and orderly; after inspection I had the Articles of War read to the men; saluted the colours; and dismissed the parade. I have ordered an European Court of Inquiry to assemble at the mess-house at eleven o'clock, the proceedings of which I will forward without any delay to you. It is 9 a.m. I have just returned from parade. All is quiet. I must close, as the *dâk* is going out.

P.S.—I will detain the guard of the 34th Regiment, Native Infantry, until I hear from you. On second thoughts I countermanded the general parade, and had only the parade of my own regiment.

From Major-General J. B. HEARSEY, C.B., *Commanding the Presidency Division, to Major* W. A. J. MAYHEW, *Deputy Adjutant-General of the Army, Calcutta—No. 86, dated Barrackpore, 2nd March 1857.*

In continuation of my letter of yesterday's date, No. 85, I have the honor to forward another demi-official communication in original on the same subject, dated the 28th ultimo, from the Officer Commanding the 19th Regiment, Native Infantry, at Berhampore, which I request may be at once submitted for the information of Government through the Military Secretary.

2. A copy of Lieutenant-Colonel Michell's letter will be transmitted to His Excellency the Commander-in-Chief by this day's *dâk*.

Demi-official from Lieutenant-Colonel W. St. L. MITHCELL, *Commanding the 19th Regiment, Native Infantry, to Major* A. H. ROSS, *Assistant Adjutant-General, Barrackpore—dated Berhampore, 28th February 1857.*

Yesterday, after my letter to your address was despatched, a Court of Inquiry was assembled at the mess-house at eleven o'clock, the proceedings of which will be continued to-day, and these proceedings will, in all probability, elucidate the whole matter.

Yesterday evening the adjutant reported to me that the men, instead of sleeping in their lines, had assembled for the purpose of sleeping by the bells-of-arms; they were however quite orderly, and made no noise, but appeared to dislike leaving their arms. I did not think it right to do anything further last night than order a parade this morning. I formed a hollow square, had out the four senior sepoys from each company, and asked them their objections to the cartridges; they said that they were doubtful about their being greased. I opened cartridges of all sorts, service and blank, left us by the 7th Regiment, Native Infantry, and some balled practice lately received from Calcutta.

I burnt them before the men, but as amongst the blank cartridges there were some made with a more highly glazed paper, they accepted the other paper as all right but mistrusted the glazed; they said they would be satisfied if both papers equally stood the test of water; of course the unglazed paper took up water readily, and they expressed their opinion the other was greased. I enclose the two different sorts of paper; one of each kind has been wetted and one not. I told the men that I would not allow them to seize the kotes, and that if they did it to-night, I would put a section of each company on duty over the kotes with double sentries. I write to you in a demi-official form for the information of the Major-General Commanding. When the proceedings of the Court of Inquiry are closed, I will then send you a statement of the whole business. I have kept a copy of this letter. I don't enter it into the letter book, as the contents would soon be spread over the lines. I had not time to take a copy of my letter to you yesterday, but will thank you to send me a copy at your leisure.

Telegram from Captain S.H. BECHER, *Assistant Adjutant-General of the Army, to Major* W. A. J. MAYHEW, *Deputy Adjutant-General of the Army—dated Roorkee, 10th March 1857.*

Your letter No. 140, with enclosure. Received also from Major-General J.B. Hearsey copy of Colonel Mitchell's letter; dated 28th February, to Major A.H. Ross. The Commander-in-Chief thinks the Government may already have issued instructions about the 19th Regiment, Native Infantry, so inform Government and state His Excellency recommends removal of this corps as soon as possible by land to Dinapore, and the 8th Regiment, Native Infantry, to be sent to Barrackpore by water, but not to start until 19th Regiment, Native Infantry, has quitted the station. In the possible event of 19th Regiment, Native Infantry, refusing to march, a European force must (the Commander-in-Chief observes) be sent from Dinapore, and this station reinforced from the provinces. If Government approves, this measure will of course be carried out direct from Calcutta. A reply by telegraph to Meerut requested.

From Major-General J. B. HEARSEY, C.B., *Commanding the Presidency Division, to Colonel* R. J. H. BIRCH, C.B. *Secretary to the Government of India, in the Military Department, Fort William—No. 94, dated Barrackpore, 5th March 1857.*

I have the honor to forward herewith a letter, in original, dated the 2nd instant, with two enclosures, from the Officer Commanding the 19th Regiment, Native Infantry, at Berhampore, which I beg you will do me the favor to submit for the information of Government.

2. This despatch only reached me an hour ago, and as there is no time to take a copy for transmission to Army Headquarters, I request that you will oblige me by causing this to be done hereafter, if considered by you to be desirable.

3. I send this by a special messenger.

From Lieutenant-Colonel W. ST. L. MITCHELL, *Commanding the 19th Regiment, Native Infantry, to Major* A. H. ROSS, *Assistant Adjutant-General, Barrackpore—dated Berhampore, 2nd March 1857.*

Enclosed I have the honor to send you a petition from the men of my regiment to the Major-General Commanding the Division. You will observe that what has now occurred has been owing to rumours they have heard during the last two or three months. The European Court of Inquiry is still sitting, and I hope their proceedings will explain the whole of this mystery.

TRANSLATION of the petition from the native commissioned and non-commissioned officers and sepoys of the 19th Regiment, Native Infantry, to Major-General J. B. HEARSEY, C.B., *Commanding the Presidency Division.*

Hitherto this regiment has been always obedient in every way, and marched and halted whenever ordered without question of any sort. For the last two months or more it has been rumoured that new cartridges have been made in the magazine at Calcutta on the paper of which bullocks' or pigs' fat was spread, and that it was the intention of Government to coerce the men to bite them. On this account we are very much afraid on the score of our religion. The colonel, on hearing this, assembled the native officers and told them that on arrival of the new muskets he would make such arrangements as would satisfy them, that is to say, that such grease as was necessary should be prepared before the sepoys by the pay-havildars of companies. With this we were perfectly satisfied.

After some time, some fresh stores arrived from Calcutta, and on the 26th of this month we received orders, on the following day to fire fifteen rounds of blank cartridge per man. At four o'clock in the afternoon the cartridges were received at bells-of-arms and inspected by us. We perceived them to be of two kinds, and one sort appeared to be different from that formerly served out. Hence we doubted whether these might not be the cartridges which had arrived from Calcutta, as we had made none ourselves, and were convinced that they were greased. On this account, and through religious scruples, we refused to take the caps. At half-past seven o'clock the colonel accompanied by the adjutant came upon parade, and very angrily gave orders to us, saying—"If you will not take the cartridges, I will take you Burma, where, through hardship, you will all die. These cartridges are those left behind by the 7th Regiment, Native Infantry, and I will serve them out to-morrow morning by the hands of the officers commanding companies." He gave this order so angrily that we were convinced that the cartridges were greased, otherwise he would not have spoken so.

The same night, about a quarter to eleven, shouts of various kinds were heard; some said there is a fire, others that they were surrendered by Europeans; some said that the guns had arrived, others that the cavalry had appeared. In the midst of this row the alarm sounded on a drum, then from fear of our lives the greater number seized their arms from the kotes.

Between twelve and one o'clock, the 11th Regiment, Irregular Cavalry, and the guns with torches arrived on the parade with the commanding officer, which still more confirmed our suspicions of the cartridges being greased, inasmuch as the commanding officer appeared to be about to carry his threats into execution by force. We had been hearing of this sort of thing for the last two months or more, and here appeared to be the realization of it. On this the colonel called all the native officers and said to them very angrily—"This is a very bad business; we don't fear to die, and will die here." Then the native officers in the most respectful manner represented to him—"The sepoys are fools, whereas you have sense and judgement. Do not a this time speak so angrily, for this is a matter affecting their religion, and that is no slight thing. Please to send the artillery and cavalry away." The colonel agreed to this, and sent each officer with his native officer to his company to soothe and explain to the men.

The sepoys represented that all men value their religion, and we believe we shall lose caste by biting these cartridges, and on seeing the artillery and cavalry we became more frightened. The officers then said to the men—"We will ask the colonel to send away the cavalry and guns," which was accordingly done. At the same time, however, the colonel said—"I will have a general parade in the morning, when I will have Governor-General's orders read out." On this the native officers again represented to him that only a short portion of the night remained, and if he had the cavalry and guns there so soon again the men would only believe that they were intended to act against them. It would be better if he only paraded the regiment alone. At first he would not agree to this, but on its again being represented to him by the adjutant, he agreed to it. The men then lodged their arms and went to their lines.

They all appeared on parade on the following morning. On the 28th again, according to orders, there was another parade, at which the cartridges which the men had refused to fire were inspected, when assuredly two kinds of cartridges were found,—one kind of white thin paper, and the other darker and thicker. On burning and submerging the two, the difference still was evident, which did not remove the distrust. The colonel put up specimens of each kind of paper, and has sent them to you. From that time onwards all duties have been properly carried on, and so shall be as long as we live. We will faithfully obey all orders. Wherever in the field of battle we are ordered to go, there shall we be found.

Therefore, with every respect we now petition that since this is a religious question, from which arose our dread, and as religion is, by the order of God, the first thing, we petition that as we have done formerly we may be now also allowed to make up our own cartridges, and we will obey whatever orders may be given to us; and we will ever pray for you.

From Major-General J.B. HEARSEY, C.B., *Commanding the Presidency Division to Colonel* R.J.H. BIRCH, C.B., *Secretary to the Government of India, in the Military Department—dated Barrackpore, 7th March 1857.*

I have the honor to forward the Proceedings of a European Court of Inquiry held at Berhampore, by order of Lieutenant-Colonel Mitchell, in regard to the mutinous conduct of the 19th Regiment, Native Infantry, which has already been reported by me to Government.

As the whole of the circumstances regarding this outbreak are fully detailed in it I do not think it requires me (unless I am called upon to do so) to offer any further opinion on this most untoward occurrence.

From Lieutenant I. F. MACANDREW, *Adjutant, 19th Regiment, Native Infantry, to Captain* W. C. ALEXANDER, *Commanding the 11th Irregular Cavalry—No. 51, dated Station Staff Office, Berhampore, 27th February 1857.*

I have honor to inform you, by direction of Lieutenant-Colonel Mitchell, commanding the station, that the Court of Inquiry, of which you are appointed President, is assembled for the purpose of investigating the cause and origin of the men of the 19th Regiment, Native Infantry, having broken open their bells-of-arms and seized their arms last night. You are authorised to summon such witnesses as you may require.

PROCEEDINGS of an European Court of Inquiry held at Berhampore, on the 27th day of February 1857, by order of Lieutenant-Colonel W. St. L. MITCHELL, *Commanding the 19th Regiment, Native Infantry, for the purpose of investigating such matter as may be laid before it.*

PRESIDENT :

Captain W.C. ALEXANDER, *11th Regiment, Irregular Cavalry.*

MEMBERS :

Captain J. B. Y. MATHESON, *52nd Regiment, Native Infantry.*

Captain E. H. C. WINTLE, *61st Regiment, Native Infantry.*

INTERPRETER :

Lieutenant J. VALLINGS, *19th Regiment, Native Infantry.*

Pursuant to Station Orders of this date, the Court assembled at 11 a.m. at the mess-house of the 19th Regiment, Native Infantry.

President, Members, and Interpreter all present.

Letter No. 51, from the Station Staff Officer, is produced and annexed to the Proceedings.

1st Witness.

Lieutenant Issac Forsyth MacAndrew, Adjutant, 19th Regiment, Native Infantry, is called into Court, and states–

Last night, about seven o'clock, a report was made to me by the sergeant-major and drill-havildar that the men of the regiment had refused to take the caps served out to them, in accordance with regimental custom, the evening before a parade for firing blank ammunition, the cartridges being served out in the morning. I immediately went to the colonel, and reported their refusal. He took me with him to the quarter-guard of the regiment, and sent for the native officers, to whom he explained that the objections of the sepoys to take the cartridges were groundless; inasmuch as these cartridges were not of a new construction, but the same as had been served to the army for years, and were made up in the regimental magazine by the sepoys of the 7th Regiment, Native Infantry.

The colonel further told the native officers that he would parade the regiment in the morning, and that the officers of companies should serve the cartridges out to the men upon the parade, according to the roll of the company; and that the first man who refused to take the cartridges should be tried by a court-martial. We then went home, and the colonel directed me to send an order to Captain W. C. Alexander, Commanding the 11th Regiment, Irregular Cavalry, to have his regiment on the parade of the 19th Regiment, Native Infantry, at six o'clock in the morning; he also directed me to bring down the post guns at the same time. About twelve o'clock, I was awoke by the colonel and havildar-major informing me that the men had broken open the bells-of-arms, seized their muskets, and were making a great noise in the lines.

The colonel directed me to assemble all the officers at his quarters, and to get out the guns immediately prepared for service. When this was done, we all went with the guns down to the parade and halted about two hundred and fifty yards in front of the sergeant-major's bungalow, and found the 11th Regiment, Irregular Cavalry, drawn up at some distance on the right of the parade. The colonel directed me to tell Captain Alexander to move up his regiment close to the guns; at this time the men were in a state of great excitement, shouting loudly. The colonel then directed me to go to the quarter-guard and sound for the Native officers to assemble in front. The drum was beat twice in my presence to call them, and I sent two sepoys of the guard for the same purpose. When I heard some of the native officers answer across the tank that they were coming, I returned to the colonel to report it.

When I approached the guard I was challenged in the usual manner some distance to the right and to the front by a man in Hindustani clothes with belt and musket. I answered to his challenge "officer," and he called out to the guard: "He is the adjutant". I went up to the guard without any further-challenge, except from the sentry there. The guard was perfectly steady, and received me as usual with shouldered arms and a drummer without hesitation obeyed my order to sound for the native officers.

The native officer in command of the guard informed me that the men in the lines had loaded, and would fire upon me if I crossed that way. When I returned to the colonel I reported this, and he ordered the guns to be loaded with grape. He then told me to remain there, and not to allow the artillery or cavalry to advance until he returned. He went towards the men, and on his return I went down to them. They offered no violence whatever, but evinced great mistrust of the cartridges, and declared they would not surrender their arms until the artillery and cavalry were removed. This was eventually done, and they lodged their arms and were quiet for the rest of the night.

This morning at seven o'clock they turned out for parade, and were orderly and obedient. Their pouches were inspected, and such as were deficient in the number of cartridges they ought to have had were marked for future proceedings. After the parade was dismissed, and I was the only officer left upon parade, the subadar-major reported to me that the men were at the kotes, and would not go to the lines; and sure enough the companies were standing there. I proceeded at once to my own company, and sent to call the colonel. In reaching my own company, I ordered them to lodge their arms at once and to their lines. They obeyed, and the others followed their example. By the time the colonel reached the parade again, they had gone. I then went home.

Question: What was the cause of the men turning out ?

Answer: When I went down among them they told me that the reason was that the artillery and cavalry was sent for, and they thought that they would be attacked.

2nd Witness

Brevet-Captain L.R. Newhouse, 19th Regiment, Native Infantry, is called into Court, and states as follows—

About a quarter-past seven in the evening of the 26th, the orderly-havildar of my company informed me that the men would not receive their caps. I told the man to go away, and that I would see about it in the morning. And as I was officer of the day, the native officer of the day reported to me that the men would not take their caps. I then told him to go and report the matter to the adjutant and commanding officer.

Question: Did either the orderly-havildar or native officer of the day give any reason for the men not taking the caps?

Answer: The orderly-havildar said that the men refused to take the caps in the evening because they were afraid of losing them.

Question: What induced you to go down to the lines to report the circumstance to the colonel of the men refusing to take their caps?

Answer: Being orderly officer, I considered it my duty to report it, and for that purpose went to his quarters. Being told that he had gone to the lines with the adjutant, I went there too, thinking the matter was something serious.

Question: Did the native officer of the day report to you that the men had broken open the kotes and seized their muskets, and did he give any reason for their doing so?

Answer: Yes, he did report that the kotes had been broken open and the muskets taken out ; but I am not exactly certain what reason he gave for their doing so.

Question: Did you at any time hear the cause of their forcibly taking the muskets, out of the kotes?

Answer: Yes. When I went to my own company to try and persuade the men to give up their arms, they refused to do so, saying that they had taken them out to defend themselves against the cavalry, which had been ordered down. Upon this I called for the subadar of the company; but the men replied with a laugh that he had been away, and had been absent since ten o'clock in the day. I remember no one in particular saying so, except Jhoolun Singh, pay-havildar. The men also said that the subadar had sent away his family and traps.

3rd Witness

Sergeant-Major John Frawley, 19th Regiment, Native Infantry, is called into Court, and questioned as follows—

Question: When did you first hear that the men of your regiment were dissatisfied ?

Answer : Yesterday evening, the 26th, after I had dismissed the evening drill, the pay-havildars of companies came to me and made me the usual reports at evening roll-call. Three of them did not come up with the others, viz., Hussen Khan of No. 5 Company, Thackoor Sing of No. 7, and Kaleechurn of No. 8. Hussen Khan came up the first of these three, as I was going to my bungalow. I asked him why he had not come up with the other havildars. He replied that he went to see if the caps had been served out, and that he found that they had not. I asked him the reason why they were not.

He told me that the men refused to take them, as they had some doubts about the cartridges. I asked him if any other companies had refused. He said he did not know but thought they had also refused. I then called all the orderly-havildars, who came up. I asked them one by one whether their companies had refused to take the caps. They all, with the exception of No. 5 orderly-havildar, replied that the men had said they would do all alike. No. 5 orderly-havildar distinctly said that they refused to take them.

Both the subadar-major and havildar-major were present, as also the drill-naick. I told the subadar-major to look after the regiment, as he was not in uniform, and explain to the regiment that there were no blank cartridges in the magazine from Calcutta, the only blank cartridges were those made over by the 7th Regiment, Native Infantry, which regiment we relieved here, and that I would go and report the circumstances to the adjutant, which I did.

Question: After your return to the lines, did anything further occur ?

Answer: Yes; after the drum-major and orderly-havildars had left after making the reports at eight o'clock roll-call, the drum-major returned immediately, and told me that he had heard that a number of men, supposed to be of the light company, got into the tank on the left front of the lines and vowed that if any man was taken out of the tank in the morning that they would rescue him. I sent the drum-major to acquaint the adjutant, as I could not then leave the lines considering the state the regiment was in.

Between ten and eleven o'clock, as I was lying awake in my bed, I heard a rush made on the bells-of-arms with shouting by the men of the regiment, the doors of which were forced open, the arms and accoutrements taken out and carried to the lines. I got up immediately, and went to see what it was all about. Shortly after this, the havildar-major came up and reported what had taken place. I directed him to report the matter immediately to the adjutant, and also sent Rampersad, sepoy of No. 3 Company and drill-instructor, who also came up with him.

As far as I can remember, between twelve and one o'clock the 11th Regiment, Irregular Cavalry, came up. When the regiment arrived, the men on discovering it rushed out of the lines shouting, and assembled near the kotes. I left my bungalow and went to the cavalry for protection. I remained there until Lieutenant-Colonel Mitchell and the officers of the regiment arrived. All the officers went to the lines, and the colonel left me in charge of the guns.

I beg further to state that on one occasion I was warned to leave, and on another not to approach my bungalow.

Question: Do you know why the men broke open the kotes and seized the arms?

Answer: No; I cannot give any reason, except that they most probably expected to be attacked by the cavalry and artillery. Had there been any other reason they would have waited till the morning, when they could have had their arms without forcing the kotes.

The Court adjourned at 4 p.m.

Saturday, 28th February 1857.

The Court re-assembled this day at eleven o'clock.

4th Witness

Shaik Kureem Bux, subadar, No. 4 Company, 19th Regiment, Native Infantry, is called into Court, and states as follows—

On the evening of the 26th after sunset roll-call, the orderly-havildar of my company reported to me that all was correct. I then went to my house. In less than half an hour after this the kote-havildar and orderly-havildar came and told me that the men would not take their percussion caps. I asked the reason why. They said that it was rumoured amongst the men that the cartridges were suspicious, and that they said "We will not lose caste by taking them". The subadar-major then summoned all the native officers at his house, and said to them you must try and settle this matter at eight o'clock roll-call, and report it also at once to the officers commanding your companies.

About an hour afterwards I heard that the commanding officer had come down to the lines and had summoned the native officers to him. At this time a considerable body of men had assembled around the colonel, who was very angry. I did not hear all that he said; but I heard him say that they must take the cartridges, otherwise they would be sent to China and Burma, where they would all die; "and recollect that I will have a parade to-morrow morning, and have the cartridges served out to you by the officers of companies, and those that refuse to take them will be imprisoned or transported". He also said the objections you make to the cartridges are perfectly groundless, as they are all ones which we received from the 7th Regiment, Native Infantry. The colonel then went to his house.

At eight o'clock roll-call I explained to my company what the colonel had said. No one made a reply to this. So I then went to my house. I doubted at the time whether they believed me. About a quarter to eleven o'clock, I heard a great noise in the lines. The orderly-havildar reported me that the men of my company and of all the rest had taken their arms and accoutrements from the kotes. I went to the men, whom I found with their arms and belts on. I asked them what was the meaning of it. Some said that Europeans were coming to kill them, others said the artillery was coming, and others the cavalry. I found I could do nothing with them, so I returned to my house and told the orderly-havildar to go and report it to the officer commanding the company.

The orderly-havildar said "The officer will be asleep". I said—"That does not signify; you must wake him up and report it". He went and did so. I remained in my house. After twelve o'clock I heard the colonel was on parade through the orderly-havildar—who said—"Be quick, the colonel has called for all the native officers". I went to him and found the artillery and cavalry were on the parade. The colonel ordered us to separate our companies from the others and call the roll. The European officers were also present, and each tried to assemble his company. Lieutenant Macdonald, in charge of my company, tried also, but without effect. All the native officers then went to the colonel. He was very angry. I said to him—"Don't be angry now, as it is of no use. Excuse the men now, as they are ignorant men. Kindly send the cavalry and artillery away, and everything will be settled in the morning". The colonel consented, but said he will have a parade of all the troops, I again begged of him to refrain from having the cavalry and artillery there; he at first refused, saying—"I command all the troops, and can assemble them when I choose." I did not think it proper to further urge him, so said nothing more. The colonel then went away.

I was, however, afraid of the consequences, as so short a time would intervene should this order be carried into effect, so spoke to the adjutant and quartermaster, and begged of them to ask the colonel not to have the artillery and cavalry on parade, as the men would be still suspicious of being forced. The adjutant then rode after the colonel, and returning shortly said the colonel has consented to have the regiment parade alone. We then all went to the lines. In the morning, the regiment was assembled on the parade at the appointed hour; the muskets and pouches were examined, and the name of those written down who had not the proper number of cartridges, or whose cartridges were broken. After this the parade was dismissed. At sunset roll-call I warned the men to be careful for the future about what they did, or else it would be the worse for them. They replied that they were in fear of their lives, and wished to keep their muskets by them or sleep by the kotes. I said—"You can do as you please, but I must report it".

At eight o'clock roll-call I went to the kotes, and found some men there sitting or lying down. I cannot say whether they had their arms or not. I told the orderly-havildar to go and report it to the officer commanding the company. I then returned to my house and slept. I was awoke by the orderly-havildar, who said—" It is the officer's orders that you go and sleep by the kote also". I told my servant to take my bed there, and went myself. A private inspection of companies had been ordered for the morning, but I was then told that there was to be a parade under the colonel, when he would arrange the cartridge business. In the morning, at parade, the colonel sent to the magazine for some of all the different kinds of cartridges, and called forward four men from each company, before whom he explained where the different kinds had come from and burnt some of the paper in which the cartridges were, to let them see if there was any smell.

Some of the men said, of the cartridges served out the paper was of two kinds, whence our suspicions. The colonel sent for these cartridges from the kotes, and said there is no difference in them. Some of the men said one paper is thicker than the other; if you will put them in water, one will soak up water more rapidly than the other. The colonel then sent for some water and immersed the paper in it, when the thinner paper soaked immediately, the thicker, on which there is "size", did not soak up the water so readily. The colonel then said to the subadar-major—"Keep this by you, and at half-past eight o'clock bring it to me. I will pack it up and send it to the General for his inspection through the post office."

Question: When the men, on the night of 26th, seized their muskets, did they assign any reason for so doing?

Answer: Yes; they said it was rumoured amongst them that Europeans were coming, and others, and that they were prepared to die rather than lose caste, and they did it to defend themselves.

Question: Have you any idea what caused the sepoys to think that the cartridges contained anything that might affect their caste?

Answer: It was first talked about after the arrival of a guard of sepoys from Calcutta escorting Government stallions, and afterwards another party of the 34th Regiment, Native Infantry, who came with European invalids, confirmed the doubts in the minds of the men, and then, the last cartridges that were about to be issued having in each bundle one or two cartridges made with paper of a different kind, led the men to suppose that there was some foundation for the report. The men had also made up their blank ammunition in every other instance themselves, and they knew that a short time before ammunition for the regiment had arrived from Calcutta.

The Court adjourned at 4 p.m.

Monday, 2nd March 1857.

The Court re-assembled this day at eleven o'clock.

5th Witness

Doolum Sing, naick, pay-havildar, Light Company, 19th Regiment, Native Infantry, is called into Court, and states—

After sunset roll-call, when the men were about to be dismissed, they asked me to petition the subadar-major that they might not have the cartridges served out to them, as they had doubts about them. He spoke to them about it, and told the orderly-havildar to report it to the sergeant-major. Later in the evening, I heard that the colonel and the adjutant had come down to the lines and summoned the native officers, when he told them that at the parade for the morning he would have the cartridges distributed by the officers of companies, and the men should be made to bite them. At a quarter to eleven o'clock, the locks of the bells-of-arms were broken, and the arms taken out by the sepoys. About twelve o'clock I was in my hut, when I heard Brevet-Captain Newhouse, commanding my company, had called for me. I went to him at the bells-of-arms; he asked me where the subadar was. I said he is probably in his hut. Then Gobind Tewary, sepoy, and others said he is taking away his family and property to the village behind the lines. When Brevet-Captain Newhouse ordered them to lodge their arms in the kote, they did so.

Question: What do you suppose was the object of the men in breaking open the kotes and seizing their arms?

Answer: Because they were apprehensive of danger, and were afraid of losing their caste by being made to take the cartridges.

Question: Have you any idea what caused the sepoys to think that the cartridges contained any thing that might affect their caste?

Answer: There have been reports flying about for the last two months, probably brought from Calcutta by travellers and command parties from Barrackpore.

6th Witness

Bijoo Sing, havildar-major, 19th Regiment, Native Infantry, is called into Court, and states—

About 11 a.m., of the 26th, at orderly hours, I received orders from the adjutant that there would be a parade on the morrow with fifteen rounds of blank ammunition. I asked whether all the companies were to have alike. He said "Yes". I then went to the lines, and at the sergeant-major's bungalow the orderly-havildars were informed of the order, which they promulgated in their respective companies. At sunset, the orderly-havildar of No. 5 Company reported to me that the sepoys would not take the percussion caps; after him the orderly-havildar of No. 7 Company reported the same, as also of the light company.

The sergeant-major then summoned all the orderly-havildars, and inquired of them what the matter was. They said, the sepoys say,—"Why should we take the caps, as we won't take the cartridges until the doubt about them is cleared up". I then went with the sergeant-major to the adjutant's quarters and reported it. He then went to the colonel's and ordered us to the lines. I heard, about half-past seven, when in the lines, that the colonel and adjutant were in the quarter-guard, and had summoned the native officers and havildars. I went there too.

The colonel enquired why they would not obey orders and take the cartridges. The subadar-major said they suspect that the paper of the cartridges is greased with pigs' and bullocks' fat. The colonel said—"There is no cause for suspicion; these cartridges were left here by the regiment we relieved". The subadar-major said—"The sepoys are suspicious, and will not believe what we say." The colonel said—"Leave them alone now, and in the morning I will have them distributed by the officers of companies," upon which he went away and we returned to the lines. After eight o'clock roll-call the men went away to their huts. About half-past ten a sepoy awoke me. By this time the kotes had been broken open. I went to the adjutant and reported it.

Question: What was the cause of the sepoys breaking open the kotes and arming themselves on the night of 26th?

Answer: There was a rumour that the cavalry were about to seize the kotes.

Question: What reason had the sepoys to suppose that there was anything objectionable in the cartridges?

Answer: I do not know.

The Court adjourned at 4 p.m.

Tuesday, 3rd March 1857.

The Court re-assembled this day at 11 a.m.

7th Witness

Beharee Sing, jemadar, 6th Company, 19th Regiment, Native Infantry, is called into Court, and states—

I was on duty at the quarter-guard on the night of the 26th, about 10-45 p.m. I was asleep, and awakened by a cry of "fire", on which I ordered the alarm to be sounded. I looked about, but could see no signs of fire. The noise increased, and I heard that the kotes were being broken open. I ordered the guard to look after the treasure and colors. The men after seizing their muskets went to their huts. The men of my guard all remained steady. The subadar-major, Subadar Kureem Bux, Subadar Mahomed Ali, and Jemadar Davee

Sing came and asked me why I had sounded the drum. I replied—"Because I heard shouts of fire".

Question: What was the cause of men breaking open the kotes?

Answer: I do not know.

8th Witness

Drum-Major James Renny is called into Court, and states—

After tattoo roll-call on the night of 26th, I went with all the orderly-havildars to make the usual report to the sergeant-major. On returning to the band lines, Heeraloll and Peter Christian and several other band boys asked me if I had seen anything. I said—"What?" They replied—"The whole of the light company and part of No. 8 Company went into the tank and took oath about something or other". I sent and reported this directly to the sergeant-major. As he had no one else to send, I volunteered to go and report to the adjutant, which I did, and then returned to the lines. About eleven o'clock, the men, with a shout that Europeans were coming, rushed on the kotes, broke them open, and seized their arms.

I assembled the band boys and drummers, and called the roll. They were all present. I sent them to the lines, telling them not to move out of them. I then went to the sergeant-major, and remained with him until the cavalry arrived upon which he joined them, and I took away his family and put them under the protection of the Nizamut guard. I then returned to the sergeant-major's bungalow. The sentry who was on duty there, whom I believe to be a nephew of the drill-naick, Dulput Sing, then said to me—"It was well that you all got away in time, as a great mob came here and searched for the sergeant-major and his family, and not finding them they broke open the pound of which he was in charge, and let all the cattle go. They even searched the pound for him".

I then went by the rear of the lines to my own house to put on my uniform. A few minutes afterwards I was called to the front, with the buglers, where the colonel was. The reason the men gave for objecting to the cartridges was that they had heard that there was bullocks' fat mixed with them.

9th Witness

Subsook Sing, jemadar, Light Company, 19th Regiment, Native Infantry, is called into Court, and states –

I was the native officer of the day on the 26th and about 6-30 p.m. it was reported to me by the orderly-havildars of each company that the sepoys had refused to receive their percussion caps. By order of the sergeant-major I went to report this to the adjutant, but not finding him, I went to the colonel's, who also was out. I then reported it to the officer of the day, Brevet-Captain Newhouse. We proceeded to the colonel's, but heard that he had gone to the lines.

I then went to the lines, and hearing they had returned, proceeded again to the adjutant's house. His servants told me he was at mess. I there found him, and made the report. At ten o'clock I went the rounds according to orders; the men at that time were all quiet. I returned to my house; about a quarter to eleven o'clock an alarm of fire was made. A sentry came and told me that the men had rushed towards the kotes. I hastily put on my uniform, and going towards the kotes, found the men had broken the locks and armed themselves. I went immediately and reported this to the colonel and the adjutant.

Question: What was the cause of the men breaking open the bells-of-arms?

Answer: I do not know.

Question: What was the reason of their refusing to take the caps ?

Answer: I went up with the other native officers to the mess, where I heard the subadar-major say that there was a rumour of bullocks' and pigs' fat being mixed with the cartridges.

10th Witness

Heeraloll, sepoy-musician, Grenadier Company, 19th Regiment, Native Infantry, is called into Court, and states—

After attending evening roll-call on the 26th, I went to my hut, and was there copying music. I heard a great noise at the tank. The drum-major came to me and said—"There are a number of men in the tank; are they taking any oath?" I replied—"They may be. I know nothing more about it".

11th Witness

Peter Christian, drummer, No. 2 Company, 19th Regiment, Native Infantry, is called into Court, and states—

After eight o'clock roll-call I heard a great noise, and on asking the other bandsmen what it was, they said that the sepoys had gone into the tank and had taken an oath, the nature of which I know not.

12th Witness

Shaik Muden Bux, tindal, 19th Regiment, Native Infantry, is called into Court, and states—

At 3 p.m. on the 26th February, I received an order to serve out fifteen rounds of blank ammunition per man to the regiment. I distributed them to the lance naicks about half-past four, and then went to my house. About half-past ten o'clock, when asleep, I was awakened by a loud noise, and heard people shouting —"Where is the tindal; bring him here; he has got the keys of the magazine." Upon this I fled out of the lines, taking the keys with me. At day break I returned.

Question: Previous to the outbreak, did you know anything about it; or had you ever been interrogated about the cartridges by the men?

Answer: No, nor was I ever questioned on the matter.

The Court adjourned at 4 p.m.

From Lieutenant-Colonel W. St. L. MITCHELL, *Commanding the 19th Regiment, Native Infantry, to Major-General* J. B. HEARSEY, C.B.,*Commanding the Presidency Division—dated Berhampore, 3rd March 1857.*

I have the honor to acknowledge the receipt of your letter of the 1st March 1857 this afternoon.

I will detain the guard of the 34th Regiment, Native Infantry, until further orders, and I will have them examined by the Court of Inquiry.

I have just read the Proceedings of the Court of Inquiry up to this date, and one of the witnesses, and subadar of my regiment, said that this uneasy feeling in the 19th Regiment, Native Infantry, originated in the information received from the guard who arrived here a short time ago, escorting Government stallions towards Buxar. This feeling was confirmed on the arrival of the guard of 34th Regiment, Native Infantry, with the European convalescents.

I heard that on Thursday, the 26th February, Friday, and Saturday, the men of the regiment fasted, taking only bhang and other exciting drugs. On Sunday I had a private interview at my quarters with a Brahmin havildar of the regiment, who asked me if I would forward a petition from the regiment to you. I replied, certainly, if there were no disrespectful terms used, and it contained a fair statement of what had occurred in the regiment and what their wishes were. I trust you have received this petition; all they ask is to be allowed to make their own cartridges and prepare the grease for them. The men are behaving very well since; they take their usual meals and perform their duties cheerfully. As far as any man can judge, the men seem in a state of alarm at what the consequences of their acts may be, but I think nothing will make them alter their opinions about the cartridges and grease. The mischievous reports spread abroad affect Hindus, Mahomedans, and Sikhs equally.

I have parades every morning, and the men are as steady and orderly as any men can be. I will continue this daily, as it brings the officers and men together, and I think will establish confidence. I have given Sergeant-Major Frawley thirty days' leave of absence, so as to keep him out of the way, as there was evidently a bad feeling towards him on the part of the men, and I think it would be as well if he was to be removed to another regiment as sergeant-major.

This appearing in G.O.s without any application for an exchange on the part of the sergeant-major, would prevent any feeling of victory on the part of the men. When the Proceedings of the Court of Inquiry reach you, you will see the necessity for the removal of the sergeant-major ; there is nothing against him ; he is a good drill, and a man of most exemplary character, perfectly steady and trustworthy, but he seems to be just now so unpopular with the men, that I thought it best that he should go away for a time.

From Lieutenant-Colonel W. ST. L. MITCHELL, *Commanding the 19th Regiment, Native Infantry, to Major* A. H. ROSS, *Assistant Adjutant-General, Barrackpore— dated Berhampore, 8th March 1857.*

All is quiet here, and the duties carried on cheerfully.

To-morrow the Court of Inquiry will re-assemble at eleven o'clock, and I hope further evidence may be obtained.

There are several inaccuracies in the evidence before the Court of Inquiry which can be explained; but there is a statement in the evidence of the fifth witness, Doolum Sing, naick, pay-havildar, Light Company, which I must contradict at once, as I never said anything of the kind. He says—

"He (meaning me) would have the cartridges distributed by the officers of companies, and the men should be *made to bite them*".

It is quite contrary to my principle to hurt the religious feelings of any man. I never made use of such a speech.

P.S. – Has the petition from the men of the regiment been received? Oblige me with an answer to this question.

From Lieutenant-Colonel W. ST. L. MITCHELL, *Commanding the 19th Regiment, Native Infantry, to Major* A. H. ROSS, *Assistant Adjutant-General, Barrackpore—No. 60 dated Berhampore, 11th March 1857.*

I have the honor to enclose, for the information of the Major-General Commanding the Division, the first and second days' Proceedings of the re-assembled Court of Inquiry. A duplicate copy will be sent by to-morrow's post.

PROCEEDINGS in continuation of an European Court of Inquiry re-assembled by order of Lieutenant-Colonel W. ST. L. MITCHELL, *Commanding the 19th Regiment, Native Infantry, to investigate such matter as may be laid before it by the Station Staff Officer—dated Berhampore, 9th March 1857.*

President, Members, and Interpreter all present.

Letter No. 58, from the Station Staff Officer, is read and attached to the Proceedings.

13th Witness

Subadar-Major Shaikh Murad Bux, Light Company, 19th Regiment, Native Infantry, is called into Court, and states—

On the 26th, at twelve o'clock or thereabouts, I heard from the orderly-havildar of the company that at the morning's parade fifteen rounds of blank cartridge were to be fired per man. About four o'clock the lance-naicks brought the cartridges from the magazine to the kotes.

After sunset roll-call I went towards my house, when the orderly-havildar came up and said to me the men want to make a petition. On enquiring of them, they said—"We are doubtful about these cartridges, and will not take them or fire them". I argued with the men, trying to explain away their doubts, saying "The rumours about the cartridges are merely about those for the new guns, these are old ones". They answered " These are of two kinds, and that one lately came from Calcutta is most likely, as stores have come. Besides, we have always been in the habit of making up our own blank cartridges, and we have made none up here".

On this I ordered some cartridges out of the kotes, and taking up a bundle I opened it and said to them there is no cause for doubt here. On this, I ordered the cartridges to be replaced in the kotes, and went and reported this to the sergeant-major. The orderly-havildars of each company were there, and made the same report respecting each company. The sergeant-major then said these cartridges are what we received from the 7th Regiment, Native Infantry, on our arrival here; only powder in barrels arrived from Calcutta. I asked the sergeant-major who should report this to the adjutant, and he said that: "The havildar-major and I will go and report it; you had better go and try and explain it to the sepoys of your companies".

I then assembled all the native officers at my quarters, and said to them at eight o'clock roll-call you must explain to your several companies that these cartridges were left behind by the 7th Regiment, Native Infantry, and that there can be no doubt about them, and that it behoves them to fire them. At half-past seven, the colonel and adjutant came to the quarter-guard and summoned the native officers there. The colonel asked us what were the doubts about the cartridges. I replied that the sepoys said: "There are two kinds of cartridges, and we have hitherto always made up our own, besides, only a few days ago some stores arrived from Calcutta, and on account of reports going about we have doubts on the subject". Upon this the colonel got very angry, and said "If the sepoys will not take their cartridges, I will take them to Rangoon or China, where they will suffer many privations and all die".

He also said at parade in the morning—"I will have the cartridges distributed by the officers commanding each company, and those who refuse to take their cartridges I will severely punish them. These are old cartridges received from the 7th Regiment, Native Infantry, and you must all explain this to the men". The colonel then went away, and I told the other native officers—"You have heard the colonel's orders, and must explain them to the men at eight o'clock". I explained it at eight o'clock roll-call to the men of my company, who heard it in silence and went away. At a quarter to eleven o'clock the orderly-havildar of my company, Alluf Khan, awoke me, and said there is a great noise. I asked him—"What noise?" He said "the men are all running towards the kotes". I then heard the drum sound.

I went out towards the kotes, and on arriving there saw some of the men armed, others arming. I asked them what they were doing, but no one gave me a reply. I then went towards the quarter-guard and saw that the other companies had done the same. I met some other native officers at the kotes, *viz.*, Subadar Shaik Kurreem Buksh, Jemadar Shaik Mohamed Ali, and Jemadar Davee Sing, and these went with me to the quarter-guard. Kurreem Buksh asked Jemadar Beharee Sing, the native officer on duty at the quarter-guard, why the drum was sounded. He said—" I heard a great uproar, some saying there was fire, some that there were Europeans coming, some that the artillery was coming, and others that the cavalry were. I then sounded the drum".

I told the Jemadar Behari Sing—"I am now going to report this. Should the colonel or adjutant come and ask for me, you will tell them where I have gone to." I then went to make the report along with the havildar, Shaik Bheekah,

No. 4 Company, who I picked up by the way. I could not find the adjutant, who had left his house, so I went to the colonel's. He also was out; so I returned to the lines in company with Alluf Khan, havildar, and Hoolass Misser, havildar, whom I met at Brevet-Captain Newhouse's bungalow. Between twelve and one o'clock I was standing at the end of the lines of No. 3 Company, when I saw lights approaching on the parade. It was very dark at this time. Shortly after this the drum sounded the native officers' call.

I went to the front with the others, and met the colonel on the road leading to the parade. The colonel said " What is this business?" and kept advancing. We prayed him not do so, but rather to retire a little; that the men were ignorant and stupid. He was excessively angry, and said "I will blow them away though I die myself". We prayed him to show clemency, and send away the guns and cavalry. On this the colonel went and spoke to the European officers, and sent them away shortly afterwards. The officers then went up to the men and began to speak to them. Shortly afterwards the colonel said to us—"I send away the cavalry and guns now, but to-morrow morning, at sunrise, I will have a general parade." We petitioned him not do so, as the men would imagine that the guns and cavalry would be used against them and they might not be obedient.

The colonel at first did not consent; but afterwards, when spoken to by the adjutant, he agreed to have the regiment paraded alone, and the orders were so issued. In the morning there was a parade, when the arms were examined as well as the pouches. Some men had not all their cartridges, and others had them broken. I wish to state that I had forgotten to say before that when the colonel declared he would have a general parade in the morning, he at the same time said that the Governor-General's orders should be read out. The parade was quietly dismissed. That same evening, after tattoo roll-call, the men went at first to their lines, but afterwards they brought out their bedding and slept at the kotes. I asked them the reason of their sleeping there, and they said —"We are afraid that the artillery and cavalry may come down on us again."

This was immediately reported and four old sepoys taken out of each company and called to the front. Orders came to the lines for a parade in the morning. At this parade the cartridges were brought out and four old sepoys taken out of each company and called to the front. When the cartridges were brought out from the kotes they were shown to these sepoys, who were asked what their objections were. They said that in each bundle there were two descriptions of cartridge, to one of which they objected, as it was made of darker paper. Both the sorts were tried both by fire and water, but a difference was manifest in both tests. The colonel then took specimens of both kinds, and having sealed them up before me sent them off to the General. After this there was an order received for the men to send in a petition to the General.

This was drawn up by delegates from the companies, and brought up to the adjutant. On the night of the 1st March some four or five sepoys in each company rushed up to the kotes, and again took out their arms, but replaced them on being ordered by the native officers. Since then all has been quiet.

BY THE COURT

Question: What are the rumours alluded to in your evidence concerning the cartridges for the new muskets ?

Answer: That they were made with the fat of pigs and bullocks.

Question: When did you first hear these rumours?

Answer: About two months ago.

Question: From whom did these rumours come?

Answer: I don't know.

Question: Since these rumours were first afloat, have your heard of anything having been received in the lines leading to confirm the rumours in the minds of the men?

Answer: No; I am not aware of any such thing.

Question: Do you think that the sepoys could hold a punchayet in the lines without the knowledge of the native officers?

Answer: No, I do not.

Question: Have there been any such meetings in the lines?

Answer: No; not that I am aware of.

Question: Do you know whether the men of your company took any oath on the night of the 26th?

Answer: No; I can swear I know nothing of it.

Question: Is not the standing in water up to the middle when taking an oath a means of making it more solemn and binding among Hindus?

Answer: Yes; especially if the water is that of the Ganges.

Question - Do not the men count the tanks in front of the lines as Ganges water, in consequence of the river water passing through them in the rains?

Answer: I do not know exactly, but some men of my company who had money transactions with a certain bunniah took their oaths to him in the river.

The Court here remarks that the river is a mile from the lines, and the tanks close to.

Question: Are you aware whether the guard of the 34th Regiment, Native Infantry, who have been lately here, have been saying anything about these rumours you speak of in the lines?

Answer: I do not know of any. On one occasion I asked the havildar of the guard now here if he had ever said anything or knew anything about it. He took his oath that he knew nothing at all about it.

Question: Are you aware that immediately previous to this outbreak on the 26th, the recruits had been in the habit of firing these blank cartridges?

Answer: Yes; the fact is that the rumours and the simultaneous arrival of stores from Calcutta filled the men's heads with these ideas. Had no stores arrived from Calcutta, they would have fired them at once.

Question: What in your opinion, do the men wish with regard to the cartridges, both now and for ever, and both for balled and blank so that their caste shall be in no danger?

Answer: I think the men will be perfectly satisfied if the cartridges are made up in the regiment, both balled and blank, and the grease required by the companies for the new rifles be supplied by the kote havildars. I do not think that the men would be satisfied now with any balled cartridge for the new rifle that came from the arsenal or a magazine.

The witness withdraws.

8th Witness recalled

Drum-Major James Renny, 19th Regiment, Native Infantry, is recalled into Court, and examined as follows—

BY THE COURT

Question: Did you see the men with your own eyes go into the tank to take an oath?

Answer: No, I did not.

Question: State exactly what you heard about it.

Answer: I was told first by Heeraloll and afterwards by Peter Christian that the light company and part of No. 8 Company had gone into the tank and taken an oath. I asked—"What about?" They told me that they did not know.

Question: Did they say that they saw the men go into the tank?

Answer: Yes.

Question: Have you observed the men previously to the 26th February congregating or discussing among themselves so as to attract your notice?

Answer: No.

Question: Have you heard anything since the 26th with reference to the cartridge question?

Answer: I have heard the men constantly saying that they do not want to lose their caste. Nothing else.

Question: Do you think that the men at this time have the same opinions about the cartridge that they had at first?

Answer: No; I do not think that they have. They seem to me to be conscious of having done wrong, and I think that they do not doubt so much as formerly.

The witness withdraws.

The Court adjourns at 4 p.m.

5th Witness recalled

Doolum Sing, naick, pay-havildar, Light Company, 19th Regiment, Native Infantry, is called into Court, and examined as follows—

BY THE COURT

Question: Since when have you heard any rumours about the cartridges?

Answer: About two months or two-months-and-a-half.

Question: What was the nature of the rumours?

Answer: That the cartridges were composed of the fat of bullocks, pigs, and jackasses.

Question: From what time did a suspicion of this become fixed in the minds of the sepoys?

Answer: From the date of the arrival of the stores from Calcutta.

Question: Why did you not report this to the captain of your company?

Answer: I was not aware till the outbreak that the doubt was so fixed in the men's minds, though I have since found out that it was an established fact from the time of the arrival of the stores.

Question: Are you aware that the recruits fired the cartridges just before the outbreak?

Answer: Yes.

Question: Have you heard the sepoys saying anything about that?

Answer: No, I have not.

Question: Have you ever heard anything from any of the command parties concerning these reasons, or have you heard that anything has been heard in the lines emanating from them?

Answer: No, I have not.

Question: Could the sepoys hold a regimental punchayet without the knowledge of the native officers and non-commissioned officers?

Answer: A few men could do so, but the regiment could not.

Question: Do you know of any such punchayet having been held?

Answer: No, I do not.

Question: Are you aware whether your company took any oath in the tank on the night of the 26th?

Answer: No.

Question: Have you heard anything about this since?

Answer: About eleven o'clock, on the 27th, some men who had been up to the captain's quarters, on their return, told me that Brevet-Captain Newhouse had asked them about it, as it had been reported by a drummer that they had done so. They denied it altogether.

Question: Were you in your house from the time the colonel came on parade in the evening until the outbreak?

Answer: I was there or thereabouts.

Question: How far is your hut from the tank on the left?

Answer: Some forty or fifty paces.

Question: Could the company have gone into the tank and taken an oath at the time alleged without your knowledge?

Answer: No.

Question: Do you think, if the sepoys had not known of the arrival of these stores from Calcutta, they would have fired the cartridges?

Answer: I cannot say.

Question: What, in your opinion, do the sepoys wish, so that they may dismiss all fears on the score of their caste from their minds, and yet use their ammunition?

Answer: I have no doubts myself, and am ready to as ordered, but I cannot answer for others.

The witness withdraws.

11th Witness recalled

Peter Christian, drummer, 19th Regiment, Native Infantry, is recalled into Court and examined as follows—

BY THE COURT

Question: Did you see the men of the light company go into the tank and take an oath on the night of the 26th?

Answer: No, I did not see them.

Question: Who told you, then?

Answer: I cannot say. I heard some of the band boys saying so, but I do not know who. I heard a noise from the water myself, and asked what it was, and was answered that it was the light company taking an oath. I don't know who told me that.

Question: Where were you when these men told you this?

Answer: At Munnyram's door.

Question: Does any one live with Munnyram?

Answer: Yes, his two sons,—Chooneelall and Kullian,—both band boys.

Question: Must a person standing at Munmnyram's door have seen the men go into the tank?

Answer: Yes.

Question: Did you see them from there?

Answer: No; they had gone out of the tank before I got there.

Question: Did you see them at all?

Answer: Yes, I saw them immediately afterwards at roll-call.

Question: Had any of the men wet clothes on them?

Answer: I did not see.

The witness withdraws.

The Court cross-examined this witness in every way it could think of, but found it impossible to elicit an answer.

14th Witness

Lieutenant James Vallings, Interpreter and Quartermaster, 19th Regiment, Native Infantry, being in Court, is asked—

BY THE COURT

Question: When did the last stores arrive from Calcutta?

Answer: On the 11th February, at four in the afternoon, I went down to the magazine, and had the things all opened before me. The sergeant-major was there, as there was a good deal to do in removing the stores from the carts and counting them. I asked several sepoys who were collected about looking on to come and help. They did not do so, but all left immediately. One man only assisted.

Question: Did you enquire anything about the reason of their going?

Answer: No; at the time it did not strike me as being a matter of any consequence. The sergeant-major said if you had wanted these men you should have obtained a fatigue party.

The witness resumes his seat in Court.

15th Witness

Munnyram, drummer, 19th Regiment, Native Infantry, is called into Court, and examined as follows—

BY THE COURT

Question- Did you see the men of the light company go into the tank on the left of the lines and take an oath on the night of the 26th February?

Answer: No, I did not.

Question: How far is your house from the tank on the left?

Answer: About forty paces.

Question: Where were you just before tattoo?

Answer: In my house.

Question: At that time, did you hear anything from the direction of the tank?

Answer: No.

Question: Did you see Peter Christian on that night?

Answer: No, I did not.

The witness withdraws.

The Court has interrogated this man in every possible way, and failed to elicit any answer from him at all bearing on the question of the oath in the tank.

16th Witness

Shaik Madar Buksh, sepoy, No. 4 Company, 19th Regiment, Native Infantry, is called into Court and examined as follows—

BY THE COURT

Question: On the 26th February, when the uproar took place, were you on duty at the sergeant-major's bungalow?

Answer: Yes, I was sentry there.

Question: Did you see the drum-major on that night?

Answer: No.

Question: Did any sepoys approach the bungalow?

Answer: No.

Question: When did you go on sentry duty?

Answer: At ten o'clock I was placed on sentry, and at twelve I was relieved.

Question: How long before your relief did the uproar break out?

Answer: It commenced about eleven.

The witness withdraws.

The Court remarks that from the manner of this witness he appears to have been intimidated.

The Court adjourns at 4 p.m.

From Lieutenant I. F. MACANDREW, *Adjutant, 19th Regiment, Native Infantry, to Captain* W. C. ALEXANDER, *Commanding the 11th Regiment, Irregular Cavalry, President, Court of Inquiry—No. 58, dated Station Staff Office, Berhampore, 9th March 1857.*

I am directed by Lieutenant-Colonel Mitchell, Commanding the Station, to inform you that the Court of Inquiry, of which you are president, is directed to re-assemble for the purpose of making a more searching enquiry into the circumstances attending the late outbreak in the 19th Regiment, Native Infantry, and to endeavour to find out the cause, origin, and progress of the uneasiness and mistrust which the men seem to have against the cartridges. You are directed to enquire into whatever has or may arise in the course of this investigation likely to throw any light upon the business or on the conduct of any one concerned therein.

From Lieutenant-Colonel W. St. L. MITCHELL, *Commanding the 19th Regiment, Native Infantry, to Major* A. H. ROSS, *Assistant Adjutant-General, Barrackpore—dated Berhampore, 11th March 1857.*

There are several mis-statements in the evidence taken before the Court of Inquiry, and I am anxious to point them out to the Major-General, as otherwise he might take my silence as acquiescence in the truth of these imputations.

First - The fourth witness, Subadar Shaik Kureem Bux, states that when I went to the quarter-guard, between 7 and 8 p.m., I told the native officers and others assembled there that the cartridges "should be served out by the officers of companies in the morning, and that those who refused to take them would be imprisoned or transported."

Secondly - From the evidence of the subadar-major and others, the Major -General might be led to suppose that I had ordered up the cavalry (distant fully three miles) and the artillery before the men took possession of their arms and accoutrements by force. Whereas I was in bed at the time, and though our lines are distant from my quarters, I heard the shout of the men—the alarm sounded on the drum. I dressed and went to the adjutant's quarters, from thence I went to Captain Alexander's house and ordered him to bring down the cavalry.

I then went to the artillery lines, roused the artillerymen, and took them with me to the magazine to get the guns. I sent two orderlies to bring the bullocks from the commissariat sheds, all which took an hour or an hour-and-a-half to effect. I have already in a former letter denied that I ever said I would make the men "bite their cartridges", as stated on hearsay by Doolum Singh, naick, the fifth witness.

The duplicate of this letter I will send you with the duplicate proceedings by to-morrow's post.

From Major-General J. B. HEARSEY, C.B., *Commanding the Presidency Division, to Colonel* R. J. H. BIRCH, C.B., *Secretary to the Government of India, in the Military Department—No. 124, dated Headquarters, Presidency Division, Barrackpore, 18th March 1857.*

I have the honor to forward, for submission to Government, the accompanying Proceedings of a Special Court of Inquiry in continuation, held at Berhampore on the 13th instant.

PROCEEDINGS in continuation of a European Court of Inquiry re-assembled by order of Lieutenant-Colonel W. ST. L. MITCHELL, *Commanding the 19th Regiment, Native Infantry, to investigate such matter as may be laid before it by the Station Staff Officer—dated Berhampore, 12th March 1857.*

President, Members, and Interpreter all present.

The Court assembled at the mess-house of the 19th Regiment, Native Infantry, at eleven o'clock.

Letter No. 58, from the Station Staff Officer, is laid on the table.

17th Witness

Hunoomunt Misser, sepoy, No. 5 Company, 19th Regiment, Native Infantry, is called into Court and examined as follows—

Question: Were you on duty as sentry at the sergeant-major's bungalow on the 26th February?

Answer: Yes; I was sentry there from twelve o'clock at night till two in the morning.

Question: Did you see the drum-major?

Answer: Yes.

Question: What passed between the drum-major and yourself?

Answer: Nothing at all. About quarter of an hour after I was put on sentry the resalah arrived. I called the sergeant-major and told him. He came out of his house, and the drum-major with him.

Question: Did any sepoys approach the bungalow?

Answer: Not while I was on sentry.

Question: Did you see the sergeant-major's family?

Answer: Yes.

Question: Where were they?

Answer: In the bungalow.

The witness withdraws.

18th Witness

Subadar Amarun Sing, No. 8 Company, 19th Regiment, Native Infantry, is called into Court and examined as follows—

Question: When did you first hear of the doubts about the new cartridges about to be issued to the army?

Answer: A long time ago, before the colonel first called us together. The colonel asked us if we had heard any such reports and what they were. The subadar-major answered that we had heard that the fat of bullocks and pigs were in the new cartridges. The colonel said that he would see that when the new muskets were served out, for which certainly some grease or oil was required, that what was necessary should be prepared by the pay-havildars of companies.

Question: Can the regiment hold a punchyayet, that is, the sepoys, without the knowledge of the native officers and non-commissioned officers?

Answer: I do not think they can.

Question: Has such a punchayet been held about this business?

Answer: No.

Question: Since these doubts first arose, or rather since these rumours were first heard, has anything been heard in the lines tending to confirm them?

Answer: Not that I know of.

Question: Have you any doubts about the cartridges?

Answer: No, I have not.

Question: Do you think the sepoys still mistrust the cartridges?

Answer: Yes, I do.

Question: What, in your opinion, is required so that the sepoys shall not fear on account of their caste, and yet do their duty by firing their muskets?

Answer: If the men made their own cartridges, they would be satisfied.

The witness withdraws.

19th Witness

Jemadar Lalla Dokehore, Grenadier Company, 19th Regiment, Native Infantry, is called into Court and examined as follows—

Question: When did you first hear any rumours about the cartridges?

Answer: About two months ago.

Question: What was the nature of the rumours?

Answer: That there was the fat of pigs and bullocks on the paper of which the cartridges were made.

Question: Were they any tidings received in the lines leading to confirm these rumours in the minds of the sepoys?

Answer: I don't exactly know, but the men were making inquiries about it on all sides after the colonel's speech to the native officers at the mess-house.

Question: Do you think the sepoys could hold a punchayet so as to arrange such an outbreak as took place on the 26th February without the knowledge of the native officers?

Answer: Yes, I do. Of course if the whole corps turned out it would be known but it might be arranged in a small punchayet without the knowledge of any one else, and spread through the regiment by agency.

Question: Do you know of any such punchayets having been held?

Answer: No.

Question: Are you aware whether any sepoys took an oath in a tank on the night of the 26th February?

Answer: No.

Question: Have the guards of the 34th Regiment, Native Infantry, been saying anything about these rumours in the lines of the regiment?

Answer: I never heard them myself, but I have heard from the sepoys that these men as they came here were talking about it.

Question: Do you know what they said?

Answer: They said that there were doubts about the cartridges at Barrackpore.

Question: Of what cartridges did these doubts arise?

Answer: Of the cartridges of the new rifles. When the stores, however, arrived from Calcutta they doubted them also.

Question: When did you first hear that they had doubts about the stores which came from Calcutta?

Answer: On the night of the outbreak.

Question: Did you hear anything about this when the stores arrived from Calcutta?

Answer: I did not.

Question: Do you think that the sepoys' doubts are now as strong as formerly?

Answer: No, I do not; they repent of what they did.

Question: What, in your opinion, would completely remove the doubts of the sepoys with regard to the cartridges?

Answer: That they should be allowed to make them themselves.

Question: What in your opinion was the cause of the outbreak on the night of the 26th February?

Answer: The men feared that they would be attacked by the artillery and cavalry.

Question: Before the outbreak, did you hear that the artillery was coming?

Answer: No, I did not.

Question: Do you know if any person or company in particular took the lead in this business?

Answer: No, I do not.

The witness withdraws.

20th Witness

Gungabissun Chowbey, subadar, No. 3 Company, 19th Regiment, Native Infantry, is called into Court and examined as follows—

Question: When did you first hear these rumours about the cartridges?

Answer: About a month or a month-and-a-half ago.

Question: What was the nature of the rumours?

Answer: That cartridges were made at Calcutta with the fat of pigs and bullocks.

Question: Was there any news received in the lines leading to confirm these rumours in the minds of the sepoys?

Answer: No, not that I know of.

Question: Do you know if there were doubts on the arrival of stores from Calcutta?

Answer: No one said so at the time, but when the outbreak took place they said that it was from the stores from Calcutta.

Question: How was it that the recruits fired those same cartridges?

Answer: Up to the time of the stores arriving from Calcutta they had no doubts about the blank cartridges; but on the night of the outbreak the idea got abroad that the blank cartridges had also come from Calcutta, and this suspicion was confirmed in the minds of the men by two kinds of paper being found in the bundle of cartridges.

Question: Do you think the sepoys could hold a punchayet, such as to get up an outbreak of this sort, without the knowledge of the native officers and non-commissioned officers?

Answer: Yes, I do.

Question: Has there been any such punchayet?

Answer: Not in my company.

Question: Do you think the outbreak took place from causes that occurred that day or night, or that it was a pre-arranged affair?

Answer: From causes that occurred that night.

Question: What in your opinion would remove all the scruples of the sepoys, and yet cause them cheerfully to their duty by the Government and fire their muskets?

Answer: That they should be allowed to make their cartridges themselves; as for the present blank cartridges if the ones of which they expressed a doubt on parade were destroyed, they would have no doubts about the others.

Question: Are the sepoys' doubts now as strong as formerly?

Answer: No, they are not.

The witness withdraws.

21st Witness

Jemadar Adjoodeah Persaud, No. 1 Company, 19th Regiment, Native Infantry, is called into Court and examined as follows—

Question: When did you first hear these rumours about the cartridges?

Answer: About twenty days before the outbreak.

Question: What was the nature of the rumours?

Answer: That the cartridges had in them the fat of bullocks and of pigs.

Question: Are you aware of any news having been afterwards received in the regiment subsequently tending to confirm these reports in the minds of the men?

Answer: No, I am not.

Question: Do you think that the sepoys of the regiment could assemble a punchayet, so as to get an outbreak such as that which occurred on the 26th February, without the knowledge of the native officers and non-commissioned officers?

Answer: Yes, I do.

Question: Do you know if any such punchayet was assembled?

Answer: No, I do not.

Question: Do you know that the recruits fired the cartridges the day before the outbreak?

Answer: Yes, I do.

Question: Do you know if the guards of the 34th Regiment, Native Infantry, who have lately arrived, have been saying anything about this?

Answer: I do not think exactly, but undoubtedly the guards and the artillery, who were lately relieved, have brought the news from Barrackpore.

Question: Do you think the sepoys entertain the same doubts now as formerly?

Answer: I really cannot say.

Question: In your opinion, what would remove all the doubts of the sepoys and at the same time cause them to do their duty to the State and fire their muskets?

Answer: That the men should make their own cartridges.

Question: What was the reason of the outbreak?

Answer: The only reason that I can give is that the men got an idea that the artillery and cavalry were to be brought against them.

Question: Do you know if the men took any oath on the night of the 26th February?

Answer: No, I do not.

The witness withdraws.

The Court adjourns at 4 p.m.

The Court re-assembled pursuant to adjournment at 11 a.m. on the 13th instant.

President, Members, and Interpreter all present.

22nd Witness

Shaik Peer Buksh, havildar, 34th Regiment, Native Infantry, is called into Court and examined as follows—

Question: Did you come from Barrackpore with a detachment of European convalescents?

Answer: Yes.

Question: Have you ever spoken to the men of the 19th Regiment, Native Infantry, about what occurred at Barrackpore, or in any way with reference to this cartridge business?

Answer: No, I have not.

Question: Had any question been raised at Barrackpore about these cartridges before you left?

Answer: I don't know. I only came off garrison duty in Fort William on the 3rd, and was sent on command on the 9th.

Question: Where were you pitched on the night of the 26th February?

Answer: On the range for target practice of the regiment.

(The Court here remarks that the range was alongside the tank in which the sepoys of the light company are said to have taken an oath.)

Question: Did you hear any men take an oath in the tank on the night of the 26th February, or indeed go into it at all?

Answer: No, I did not.

Question: When the outbreak took place were your men all present?

Answer: Yes, they were asleep. When awakened by the noise they got up and asked what it was. I told them that it was no business of ours.

Question: At what time do you change your sentries?

Answer: At the even hours.

Question: Who was sentry from six to eight o'clock on the night of the 26th.

Answer: Sepoy Shaik Rujjub Ali.

The witness withdraws.

The Court successively called in a number of the guard of the 34th Regiment Native Infantry, and asked them if they had ever had any communication with the men of the 19th Regiment, Native Infantry, regarding the Barrackpore affair, or on the question of the cartridges. They all denied having had any such communication or knowing anything about it at all.

23rd Witness

Bhowany Deen, subadar, 3rd Company, 9th Battalion, Artillery, is called into Court and examined as follows—

Question: Before you left Dum Dum, did you hear anything of the discontent at Barrackpore among the sepoys on the subject of the cartridges? Have you ever had any conversation with the men of the 19th Regiment, Native Infantry, on this subject?

Answer: Never.

The witness withdraws.

24th Witness

Sewsahoy, pay-havildar, 3rd Company, 9th Battalion, Artillery, is called into Court and examined as follows—

Question: Before you left Dum Dum, did you hear anything of the discontent at Barrackpore among the sepoys on the subject of the cartridges?

Answer: I heard some vague reports, but paid no attention to them, and don't know what they were.

Question: Have you ever had a conversation with any of the men of the 19th Regiment, Native Infantry, on this subject?

Answer: Never.

The witness withdraws.

25th Witness

Shaik Rujjub Ali, sepoy, 34th Regiment, Native Infantry, is called into Court and examined as follows—

Question: Were you on sentry duty over your guard arms on the night of the 26th February between six and eight o'clock?

Answer: Yes.

Question: During your tour of sentry duty, did you hear any noise, especially from the direction of the tank?

Answer: No noise whatever.

Question: Have you ever had any conversation with the men of the 19th Regiment, Native Infantry, regarding cartridges?

Answer: Never.

Question: Did you hear anything about cartridges before you left Barrackpore?

Answer: No.

The witness withdraws.

The Court having no further evidence before it, adjourned at 2 p.m.

From Major-General J. B. HEARSEY, C.B., *Commanding the Presidency Division, to Colonel* R. J. H. BIRCH, C.B., *Secretary to the Government of India, in the Military Department—dated Barrackpore, 18th March 1857.*

Having received the reports from Brigadier Grant and the officers commanding regiments at this station that the native commissioned officers warned for court-martial duty at Calcutta had left this cantonment, I ordered the Brigade to parade in contiguous quarter distance columns for my inspection, and having received their salute, I addressed them and told them to call to mind what I had said to them on a former occasion, *viz.*, that men of bad character had got amongst them and were endeavouring to mislead them; that two such men in the 2nd Grenadiers had been detected at Calcutta, who had tried by lies to induce the subadar of the 34th Regiment, Native Infantry, and his guard to quit their post, but that officer was not to be deceived, and had seized and confined the two offenders, reporting to superior authority the whole circumstance the next morning, and that these two sepoys were now under trial for mutiny. I again bid them beware of such characters, who endeavour to take the bread from the mouths of good sepoys by making them the instruments of their bad designs.

I then spoke of the discontent still prevailing in regard to the cartridge paper having grease of any kind in it, and that its glossy appearance had caused this supposition. I explained to them that this shining of the paper was caused by the starch mixed with the pulp of cotton and hemp to make the paper tough and consistent, that it was to be found in all writing and fine paper made by the natives of Hindoostan. I then took a letter I received many years ago from Maharajah Golaub Sing from a gold tissue *khareeta*, and handed it successively to all the native officers and bid them open it and look at it and tell me if it was not more glossy than the cartridge paper they suspected, and to go into the ranks and show it to their men. Having done this, I asked the native officers and men if it was likely a Dogra Brahmin or Rajpoot, who so strictly protected kin, would himself write on paper that had grease in it or such nature. I then asked them if during their festivals they did not make lanterns of oiled and greased paper, and having so oiled and greased it, whether they could get the grease out of it again; nay, that if even one drop of grease fell on paper it would be spoilt, and any child could detect that part of the paper on which it had fallen. In conclusion, I told them if they did not believe me I would give them leave to visit the paper manufactory at Serampore and watch the process of making it, and they would find that alum and starch of rice or potatoes was used, which gave it the shiny appearance they had so strongly objected to.

I then said this silly view of the manufacture of paper had caused much annoyance to them, and had I not so fully explained to them on a former occasion that grease being mixed with it was a falsehood, they might have been misled by designing men; that such had unfortunately occurred in the 19th Regiment, Native Infantry, at Berhampore; that corps had "mutinied",—had turned out in a disorderly manner at 11 p.m., had broken open their bells-of-arms and had seized their muskets, belts and pouches, and would not lodge them again though repeatedly ordered to do so by their commanding officer, Colonel Mitchell. That the investigation of this disturbance had been sent to me, and that I had laid it before Government. That Government was exceedingly angry, and would, in my opinion, order me to disband the regiment. That the 19th Regiment, Native Infantry, had been ordered to march to this cantonment, and if I received orders to disband it, all the troops of this division within two marches would be assembled here to witness the disbandment, whether artillery, Europeans or cavalry, and that the ceremony of striking the name and number of the regiment (the 19th Regiment Native Infantry) from the list of army would be carried out exactly in the same manner as the old 34th Regiment, Native Infantry, was disbanded at Meerut.

I said I inform you of this beforehand, because your enemies are trying to make you believe that European troops with cavalry and artillery will be sent here suddenly to attack you; these and such lies are fabricated and rumoured amongst you to cause trouble. That no European or other troops would come to Barrackpore until ordered to do so by me and that I would give them timely intelligence of their coming here.

I finished by telling them no fault had been proved against them, then why should they dread being attacked.

But that I expected them to obey orders and keep clear of any act that could be construed into mutiny; that the officers and I myself were open to all representations made in a proper manner; that their caste and religious prejudices were safe under my protection; and that any endeavour to interfere with such would meet with most severe punishment.

I then deployed the columns, opened the ranks to double distance, and rode my horse slowly and quietly up and down them, speaking to the men wearing medals, and asking them in what actions they had earned them. The brigade was then dismissed in the usual manner to its lines.

From Major-General J. B. HEARSEY, C.B., *Commanding the Presidency Division, to Colonel* R. J. H. BIRCH, C.B., *Secretary to the Government of India, in the Military Department, Fort William—No. 126, dated Headquarters, Presidency Division, Barrackpore, 20th March 1857.*

I have the honor to forward herewith, for the information of Government, the enclosed letters in original from the Officer Commanding the 19th Regiment, Native Infantry, dated respectively the 16th and 18th current.

Demi-official from Lieutenout-Colonel W. ST. L. MUTCHELL, *Commanding the 19th Regiment, Native Infantry, to Major* A. H. ROSS, *Assistant Adjutant-General, Barrackpore—dated Barrackpore, 16th March 1857.*

All is quiet here, and everything going on as usual.

I will now leave off writing to you daily, but will re-commence should there be the least signs of uneasiness in the regiment.

Demi-official from Lieutenant-Colonel W. St. L. MITCHELL, *Commanding the 19th Regiment, Native Infantry, to Major* A. H. ROSS, *Assistant Adjutant-General, Barrackpore—dated Berhampore, 18th March 1857.*

The guard of the 34th Regiment, Native Infantry, started this morning in progress to Barrackpore.

I will leave this on Saturday morning, the 21st March, if I can get only the amount of carriage as laid down in the Military Regulations.

The Proceedings of the Court of Inquiry are closed, as the evidence is exhausted. I will now dissolve the Court. I only waited to know what the Major-General's wishes were.

I will report my departure from this station and the probable date of arrival at Barrackpore the day before I commence the march.

I had a parade this morning, and told the regiment that their petition had been laid before Government and no more.

I will return the petition to-morrow with an explanatory letter.

From Colonel R.J.H. BIRCH, C.B., *Secretary to the Government of India, in the military Department, to Major-General* J. B. HEARSEY, C.B., *Commanding the Presidency Division, Barrackpore—No. 409, dated Fort William, 14th March 1857.*

*** A Persian Petition from the 19th Native Infantry, with a translation in English. (Vide page 45.)**

instant, and to request that you will transmit them to Lieutenant-Colonel Mitchell for explanation of his conduct as affected by the statement in the petition of the men of the 9th Regiment, Native Infantry.

2. I am also desired to request that you will cause the men of the 19th Regiment, Native Infantry, to be informed that their petition has been laid before Government.

From Lieutenant-Colonel W. St. L. MITCHELL, *Commanding 19th Regiment, Native Infantry, to Major* A. H. ROSS, *Assistant Adjutant-General, Barrackpore—No. 17, dated Berhampore, 18th March 1857.*

I have the honor to acknowledge the receipt of a letter, No. 409, to Major-General J. B. Hearsey, Commanding the Presidency Division, from Colonel R. J. H. Birch, Secretary to the Government of India, Military Department, dated Council Chamber, Fort William, the 14th March 1857, and in reply I beg leave to state as follows—

The first statement in the petition in which I am mentioned is regarding the meeting at the mess-house on the 16th February. On that subject I need say nothing; the Major-General has received has received my report and approved of my proceedings.

The petition then goes on to state,— "after some time fresh stores arrived from Calcutta...". this statement is not true: the stores arrived on the 11th February, five days before the meeting at the mess-house, and subsequently none have been received.

The petition then states that I spoke angrily on parade, saying: "If you will not take the cartridges, I will take you to Burma, where, through hardship, you will all die." I certainly did not make use of the expression above quoted. I explained to the regiment that the cartridges were made by the men of the 7th Regiment, Native Infantry, and had been in store for a long time, and therefore they should be served out by the officers commanding companies. It is true I cautioned the regiment against the serious consequences which would ensue from their persisting to disobey orders in refusing to take the cartridges.

It is stated in the petition that I said: "This is a very bad business; we do don't fear to die, and will die here." I don't remember exactly the words I made use of on the occasion above referred to, but they were to the effect that "We" (the officers) "were prepared to do our duty should the men of regiment not yield obedience."

It was not until after the men of the regiment had broken into the kotes, had armed themselves, and were in a state of mutiny that I called out the artillery and cavalry.

The adjutant, who went by my orders to the quarter-guard to sound the call for the native officers, came back with a report that the native officer at the quarter-guard had warned him not to go onwards, as the men were loaded and would fire. When I arrived with the guns on parade there was much shouting on the part of the men and the rattling of ramrods in the barrels of the muskets, such a noise as is made in loading.

It is further stated in the petition that I sent away the cavalry and guns, but said that they should come to a general parade in the morning, but that, on the native officers having requested me to dispense with the presence of the artillery and cavalry, and on the representation of the adjutant, I did so. I at first thought it advisable to parade all the troops together in the morning, thinking that the presence of the cavalry and artillery would hold the 19th Regiment, Native Infantry, in check in case of any further outbreak, but subsequently on its being reported to me that three or four companies had given up their arms, and that the rest were doing so, and as I saw a disposition on the part of the men to return to obedience, and in order to restore confidence, I took away the guns and ordered off the cavalry, and all was quiet in the lines.

At first I objected to parade the 19th Regiment, Native Infantry, alone for the reasons above assigned, but on hearing from the adjutant that the native officers had told him that the men could not be divested of the idea that the other troops were to be called out to act against them, I relinquished my intention of parading all the troops in the morning, and directed that the 19th Regiment, Native Infantry, should be paraded alone, which was done, and the regiment behaved quietly, respectfully, and obediently.

I feel certain that the mutinous proceedings of the 19th Regiment, Native Infantry, on the night of 26th February, did not arise from anything that took place on parade that evening, but that the men were ripe for an outbreak, owing to communications which they had been receiving for days and weeks previously from some of their comrades in the regiments at Barrackpore.

I am sure it will be readily admitted by the Major-General that my position was a very trying and a very difficult one, and I cannot help thinking that if I had adopted measures less prompt and vigorous, lamentable results might have ensued.

From Lieutenant-Colonel W. St. L. MITCHELL, *Commanding the 19th Regiment, Native Infantry, to Major* A. H. ROSS, *Assistant Adjutant-General, Barrackpore—No. 22, dated Barrackpore, 20th March 1857.*

I have the honor to report, for the information of the Major-General Commanding the Presidency Division, that 19th Regiment Native Infantry, under my command, will commence its march to-morrow morning towards Barrackpore, agreeably to instructions received from the Deputy Quartermaster-General of the Army.

Herewith I have the honor to forward a present state.

Forwarded for the information of Colonel R. J. H. Birch, Secretary to the Government of India, Military Department.

BARRACKPORE (Sd.) J. B. HEARSEY, *Maj-Genl.,*
The 24th March 1857. *Comdg. The Presy. Divn.*

From Major-General J. B. HEARSEY, C.B., *Commanding the Presidency Division, to Colonel* R. J. H. BIRCH, C.B., *Secretary to the Government of India, in the Military Deopartment, Fort William—No. 141, dated Barrackpore, 27th March 1857.*

In forwarding, for your information, the enclosed progress report from the Officer Commanding the 19th Regiment, Native Infantry, dated the 25th instant, I have the honor to request that you will favor me as early as possible with the orders of Government regarding this regiment, as it may be expected to reach Barrackpore on the morning of the 31st current.

From Lieutenant-Colonel W. ST. L. MITCHELL, *Commanding the 19th Regiment, Native Infantry, to Major* A. H. ROSS, *Assistant Adjutant-General, Barrackpore—dated Camp Kishnagurh, 25th March 1857.*

I have the honor to report, for the information of the Major-General Commanding the Presidency Division, that the 19th Regiment, Native Infantry, under my command, has made the following movements since my last report dated Berhampore, 20th March 1857—

Dates.		Stages.		M. F.
21st March 1857	...	Burruah	... ...	11. 0
22nd March1857	...	Plassey	... ...	11. 0
23rd March 1857	...	Bickrampore	... ...	13. 2
24th March 1857	...	Buleea	... ...	11. 6
25th March 1857	...	Kishnagurh	... ...	7. 4

And that I purpose resuming my march to-morrow morning towards Barrackpore.

Herewith I have the honor to forward a present state.

From Colonel R. J. H. BIRCH, C.B., *Secretary to the Governmetn of India, Military Department, to the Secretary to the Government of Bengal—No. 884, dated Council Chamber, Fort William, 27th March 1857.*

I am directed to advise you that it is the intention of Government to disband the 19th Regiment, Native Infantry, on its arrival of Barrackpore, where the corps may be expected on or about the 31st instant.

It is very advisable that this should not be prematurely published; but the information is afforded, in order that such instructions may be issued to the several civil authorities to put police on their guard, as may be considered necessary to obviate the possible evil effect of so many discharged men being for a time at large in the neighbourhood of the presidency.

Minute on the Mutiny at Barrackpore of the 19th Regiment, Native Infantry.

The time has arrived at which it is necessary to place upon record connectedly the principal facts in the recent conduct, of the 19th Regiment, Native Infantry, at Berhampore, and the measures adopted, or about to be adopted, by the Governor-General of India in Council in consequence thereof.

On the 22nd of January last, Captain Wright, one of the officers attached to the School of Musketry at DumDum reported that a feeling of uneasiness had manifested itself amongst the sepoys regarding the ingredients used in the arsenal for greasing the cartridges of the new Enfield rifle.

Enquiry was immediately made as to the composition of the grease. The tallow used had been supplied by a contractor, and it was ascertained that no sufficient precautions had been taken in the arsenal to insure the absence from it of all matter which might be objectionable to the sepoys. Hereupon the Government, on 27th of January, authorised the officer commanding the depot to obtain from the bazar the proper ingredients, and directed that the men themselves should apply the grease to the cartridges. The cartridges to which the grease had been applied were withdrawn, and ungreased cartridges were supplied.

Nothing at this time had been said about the paper of which the new cartridges were made.

This paper is received from England. It is finer than the paper heretofore used for cartridges, is of a lighter colour, and has a glossy surface.

On the 28th January, Major-General J. B. Hearsey, Commanding the Presidency Division, reported that an ill-feeling existed amongst the troops at Barrackpore, and that sepoys believed that the new paper was greased with the fat of cows and pigs.

Some men of the 2nd Regiment, Native (Grenadier) Infantry, having raised objections to the paper, a Court of Inquiry was assembled. The men examined stated that their doubts regarding the paper were caused by its being different in appearance from that which had formerly been used; that when burnt it gave out a noise and smell as if there were grease in it; and that they objected to use it, because it was the general opinion that it was made up with grease.

The paper was sent to the Chemical Examiner for analysis. After a careful examination Dr. Macnamara reported, "The paper has not been greased or treated with any greasy or oily matters during or since its manufacture."

Major-General J. B. Hearsey explained to the troops at Barrackpore assembled on parade the cause of the glossy appearance of the paper, and that there was no grease in it; and he assured them, apparently with good effect, that there was no intention to lead them to use anything to which they could object.

It having, however, been represented that a messenger had been despatched from certain men at Barrackpore to the regiments at Dinapore and Berhampore, giving intelligence of what was doing at the first-named station, a communication was made to the officers commanding at Dinapore and Berhampore.

Lieutenant-Colonel W. St. L. Mitchell, Commanding the 19th Regiment Native Infantry, at Berhampore, replied in a letter, dated the 17th of February, that the 19th Regiment, Native Infantry, the only infantry regiment at that station, had shown no feeling of uneasiness, and that he had explained to the native officers that he would apply to the General Officer Commanding the Division to allow the pay-havildars to prepare the grease required for the new rifles.

It appears by a letter from Lieutenant-Colonel Mitchell to Major Ross that a fortnight before the above date a Brahmin pay-havildar had brought to his notice the report in circulation that the Government intended to make the native army use cows' and pigs' fat with the ammunition of the new rifles.

On the 26th February, Lieutenant-Colonel Mitchell ordered the 19th Regiment, Native Infantry, to parade the following morning for exercise with fifteen rounds of blank ammunition per man.

It has been the custom in the 19th Regiment, Native Infantry, to serve out the percussion caps over night, and to give the ammunition to the men in the morning. When the percussion caps were about to be issued, the men refused to receive them saying that there was some doubt as to how the cartridges were made. This was reported between 7 and 8 p.m. to Lieutenant-Colonel Mitchell, who immediately went to the lines, sent for the native officers, and explained that the cartridges about to be served out had been made up by the 7th Regiment, Native Infantry, about a year before. He then desired the native officers to tell their men that those who refused to obey their officers were liable to severe punishment. Lieutenant-

Colonel Mitchell says that he ordered a general parade in the morning of all the troops at the station. It appears from the evidence of the adjutant that, on returning from speaking to the native officers, Lieutenant-Colonel Mitchell directed him to order Captain Alexander, Commanding the 11th Regiment of Irregular Cavalry, to have his regiment on the parade of the 19th Regiment, Native Infantry, at six o'clock the following morning, and that the post guns should also be present at the same time.

Between ten and eleven o'clock the men of the 19th Regiment, Native Infantry, broke open the bells-of-arms, took possession of their muskets and ammunition, and carried them to their lines.

On hearing that the men had taken their arms, Lieutenant-Colonel Mitchell called out the cavalry and the guns at once. When the cavalry arrived on the parade, between twelve and one o'clock at night, the men of the 19th Regiment, Native Infantry, rushed out of their lines shouting, and assembled near their bells-of-arms.

As soon as the guns were ready, Lieutenant-Colonel Mitchell proceeded with the officers of the regiment to the parade ground, where he found the men in undress but armed, formed in line, and shouting. Some voice from among the men called out—"Do not come on, the men will fire."*

The guns having been loaded, the native officers were called to the front. They made excuses for the men. After addressing the men, Lieutenant-Colonel Mitchell told the officers that they must call upon the men to lay down their arms immediately. The native officers said that the men would not do so in the in the presence of the artillery and cavalry, but that if these were withdrawn, they would go quietly to their lines. The guns and cavalry were accordingly ordered away, and the men dispersed to their lines. This took place about 3 a.m. At six o'clock the same morning there was a parade, when the regiment turned out as usual. The men were quiet and orderly. The arms and ammunition were examined. It was found that some of the men had in their pouches only nine rounds of ammunition the proper complement being ten rounds; whilst with others, who had their ten rounds complete, one of the rounds bore the mark of the worm in the bullet, as if it had been drawn from the musket.

***This is Lieutenant-Colonel Mitchell's account in his letter of the 27th February, but it appears from the evidence before the Court of Inquiry that the men had assembled without any regular order; that after Lieutenant-Colonel Mitchell's arrival the officers were ordered to separate their companies and to call the roll, and that they tried but were unsuccessful.**

On the night of the 27th the men, instead of sleeping in their lines, assembled round the bells-of-arms. They were quiet and orderly, but seemed afraid to leave the neighbourhood of their arms.

The regiment was paraded on the morning of the 28th, and the men were asked what objections they had to the cartridges. They said they were doubtful whether the cartridges were not greased. Several cartridges were produced and opened before the men, the paper of some being burnt. Among the blank cartridges which had been left at Berhampore by the 7th Regiment, Native Infantry, some were made of a paper differing somewhat in color and appearance from that of the rest; with one kind, of a brownish tint, the men were satisfied, but the other they mistrusted.

The paper used for the last eight years has been made at Serampore. The cartridges left by the 7th Regiment, Native Infantry, were all made of this paper.

The reason assigned by the men for arming themselves is that they were afraid that cavalry and the guns and European troops were coming, and they said they were prepared to die rather than lose caste.

On the 5th of March a petition addressed by the men of the 19th Regiment, Native Infantry, to Major-General J. B. Hearsey was received by that officer. In this they solicited permission for the men to make up their ammunition as formerly. This petition was submitted to Government, but was returned to the Major-General, in order that Lieutenant-Colonel Mitchell might be called upon for any observations he might have to offer on the statements made by the men. Some of the statements bore upon Lieutenant-Colonel Mitchell's conduct towards them.

Upon the whole the petition contains a fair account of what took place on the occasion of the outbreak, the main points being borne out by the evidence at the Court of Inquiry.

It appears that on the 25th of February, the day before the outbreak, a party of European convalescents arrived at Berhampore accompanied by a havildar's guard from the 34th Regiment, Native Infantry, at Barrackpore. This guard was relieved by a detachment from the 19th Regiment, Native Infantry. Some time previously another party from the 34th Regiment, Native Infantry, had reached the station in charge of Government stallions. It was about the time of the arrival of the first guard that the subject of cartridges was first talked about. Subadar Kurreem Bux states that the doubt which the men felt about the cartridges was confirmed on the arrival of the second guard with the convalescents.

Lieutenant-Colonel Mitchell denies that he made use of the expression attributed to him by the petitioners, *viz.,* "If you will not take the cartridges, I will take you to Burma, where through hardship you will all die." He says that he cautioned the men against the serious consequences of refusing to obey orders. The adjutant in his evidence before the Court says that Lieutenant-Colonel Mitchell told the native officers that he would parade the regiment in the morning; that the officers of companies should serve out the cartridges to the men according as their names stood on the rolls; and that the first man who refused to take the cartridges should be tried by a court-martial.

Subadar Kurreem Bux says that Lieutenant-Colonel Mitchell told them that the men must take the cartridges, "otherwise they would be sent to China and Burma, where they would all die"; and he testifies to what was reported by the adjutant as having been said of the cartridges being distributed by the officers on parade.

Subadar-Major Shaikh Murad Bux says the men were threatened with Rangoon and China; and gives the same evidence as the other respecting the distribution of the cartridges by the officers.

Two other witnesses, Doolum Sing, pay-havildar, and Bijoo Sing, havildar-major, repeat what has been said about the cartridges being distributed by the officers, but say nothing about China and Rangoon. With reference to the expression attributed to Lieutenant-Colonel Mitchell - "this is a very bad business; we don't fear to die, and will die here", that officer observes that he does not remember exactly the words which he used, but that they were to the effect that "we, the officers of the regiment, were prepared to do our duty should the men of the regiment not yield obedience".

Lieutenant-Colonel Mitchell says that it was not until after the regiment had broken into the kotes and armed themselves and were in a state of mutiny that he called out the artillery and cavalry.

The artillery and cavalry were ordered to parade at six o'clock the following morning on Lieutenant-Colonel Mitchell's return from the lines between 7 and 8 p.m. The cavalry lines are distant about three miles from the lines of the infantry.

Between 10 and 11 p.m., when it must have been known that the cavalry and artillery were to be present in the morning, the men broke open the bells-of arms and took their arms and ammunition with them to their huts. On hearing this, Lieutenant-Colonel Mitchell ordered out the artillery and cavalry at once; and it was on the cavalry reaching the parade that the men ran out of their lines to the parade armed.

Lieutenant-Colonel Mitchell says that it was only when those four companies had given up their arms and the rest were doing so that he ordered away the artillery and cavalry.

Lieutenant-Colonel Mitchell feels certain that the mutinous proceedings did not arise from anything that took place on parade; but that the men were ripe for an outbreak owing to the communications which they had received for some time from their comrades in regiments at Barrackpore.

These are the principal features of this unfortunate event.

With respect to the share borne in it by Lieutenant-Colonel Mitchell, I think it essential to a right judgment of that officer's conduct that further investigation should be ordered, and I propose that directions be given to Major-General J. B. Hearsey to this effect, with the view to the institution of a Court of Inquiry of field officers so soon as Lieutenant-Colonel Mitchell shall reach the presidency. The demeanour of Lieutenant-Colonel Mitchell to his men, and the circumstances under which the artillery and cavalry were withdrawn, have not been satisfactorily established.

But as to the conduct of the regiment the case is simple.

From the moment when the main facts of the outbreak were established, it was clear that no penalty short of disbandment would meet the case. Additional guilt might possibly by closer enquiry be fixed upon individuals as instigators or ringleaders, and to these additional punishment might be found to be due; but the open refusal of the whole regiment to obey orders, the seizure of arms with violence, and a tumultuous but combined resistance of the authority of its officers with arms loaded is an offence for which any punishment less than dismissal from the service of the State would be inadequate. Mutiny so open and defiant cannot be excused by any sensitiveness of religion or caste, by fear of coercion, or by the seductions and deceptions of others.

It must be met promptly and unhesitatingly, and without the delay of a day more than may be necessary.

Accordingly, it has been resolved by the Governor-General of India in Council that the 19th Regiment, Native Infantry, shall be disbanded immediately; and regard being had to the situation of Berhampore relatively to other military stations, and to the actual distribution of regiments, especially European regiments, it is determined that the disbandment shall take place at the headquarters of the Presidency Division.

The 19th Regiment, Native Infantry, has therefore received orders to come to Barrackpore, and is on its march. Its arrival may be expected on the 31st instant, and I propose that instructions should now be sent to Major-General Hearsey to disband it as soon as it shall reach the parade ground of the situation.

I propose that this shall be done in the presence of all the troops of all arms which are within two days' march of the station. There are many indications that the seeds of insubordination which have grown to a head in the open mutiny of the 19th Regiment, Native Infantry, were first sown in some of the regiments now quartered at Barrackpore. Unfortunately the acts of incendiarism and the tendency to insubordination which during the last two months have prevailed at Barrackpore have not been traced to the individual agents, but whoever these may be, I believe that no more effective warning can be given to them of the danger to which their present courses expose themselves and their comrades than that of the 19th Regiment, Native Infantry, in the guilt of which there is reason to believe they have a large share, should receive its sentence and its punishment before their eyes.

I anticipate no show of resistance or disaffection from selecting Barrackpore as the scene of the measure.

The presence of a considerable force of artillery now at Dum Dum, of the Body Guard, and of the main portion of two European regiments, one of which, the 84th, has been brought from Rangoon for the purpose, will be sufficient to repress any tendency of the kind,—even if the bad feeling to which I have referred were much more widely spread than I believe it to be. I propose that the accompanying General Order be read to the 19th Regiment, Native Infantry, and to the troops assembled at Barrackpore, upon the occasion of the disbandment of that regiment, by the Major-General Commanding the Presidency Division.

The 27th March 1857.	(Sd.)	CANNING.
The 28th March 1857.	"	J. DORIN.
The 28th March 1857.	"	J. P. GRANT.
The 28th March 1857.	"	B. PEACOCK.

GENERAL ORDER by the Right Hon'ble the Governor-General of India in Council, dated Fort William, 27th March 1857.

No. 470 of 1857—The 19th Regiment, Native Infantry, has been brought to the head-quarters of the Presidency Division, to receive, in the presence of the troops there assembled, the decision of the Governor-General in Council upon the offence of which it has been guilty.

On the 26th of February, the 19th Regiment, Native Infantry, was ordered to parade on the following morning for exercise, with fifteen rounds of blank ammunition for each man.

The only blank ammunition in store was some which had been made up by the 7th Regiment, Native Infantry, the regiment preceding the 19th Regiment, Native Infantry, at Berhampore, and which had been left at that station of the Regiment, Native Infantry. This ammunition had been used by the recruits of the 19th Regiment, Native Infantry, up to the date above mentioned.

When the quantity of ammunition required for the following morning was taken to the lines, it appears that the men objected to the paper of which the cartridges were made, as being of two colors; and when the pay-havildars assembled the men to issue the percussion caps, they refused to receive them, saying that they had doubts about the cartridges.

The men have since stated, in a petition addressed to the Major-General Commanding the Presidency Division, that for more than two months they heard rumours of new cartridges having been made at Calcutta, on the paper of which the fat of bullocks and pigs had been spread, and of its being the intention of the Government to coerce the men to bite these cartridges; and that therefore they were afraid for their religion. They admit that the assurance given to them by the colonel of their regiment satisfied them that this would not be the case; adding, nevertheless, that when on the 26th of February, they perceived the cartridges to be of two kinds, they were convinced that one kind was greased, and therefore refused them.

The commanding officer on hearing of the refusal went to the lines, assembled the native commissioned and non-commissioned officers, and explained that the cartridges were unobjectionable, and had been left at Berhampore by the 7th Regiment, Native Infantry. He instructed them to inform their men that the cartridges would be served out in the morning by the officers commanding companies, and that any man who refused to take them would be tried by a court-martial and punished.

This occurred at eight o'clock in the evening.

Between ten and eleven o'clock a rush was made by the sepoys to the bells-of-arms; the doors were forced open; the men took possession of their arms and accoutrements, and carried them to their lines.

On learning what has occurred, Lieutenant-Colonel Mitchell ordered out the 11th Regiment of Irregular Cavalry and the post guns.

When the cavalry reached the parade, the men of the 19th Regiment, Native Infantry, rushed out of their lines with their arms, shouting, and assembled near the bells-of-arms, where many loaded their muskets.

Upon Lieutenant-Colonel Mitchell and the European officers approaching the men, they were warned no to go on, or the men would fire.

The native officers were assembled, and Lieutenant-Colonel Mitchell, after addressing the men, directed the officers to separate the companies, and to require them to give up their arms. The men hesitated at first, but eventually gave up their arms and retired to their lines.

These are the principal features of the outbreak at Berhampore on the 26th of February.

The men of the 19th Regiment, Native Infantry, have refused obedience to their European officers. They have seized arms with violence. They have assembled in a body to resist the authority of their commander.

The regiment has been guilty of open and defiant mutiny.

It is no excuse for this offence to say, as has been said in the before-mentioned petition of the native officers and men of the regiment, that they were afraid for their religion, and that they apprehended violence to themselves.

It is no atonement of it to declare, as they have therein declared, that they are ready to fight to their Government in the field, when they have disobeyed and insulted that Government in the persons of its officers, and have expressed no contrition for their heavy offences.

Neither the 19th Regiment, Native Infantry, nor any regiment in the service of the Government of India, nor any sepoy, Hindu or Mussulman, has reason to pretend that the Government has shown, directly or indirectly, a desire to interfere with the religion of its troops. It has been the unvarying rule of the Government of India to treat the religious feelings of all its servants, of every creed, with careful respect; and to representations or complaints put forward in a dutiful and becoming spirit, whether upon this or upon any other subject, it has never turned a deaf ear.

But the Government of India expects to receive, in return for this treatment, the confidence of those who serve it.

From its soldiers, of every rank and race, it will, at all times, and in all circumstances, enforce unhesitating obedience. They have sworn to give it, and the Governor-General of India in Council never ceases to exact it. To no men who prefer complaints with arms in their hands will he ever listen.

Had the sepoys of the 19th Regiment, Native Infantry, confided in their Government, and believed their commanding officer, instead of crediting the idle stories with which false and evil-minded men have deceived them, their religious scruples would still have remained inviolate, and themselves would still be, as they have hitherto been, faithful soldiers, trusted by the State, and laying up for future years all the rewards of a long and honorable service.

But the Governor-General of India in Council can no longer have any confidence in this regiment, which has disgraced its name, and has lost all claim to consideration and indulgence.

It is therefore the order of the Governor-General of India in Council that the 19th Regiment, Native Infantry, be now disbanded; that the native commissioned and non-commissioned officers and privates be discharged from the Army of Bengal, that this be done at the headquarters of the Presidency Division, in the presence of every available corps within two days march of the station; that the regiment be paraded for the purpose; and that each man, after being deprived of his arms, shall receive his arrears of pay and be required to withdraw from the cantonments.

The European officers of the regiment will remain at Barrackpore until orders for their disposal shall be received from his Excellency the Commander-In-Chief.

This order is to be read at the head of every regiment, troop and company in the service.

From Colonel R.J.H. BIRCH. C.B., *Secretary of the Government of India, in the Military Department, to Major-General* J.B. HEARSEY, C.B., *Commanding the Presidency Division—No. 925, dated Fort William, 28th March 1857.*

With reference to recent correspondence regarding the conduct of the 19th Regiment, Native Infantry, on the 26th and 27th of February last, I am directed to acquaint you that the Proceedings of the Court of Inquiry which was assembled at Berhampore to investigate the circumstances connected with the outbreak in that regiment, the petition to your address from the men of that corps, and the correspondence upon the subject having been fully considered by the Government of India, the Right Hon'ble the Governor-General of India in Council is of opinion that no penalty, short of disbandment, can meet the case, and he has accordingly resolved that the regiment shall be disbanded.

2. I am instructed to request that will carry into effect the resolution of the Government of India in the following manner—

   You will ascertain from Lieutenant-Colonel Mitchell the exact day and hour on which the regiment will reach Barrackpore.

   The Governor-General of India in Council desires that all available troops of all arms within two days' march of Barrackpore shall be present at the station by the time that the 19th Regiment, Native Infantry, arrives there. This enables you to have present, in addition to the Barrackpore Brigade, two field batteries with their European reserve companies, a portion of the 9th Battalion of Artillery, a wing of Her Majesty's 53rd Foot, and the depot of musketry from Dum Dum, the Governor-General's Body-Guard from Ballygunge, and her Majesty's 84th Foot from Chinsurah. The Native Infantry guards on duty in Calcutta cannot be withdrawn, and the wing of Her Majesty's 53rd Foot in Fort William must therefore stand fast.

3. The whole of the troops above detailed are to be paraded on the arrival at Barrackpore of the 19th Regiment, Native Infantry, which is to be disbanded immediately after it reaches the parade.

4. The process of disbandment is to be the same as was observed on the occasion of the dismissal of the 34th Regiment, Native Infantry, at Meerut, with the exception that the men are not be turned out of cantonments with ignominy, and that the number of the 19th Regiment, Native Infantry, will not be erased from the Army List.

   G.O.C.C, 20th March 1844.

5. The Governor General of India in Council leaves it to you to make such disposition of the troops as may enable you to carry out the resolution of the Government in the manner you consider best; and in the improbable event of any opposition, you are directed to make such use of the troops as may be necessary. Any show of resistance to your authority must be put down at once, and the measure must be carried out any cost.

6. Arrangements will be made in the Military Department for sending up, with the Body-guard, sufficient money to pay up the men immediately after they have delivered up their arms and the uniform, the property of the State, and you are requested to take proper steps to cause every man connected with the 19th Regiment, Native Infantry, to quit the cantonments immediately after the regiment is paid up, and to prevent the return of any of them within the limits of cantonments.

7. A copy of a G.O. issued this day is enclosed, and you are requested to cause it to be read to the 19th Regiment, Native Infantry, as well as the other corps on parade.
8. When you may consider it right to dispense with the troops brought to Barrackpore, you are requested to direct their return to their proper stations bearing in mind that the season is far advanced to detain Europeans in tents for longer than necessary.
9. The Inspector-General of Ordnance and Magazines will be instructed to cause the tents required for the Europeans troops to be sent to Barrackpore on such date as you may name, and you are requested to communicate with Colonel A. Abbott accordingly.

From Lieutenant Colonel W. St. L. M ITCHELL, *Commanding the 19th Regiment, Native Infantry, to Major* A. H. ROSS, *Assistant Adjutant-General, Barrackpore, dated—Baraset, 30th March 1857.*

I think it best to march the regiment into Barrackpore to-morrow morning. It is evident that the men know their fate, and I think it best to tell them the plain truth that the regiment is to be disbanded, as they have strange thoughts on the subject.

I have just received your letter of the 29th, 5 p.m., enclosing notes from the Major-General and Colonel Birch. I have anticipated these orders.

I have just had a meeting of the native officers in my tent. I told them, (what they knew before) that the regiment was to be disbanded. They said that two batteries of guns and Europeans were to be brought out against them. I replied if they behaved properly and everything took place as on an usual parade, nothing would happen to the regiment beyond paying them up and dismissing them; that I had issued my orders for the day, and they must be obeyed; that I had nothing to do but to carry out strictly the orders of the Major-General; that their business was to explain to the men to remain obedient. They told me that it was hard upon them, after so many years' service, to lose their bread, and hoped that I would represent their case to the General. I told them that any petition they wished to forward I would present it to the Major General on parade in their presence.

Telegram from Major General J. B. HEARSEY, c.b., *Commanding the Presidency Division, to Colonel* R. J. H. BIRCH, c.b., *Secretary to the Government of India, in the Military Department, Calcutta—dated Barrackpore, 31st March 1857.*

All has gone off well and quietly. The 19th Regiment, Native Infantry, has been paid up and marched to Fultah Ghat under escort of a wing, 84th, and the Body-Guard. The whole will cross to the right bank during the day, and thence to Chinsurah.

From Colonel R. J. H. BIRCH. C.B., *Secretary of the Government of India, in the Military Department, to Major-General* J. B. HEARSEY, C.B., *Commanding the Presidency Division—No. 976, dated Fort William, 31st March 1857.*

I am directed to request that you will without delay convene a Special Court of Inquiry composed of four European officers (field officers) to investigate in the fullest manner into the conduct of Lieutenant-Colonel W. St. L. Mitchell, Commanding the 19th Regiment Infantry, at Berhampore, in connection with the occurrences at that station on the 26th ultimo and subsequently, which have led to the disbandment of the regiment.

From Major General J. B. HEARSEY, C.B., *Commanding the Presidency Division, to Colonel* R. J. H. BIRCH, C.B., *Secretary to the Government of India, in the Military Department, Calcutta—dated Barrackpore, 31st March 1857.*

I have the honour to report, for the information of the Most Noble the Governor-General of India in Council, that agreeably to the instructions received from you under date, I this morning paraded all the troops now at this station at gun-fire, or at quarter after 5 a.m., and then, accompanied by Major A. Ross and my Aide-de-Camp, Captain J. Hearsey, proceeded about one mile on the road towards Baraset to meet the 19th Regiment, Native Infantry, under the command of Lieutenant-Colonel W. St. L. Mitchell as it marched into this cantonment, and placing myself between the advanced guard and head of the column, I directed Lieutenant-Colonel Mitchell to proceed towards the parade ground, and on reaching the open space to the right of the Body-Guard, the regiment from sections was formed into open column of companies which were closed to quarter distance, and in that formation were brought in the front of two field batteries of artillery, and then wheeled to the left, so as to face them at about 80 yards distance.

I then made a short address to the 19th Regiment, Native Infantry, in Hindustani, informing the men and native officers of the reason of their being ordered to this the head-quarters of the Presidency Division of the Army, and directed Lieutenant F.E.A. Chamier, Interpreter and Quartermaster, 34th Regiment, Native Infantry, to read out in a loud voice the translation he had prepared of the orders of Government for the disbandment of the corps.

This being done, Lieutenant-Colonel Mitchell solicited me to permit the native officers to address a petition to Government. I replied I could receive no petition until the regiment had laid down its arms and obeyed such orders as I gave it.

The ranks were then opened, and the order distinctly given by Lieutenant-Colonel Mitchell to pile arms. This being done, the next order to take off their belts and hang them on their bayonets was given, and immediately complied with. The colours were then brought to the front of the columns (encased), a pile of three muskets put in front, and the colors placed resting on them. The order was then given—Left face (to the open ranks), file to your left, march, and instantly complied with. The men having gone about one hundred and fifty paces from their arms, the column was halted and fronted, ranks closed, and the tumbril with pay was brought to its front, and orders given to Lieutenant-Colonel Mitchell for the native officers and the men to be paid to this date.

I then made known to the native officers of the regiment any petition they chose to send to me would be forwarded by me to Government, but I could give them no hope. I told the men that Government, that though it had punished them by summary dismissal from the service, did not wish to disgrace them by stripping them of their uniform but all clothing belonging to the State, agreeably to the Clothing Regulations, must be given up. This evidently affected them. I continued: Since you have behaved so well and so penitently during your march from Berhampore and since the occurrence for which you have now been punished, I have further to inform you the Government, though forced to correct, was merciful and just, and that the hackery hire and hire of cattle for their journey, and also the hire of the boats that had brought down their families and heavy baggage from Berhampore, would be defrayed by the Government. This gracious act was keenly felt, and they loudly bewailed their fate, many men saying the regiment had been misled (and as I understood) by the 34th Regiment, Native Infantry, on which corps they vowed vengeance.

Whilst their accounts were being settled and the men receiving their pay I narrowly inspected the troops that had marched in yesterday.

The Government orders disbanding the 19th Regiment, Native Infantry, were read by the interpreters to the 2nd (Grenadier), the 34th, the 43rd, and 70th Regiments, Native Infantry in their formation of contiguous close columns at quarter distance. I then addressed this brigade, pointing out the mercy and justice of the Government, and pressing on their attention that no attempt had been made from any quarter to injure their caste or interfere in their religious prejudices in any way. That the 19th Regiment, Native Infantry, in which there were 409 Brahmins and 150 Rajputs, were now sent to their homes, paid up to the uttermost farthing of their claims, and were at liberty to visit any shrine they chose, or to go and worship at the temples of the villages where they were born, and where their fathers had worshipped before them, without hindrance or molestation, making a strong proof that the reports so industriously circulated of the intention of Government to interfere with their religion was a base falsehood, intended by their enemies to ruin their prospects in life and to take the bread from the mouths of their parents, the widows of their lost companions, and from their own wives and children. I again pointed out to them that our Government and their officers were Christians of *" The Book "*, and that no adult person could be baptised to our system of religious faith out of his own full consent, and then only after being strictly examined in the tenets written in *" The Book "* we put our faith and trust on.

I was listened to most attentively.

This discourse I repeated a second time to the Barrackpore Brigade before it was dismissed.

The 19th Regiment, Native Infantry, was paid up by 8.40 a.m.

The morning was cool with a fresh breeze. I had, during the night, made every arrangement for five companies of Her Majesty's 84th Foot to encamp on the other side of the Ganges at Ghyretty, there being no encamping ground at Fultah on this side.

A gharry as sent on with tents, & c, and provisions had been also despatched; a fatigue party of 50 men and a large-body of *khalasis* had proceeded to have their camp ready.

Captain J. Hearsey showed these men the road, and had returned from Fultah just as the 19th Regiment, Native Infantry, and their escort left the parade here, so I hope there has been no unnecessary exposure to the sun. The Europeans were directed to take off their stocks, and were in a light white linen marching dress. The men of the disbanded regiment, the 19th Regiment, Native Infantry, cheered me and wished me long life as they marched off, and I returned the compliment, making them promise me they would behave properly on their way to their homes, and I forbidding them under severe punishment going to Calcutta or returning to this cantonment.

The Body-guard will wait at Fultah Ghat until the 19th Regiment, Native Infantry, cross the river. The officers of the 19th Regiment, Native Infantry, have been sent with them to see them across, and I have directed all their baggage to be sent on to Chinsurah, from whence they will be permitted to disperse to their homes and proceed to the different shrines of Hindu worship the large number of Brahmins are desirous of visiting. All has ended to my complete satisfaction, and either to-morrow or on Thursday, the force sent here will return to Chinsurah, Dum Dum, and Calcutta as soon as arrangements can be made for it to do so.

In making this report I hope all I have done will meet the approbation of Government.

TRANSLATION of the first petition of the faithful officers and sepoys of the discharged 19th Regiment, Native Infantry, to Major-General J. B. HEARSEY, C.B., *Commanding the Presidency Division, dated Fultah Ghat, the 31st March 1857.*

That your humble petitioners' regiment has been raised nearly a hundred years, since which time no disturbance has occurred: they have always done their duty faithfully and have marched on service wherever they have been ordered, but unfortunately through the advice of some wicked men, on the 26th February, the regiment committed a very great crime, for which the Government issued the following order: "That they were to march immediately from Berhampore to Barrackpore". Accordingly, we marched and arrived at Barrackpore on the 31st March 1857, where we were punished by receiving our discharge before the whole force, after which we confessed our fault to the Major-General, and also before our arrival at Barrackpore we agreed in case we were pardoned to become a general service regiment and go wherever we were ordered.

Should our fault be pardoned through your kindness, we hope to be re-embodied and accounted as faithful servants, because this is our first fault, and the Government may be kind enough to pardon it.

We shall ever pray for your welfare.

TRANSLATION of Major-General J. B. HEARSEY'S *answer to the above.*

I have received the petition of the officers and sepoys of the late 19th Regiment, Native Infantry, and understand all that you have written but until you can give me full information of the rank and names of those people who have misled you, either through bribes or any other way, and can prove and confirm it by good testimony, I cannot intercede for you. If you do so I say, I will intercede with the Government as much as lies in my power.

But Government will do as it thinks fit. And in my judgment, without doubt, someone has misled you; you ought not to hide the name and rank, or be on friendly terms with those who have ruined your livelihood, because they have brought you and your families to the dust. I give you this advice, as I feel for you; you can do what you like. I can neither do or say anything more.

TRANSLATION of the second petition from the officers and men of the late 19th Regiment, Native Infantry, to Major-General J. B. HEARSEY, C.B., *Commanding the Presidency Division, dated Ghyretty the 2nd April 1857.*

We received your honor's answer to our petition, dated 31st March, yesterday evening, regarding our giving up the names and rank of those wicked men who have misled and ruined us, and thoroughly understand the good advice you have written in our behalf. Alas, if we had known the names and rank of those who have misled us, we should have handed them up immediately before this misfortune overwhelmed us.

Firstly: The men who are acquainted with the names and rank of those instigators are at enmity with us and friendly with them, because, being young, they are independent of the Hon'ble Company's service, and they began with this mutiny with a view to our ruin only, and this is the reason they do not tell us.

Secondly: On the night that this conspiracy took place, we left them and went to our colonel. By so doing we placed ourselves in opposition to them, neither did they consult us nor tell us their plot; even now they do not trust us. When this is the case, they will never assist us in our miserable state by giving up the names of the instigators. For these reasons we are unable to give up their names and rank. In our opinion the guard of the 34th was the cause of this mutiny. But we cannot recognise any of the guards who kindled it, that we may prove it against them. We have given you a true statement. You can use it as you like, with a view to our long service and old age, to keep us from starving.

Hoping for a speedy answer. We shall ever pray.

TRANSLATION of Major-General J. B. HEARSEY'S *answer to the above.*

To the disbanded officers and sepoys who were in the 19th Regiment, Native Infantry.

I have received your petition, dated 2nd April, and thoroughly understand it. I write now as I wrote before, that without giving up the names and rank of the wicked instigators, I am unable to help you, for most likely the Government will not listen to it. For the Government has granted your commissions and rank to keep the privates in subjection, and not allow them to mutiny, and it is known to all that a sepoy cannot even cough without the knowledge of his native officers. When this is the case, how will they believe that such a mutiny could take place without their knowledge. In short, nothing can be done without giving up the names and rank of the wicked instigators, either by me or Government. In the event of your being unable to inform and prove what you say, it is no use troubling me with petitions. Do as you think best.

From Colonel R. J. H. BIRCH, C.B., *Secretary to the Government of India, in the Military Department, to Colonel* C. CHESTER, *Adjutant -General of the Army—No. 158, dated Fort William, 4th April 1857.*

The Right Hon'ble the Governor General of India in Council having received a report, a copy of which is enclosed, by Major-General J. B. Hearsey, Commanding the Presidency Division, of the proceedings which took place at Barrackpore on the 31st ultimo, on the occasion of the disbandment of the 19th Regiment, Native Infantry, I am directed to acquaint you, for the information of His Excellency the Commander-in-Chief, that His lordship in Council considers that Major-General J.B. Hearsey has discharged the difficult task assigned to him in a manner which well deserves the thanks of the Government of India.

2. With the firmness of a soldier executing imperative instructions, he has shown towards the men who received their sentence from him a kindliness of feeling and in consideration, the effect of which upon them was, the Governor- General of India in Council is assured, very apparent. This combined with good judgement, a thorough knowledge of the character and feelings of those with whom he had to deal, and unusual familiarity with their language, has enabled the Major-General to carry out with perfect success one of the most trying duties which can be imposed upon a commandant.

3. The Governor General of India in Council requests that His Excellency will be so good as to convey to Major-General Hearsey, the entire approbation and cordial thanks of the Government of India.

4. The Governor General of India in Council has receicved with pleasure Major-General J.B. Hearsey's testimony* to the great value of the services rendered to him by Major A. H. Ross, Assistant Adjutant-General of the Presidency Division, during the late proceedings at Barrackpore, and His Lordship in Council desires to convey, through His Excellency, to Major Ross, the approval and thanks of the Government of India for the manner in which he discharged his duties, and for the assistance which he gave to Major- General J.B. Hearsey on the occasion.

***Letter dated 1st April,— a copy enclosed**

No. 159

Copy of the above forwarded to Major- General J.B. Hearsey, for information, with reference to his letters of the 31st ultimo and 1st instant.

By order of the Right Hon'ble the Governor General of India in Council.

MILITARY DEPARTMENT
FORT WILLIAM; (Sd.) R. J .H. BIRCH Col.,
The 4th April 1857. *Secy. to the Govt. of India.*

From Major General J. B. HEARSEY, C.B, *Commanding the Presidency Division, to Colonel* R. J. H. BIRCH, C.B, *Secretary to the Government of India, in the Military Department, No. 151—dated Barrackpore, 6th April 1857.*

In forwarding for the approval and confirmation of Government the accompanying copy of my Division Order, dated 5th instant, No. 1, I beg that you will do me the honour to submit my earnest recommendation that the energetic and gallant conduct of Lieutenant and Adjutant B.H. Baugh and of Sergeant-Major J. T. Hewson, on the occasion in question may be favorably noticed in G.O.s; and further, that the promotion to a supernumerary havildar of Shaik Pultoo, sepoy, may be confirmed, and the Order of Merit bestowed on him by Government as a reward for his fidelity and bravery in defending the life of his European officer under most trying circumstances, in which act he was severely wounded.

PRESIDENCY DIVISION ORDERS by Major General J. B. HEARSEY, C.B, *Commanding the Presidency Division, dated Headquarters, Barrackpore, 5th April 1857.*

No. 1 of 1857.—The Major General cordially congratulates Lieutenant and Adjutant B. H. Baugh and Sergeant-Major J. T. Hewson, both of the 34TH Regiment, Native Infantry, for the personal gallantry displayed by them in the conflict with the sepoy, Mungul Pandy, of No. 5 Company, 34th Regiment, Native Infantry, who, in a state of religious frenzy, endeavoured to raise a mutiny in that regiment on Sunday afternoon, the 29th ultimo.

The Major-General will have much pleasure in bringing their praiseworthy conduct on this occasion to the notice of the Government and His Excellency the Commander-in-Chief.

Shaik Pultoo, sepoy, Grenadier Company, 34th Regiment, Native Infantry (the orderly who accompanied Lieutenant Baugh), is promoted to havildar from the 29th March ultimo, and is to be borne on the rolls of the 34th Regiment, Native Infantry as supernumerary from that date for the loyal and gallant conduct shown by him on that occasion, and application will be made by the Major-General to Government and His Excellency the Commander-in-Chief that he, Shaik Pultoo, Grenadier sepoy, may be further rewarded with the Order of Merit for being instrumental in saving the life of his officer.

This order is to be translated and read to all the native corps assembled on their regimental parades for that purpose, and afterwards to be read at the head of each company.

From Major General J. B. HEARSEY, C.B, *Commanding the Presidency Division, to Colonel* R. J. H. BIRCH, C.B, *Secretary to the Government of India, in the Military Department—dated Barrackpore, 8th April 1857.*

I have the honour to report, for the information of the Governor-General, that Mungul Pandy, sepoy 5th Company, 34th Regiment, Native Infantry, who was found guilty by a native General Court-martial of mutiny and murderous assault on Lieutenant and Adjutant B. H. Baugh and Sergeant-Major J. T. Hewson of that regiment, on Sunday, the 29th of March (ultimo), and sentenced to be hung by the neck till dead, was executed this morning in presence of the native brigade stationed here and all other troops, Europeans and Native, within two marches of Barrackpore, drawn up on parade.

The columns of native infantry were then advanced close to the gallows, and I addressed the men, telling them they had now witnessed the punishment for mutiny, and I bid them to take warning by it.

All was conducted with strict order and agreeable to military law, and everything went off quietly.

The 84th Queen's arrived at Barrackpore from Chinsurah at 6 p.m. yesterday evening, during a most violent storm. I kept them on board the steamers and flat that the men might not be exposed to the severity of the weather, and when the storm had passed over, or about midnight, the corps was moved up to camp, where they found dry ground to sleep-upon till morning. I shall order the corps back to Chinsurah, after the men have had their breakfast, by the steamers and flat.

From Captain G. C. HATCH, *Deputy Judge Advocate-General, to Colonel* R. J. H. BIRCH, C.B, *Secretary to the Government of India, in the Military Department—No. 131, dated Calcutta, 9th April 1857.*

Under instructions from Major-General Hearsey, Commanding the Presidency Division, I have the honor to forward, for the information of Government, a copy of the Proceedings of a native General Court-martial, held at Barrackpore on the 6th instant, upon the trial of Sepoy Mungul Pandy, 34th Regiment, Native Infantry, on charges for mutiny and violence to the adjutant and sergeant-major of his regiment, and upon whom sentence of death has been carried out.

Agreeably to instructions received from the Brigade-Major, the Field Officer and Interpreter of the week having proceeded to the quarter-guard of Her Majesty's 53rd Regiment, put the following questions to, and received the following answers from, the prisoner of the 34th Regiment, Native Infantry—

Question: Have you anything to disclose, or do you wish to say anything?

Answer: No.

Question: Did you act on Sunday last by your own free will, or were you instructed by others?

Answer: Of my own will. I expected to die.

Question: Did you load your own musket to save your life?

Answer: No, I intended to take it.

Question: Did you intend to take the adjutant's life, or would you have shot any one else ?

Answer: I should have shot any one who came.

Question: Were you under the influence of any drugs?

Answer: Yes, I have been taking *bhang* and opium of late, but formerly never touched any drugs. I was not aware at the time of what I was doing.

The prisoner was asked frequently if he would give up the names of any connected with the occurrence, and was given to understand that he had nothing to fear from his own regiment by disclosing anything, but he refused to state more than the above.

The sepoy attending him was removed from the tent during the investigation.

(Sd.) W. A. COOKE, *Major,*
Field Officer of the week.

(Sd.) F. E. CHAMIER, *Ensign,*
Interpreter and Qr. – Mr. of the week.

(Sd.) C. GRANT, *Brigr.,*
Comdg. at Barrackpore.

BARRACKPORE,

The 4th April 1857.

From Captain G. C. HATCH, *Deputy Judge Advocate-General, to Major-General* J. B. HEARSEY, C.B., *Commanding the Presidency Division—dated Barrackpore, 6th April 1857.*

I have the honor to make the following reports to you in regard to the state of the votes of the officers forming the general court-martial on the trial of Sepoy Mungul Pandy, 34th Regiment, Native Infantry—

1st- That the verdict was carried by the votes of fourteen officers on the first charge; and by the votes of fourteen officers on the second charge.

2nd-That eleven officers voted for the sentence of death.

From Major-General J. B. HEARSEY, C.B, *Commanding the Presidency Division, to Colonel* R. J. H. BIRCH, C.B, *Secretary to the Government of India, in the Military Department—dated Barrackpore, 9th April 1857.*

I have the honor to report that I have directed Captain G. C. Hatch, Deputy Judge Advocate-General, Presidency Division, to wait on you at your office this day, and to lay before you, for the information of Government, the Proceedings of the Court convened by my order to investigate into the circumstances attending the mutinous conduct of Mungul Pandy, late sepoy, No. 5 Company, 34th Regiment, Native Infantry, on the afternoon of the 29th March 1857; also the Proceedings of a native General Court-martial assembled by my orders at Barrackpore for the trial of the sepoy.

These documents will fully elucidate the whole of the occurrence as regards Lieutenant and Adjutant B. H. Baugh and Sergeant-Major J. T. Hewson, 34th Regiment, Native Infantry, but I deem it my duty to lay before Government officially a narrative of the circumstances that came to my knowledge on that afternoon, and also my own conduct on that occasion.

At 5.10 p.m., of the 29th of March (ultimo), one of the orderlies on duty at my quarters, a sepoy of the 34th Regiment, Native Infantry, ran to the portico of my house to inform me that all the sepoys of the brigade were turning out on their parades, and men were running in that direction from all quarters of the cantonment.

I immediately ordered my horse to be saddled, and put on my uniform, directing my son to load my revolvers and place them in the holsters of my saddle. Whilst this was being done, I went to my desk and wrote two short notes, one addressed to Colonel Reed, Commanding Her Majesty's 84th Foot, at Chinsurah, the other to Colonel Amsinck, Commanding at DumDum, to the purport that on receipt of those notes, they were instantly to move with the troops at their posts to Barrackpore, for it was my intention had the brigade all turned out in the mutinous manner, to have taken post in the Governor-General's house with the 50 Europeans who were at the Flag-staff Ghat, and with the officers of the force and any men who might prove true to Government and join us to have defended that position until relieved or supported.

I had just sealed these notes and put them into my pocket to despatch by mounted officers if I should find matters serious on my arrival at the parade ground, when Lieutenant and Adjutant Powell, of the 43rd Regiment, Native Infantry, arrived at my quarters on horseback, with his hands and his clothes partly covered with blood, and he informed me that Lieutenant and Adjutant Baugh, 34th Regiment, Native Infantry, had been fired upon on the parade of the 34th Regiment, Native Infantry, and his horse had been shot, and that the Adjutant, Lieutenant Baugh, had been cut down, as well as the Sergeant-Major J.T. Hewson of that corps, by a sepoy.

Major H. W. Mathews, 43rd Regiment, Native Infantry, the field officer of the week, then came and reported that all the men of the brigade had assembled in front of their bells-of-arms. I asked him—"Has no attempt been made to seize or shoot down the mutineers?" Major Mathews replied —"Lieutenant-Colonel Wheler and Lieutenant and Adjutant Drury,* of the 34th Regiment, Native Infantry, were on parade, and had gone to the quarter-guard of that regiment to move with it and seize the mad man." I told him to ride off instantly, and direct Lieutenant-Colonel Wheler he had my orders to shoot the mutinous sepoy if he made any resistance to his seizure. (I have since been told Lieutenant-Colonel Wheler could not get the jemadar, Issuree Pandy, or the men of the guard, to obey him).

I then mounted my horse and accompanied by my two sons, Captain John Hearsey, 38th Regiment, Native Infantry, and Lieutenant Andrew Wm. Hearsey, 57th Regiment, Native Infantry (who is residing with me, being on leave from his regiment under medical certificate), as fast as our horses could carry us to the parade of the 34th Regiment, Native Infantry. The Assistant Adjutant-General, Major A. H. Ross, had just arrived there before me. I saw the whole front of the bells-of-arms crowded with sepoys in their undress and unarmed, the native officers of the 43rd Regiment, Native Infantry, with them, and endeavourijng to keep them in order. The men of the 34th Regiment, Native Infantry, had also turned out unarmed to the right and rear of their quarter-guard.

I asked Major Ross what was the matter, and was answsered by many officers who were standing there,—*viz.,* Brigadier C. Grant, Major H. W. Mathews, and others, some were mounted, many on foot,—that a sepoy of the 34th Regiment. Native Infantry, had cut down Lieutenant Baugh and the sergeant-major of that regiment, and that he (the sepoy) was pacing up and down about eighty or ninety paces in front of the quarter-guard of that regiment, calling out to the men of the brigade to join him to defend and die for their religion and their caste. "For the Europeans had arrived" (he alluded to a small party of fifty men of Her Majesty's 53rd Foot, then at the Flag-staff Ghat, that had been sent by Major A. Sanders, Deputy Quartermaster-General of the Army, and who were landing from the steamer that had arrived there from Calcutta). He called aloud to them— "You have incited me to do this, and now you *bhainchutes* (an abusive term), you will not join me."

* "Lieutenant and Adjutant Drury"—*Sic* in original. But General Hearsey evidently committed an error for Lieutenant Baugh was the Adjutant, and the officer mentioned was Captain C.C. Drury,— *See Quarterly Bengal Army List, January 1857.*

On seeing this man I immediately rode to the quarter-guard of the 34th Regiment, Native Infantry, and saw the jemadar, Isssuree Pandy, and about ten or twelve men had turned out, and were standing before the quarter-guard house.

My two sons and Major Ross accompanied me. I heard an officer shout out to me—"His (the mutineer's) musket is loaded." I replied—"Damn his musket."

I ordered the jemadar and his guard to follow me. The jemadar said, as I then understood, "The men are loaded," but I have since been told his answer was—"*He* is loaded" (meaning the mutineer had his musket loaded) and "he will shoot us". I again (shaking my revolver and pointing it partly towards him) sharply repeated the order. The jemadar looked askance at me and replied "The men of the guard are putting caps on the nipples." I said in a commanding and peremptory voice—"Be quick and follow me," and rode out in front towards the mutineer.

The guard followed, my aide-de-camp on horseback close to the jemadar armed with his revolvers, my other son also close to the native officer similarly armed, Major Ross in rear of myself. As we approached the mutineer we quickened our pace. My son, Captain J. Hearsey, called to me—"Father, he is taking aim at you, look out sharp" (meaning the mutineer). I replied—"If I fall, John, rush upon him, and put him to death." Immediately after the mutineer, Mungul Pandy, fired his musket, the whistle of the bullet was heard by the guard, for all but three men of it bent down apparently to avoid being struck by it. It appeared the mutineer had suddenly altered his mind, I suppose, seeing there was no chance of escape (for a body of officers had either joined, or were coming up armed, and close to the left rear of the guard). He turned his musket muzzle towards his own breast hurriedly, touching the trigger with his toe. The muzzle must have swerved, for the bullet made a deep graze, ripping up the muscles of the chest, shoulder and neck, and he fell prostrate; we were on him at once. The guard calling out—"He has shot himself", a Sikh sepoy of the guard took his bloody *tulwar* (native sword) from under him, for in falling he partly covered his sword with his body. His regimental jacket and clothes were on fire and smoking. I bid the jemadar and the sepoy to put the fire out, which they did.

I then (thinking the mutineer was dying, for he was shivering and convulsed) directed Brigadier Grant (who had come up on foot) to form a court of inquest from the officers assembled there. Dr. Hutchinson being present, it was soon ascertained that the wound, though severe, was superficial, and the man was conveyed to the hospital of the 34th Regiment, Native Infantry, for medical treatment. He was handcuffed, and a guard placed over him. Before I quitted to go to my quarters, I rode amongst the sepoys of the 43rd Regiment, Native Infantry, and re-assured them that no person should be permitted to interfere with their religion and caste prejudices whilst I commanded them. I then went accompanied by Major Ross and my two sons amongst the crowd of sepoys of the 34th Regiment, Native Infantry (the regiment of the mutineer, Mungul Pandy), and also re-assured them telling them they had not done their duty in allowing their fellow-soldier, Mungul Pandy, to behave in the murderous manner he had done.

They answered in one voice—"He is mad, he has taken *bhang* (intoxicating drug) to excess." I replied—"Could you not have seized him, and if he resisted have shot him or maimed him. Would you not have done so to a mad elephant or to a mad dog, and what difference was there in the dangerous madness of a man and the same in an elephant or a dog." They said—"He has loaded his musket." "What," I replied, "are you afraid of a loaded musket?" They were silent. I bid them go quietly to their lines, and they did so, immediately obeying my orders.

P.S.—As I was not present when Lieutenant and Adjutant B. H. Baugh and Sergeant-Major J. T. Hewson were wounded by Mungul Pandy, sepoy, the Proceedings of the Court of Inquiry and Court-martial will make fully known all the circumstances regarding the murderous assault of Mungul Pandy, sepoy on those officers.

Sepoy Mungul Pandy has not improved in health since he came under my charge; he has been gradually becoming weaker, and is now much debilitated. The wound also presents an unhealthy appearance. I still, however, consider him in a fit state to be removed to the mess-house of the 34th Regiment, Native Infantry.

CAMP BARRACKPORE — (Sd.) T. B. REID
The 6th April 1857 — *Asst. Surgeon, 53rd Regt.*

I, James Allen, F. R. C. S., Assistant Surgeon, 34th Regiment, Native Infantry, do hereby certify, that Mungul Pandy, sepoy, No. 1446, 5th Company, 34th Regiment, Native Infantry, is in a fit state to undergo his trial this day.

PROCEEDINGS in continuation of a native General Court–martial assembled at Fort William, by order of Major-General J. B. HEARSEY, C.B., *Commanding the Presidency*

Division, for the trial of sepoys BOODHELALL TEWARY *and* BAHADOOR SING, *2nd Regiment, Native (Grenadier) Infantry, and all such prisoners as may be duly brought before it, and are re-assembled at Barrackpore on Monday, 6th April 1857, by order of the Major-General, for the trial of Sepoy* MUNGUL PANDY, *34th Regiment, Native Infantry, and all prisoners who may be brought before it.*

PRESIDENT:

Subadar-Major JOWAHIR LALL TEWARY, *43rd Regiment, Native Infantry.*

MEMBERS:

Subadar BHOLA OPUDEAH, *17th Regiment, Native Infantry.*

Subadar HURRUCK SING, *40th Regiment, Native Infantry.*

Subadar RAM SING, *9th Battalion, Artillery.*

Subadar AMANUT KHAN, *37th Regiment, Native Infantry.*

Subadar SEWUMBUR PANDY, *34th Regiment, Native Infantry.*

Subadar DIRGA RAM, *70th Regiment, Native Infantry.*

Subadar KHOODA BUKSH, *2nd Regiment, Native (Grenadier) Infantry.*

Subadar MEERWAN SING *70th Regiment, Native Infantry.*

Subadar SOOKHLAL MISR, *43rd Regiment, Native Infantry.*

Subadar AJOODHIA TEWARY, *70th Regiment, Native Infantry.*

Subadar JALIM SING, *43rd Regiment, Native Infantry.*

Subadar DEWAN ALLIE, *9th Battalion, Artillery.*

Subadar MOHUN SING, *65th Regiment, Native Infantry.*

Subadar LALLA RAM BUKSH, *8th Regiment, Native Infantry.*

JUDGE ADVOCATE :

Captain G.C.HATCH, *Deputy Judge Advocate-General, Presidency Division.*

INTERPETER:

Lieutenant JAMES VALLINGS, *19th Regiment, Native Infantry.*

The Court re-assembled at the Mess House of the 34th Regiment, Native Infantry, at Barrackpore, at 11 a.m., the President, Members, Judge Advocate, Interpreter all being present.

Lieutenant and Brevet-Colonel S. G. Wheler, Commanding the 34th Regiment, Native Infantry, being appointed Prosecutor, takes his place in Court.

Mungul Pandy, sepoy, No. 1446, 5th Company, 34th Regiment, Native Infantry, is brought a prisoner into Court.

The Division Orders directing the re-assembly of the Court-martial at Barrackpore, and the Station Order directing the hour and place of the Court's assembly, are produced and read.

The names of the President and Members of the Court are read over to the prisoner.

BY THE JUDGE ADVOCATE

Question: Sepoy Mungul Pandy,—Do you object to being tried by the President or by any of the Members of this Court- martial?

Answer: No, I do not object.

The Interpreter, President, Members, and Judge Advocate make the prescribed solemn affirmation.

The following charge is read—

Mungul Pandy, sepoy No. 1446, 5th Company, 34th Regiment, Native Infantry, confined by the order of the of Major-General J. B. Hearsey, Commanding the Presidency Division, on the following charges—

1st— For mutiny, in having at Barrackpore, on the 29th March 1857, gone on to the parade ground in front of the quarter-guard of his regiment armed with a sword and musket, and then there used words tending to incite the men of his regiment to turn out and join him in resistance to lawful authority.

2nd— For having, on the occasion set forth in the first charge, used violence against his superior officers Sergeant-Major James Thornton Hewson and Lieutenant and Adjutant Bempde Henry Baugh, of the 34th Regiment, Native Infantry, by discharging at them, severally his loaded musket, and then and there striking and wounding with his sword the said Lieutenant, B.H. Baugh and Sergeant-Major J. T. Hewson.

By order of the Major General Commanding Presidency Division.

ASST. ADJT-GENL'S OFFICE,
BARRACKPORE
The 5th April 1857.

(Sd.) A. H. ROSS, *Major*
Asst. Adjt.-Genl., Presy. Divn.,

BY THE JUDGE ADVOCATE

Question: Sepoy Mungul Pandy, No.1446, 5th Company, 34th Regiment, Native Infantry,—How say you, are you guilty, or not guilty, of these charges?

Answer: Not guilty.

The handcuffs are removed from the prisoner.

PROSECUTION

1st Witness

Lieutenant and Brevet-Colonel S.G. Wheler, Commanding the 354th Regiment, Native Infantry, the Prosecutor, is sworn.

BY THE JUDGE ADVOCATE

Question: You commanded the 34th Regiment, Native Infantry?

Answer: Yes.

Question: On the 29th March last, did you go down to the quarter guard of your regiment?

Answer: Yes.

Question: Drury drove up to my house in the afternoon of that day, informing me that a man, a sepoy, had gone out in front, inciting the men to mutiny. I proceeded with him to the parade—the lines I mean.

Question: What did you observe there ?

Answer: I observed the sepoy in front, the prisoner, walking parallel with the lines in front of the quarter-guard armed with a musket and sword. I proceeded in rear of the bells-of-arms to the quarter-guard. I did so, as several men about told me if I went in front of the bells-of-arms I should be shot. On arriving at the quarter-guard, it having been reported to me that the prisoner had wounded Lieutenant Baugh and the sergeant-major, I directed three or four men of the quarter-guard to load. They did load. I then directed the whole of the guard to load, and ordered the native officer in command of the guard to seize the prisoner. He hesitated, and said that the men would not touch the prisoner.

I repeated the order two or three times, when he gave the order to advance. The guard did so a few paces, and then halted, and he, the native officer, returned and said the men would not advance. As the Brigadier was on the parade, I went and reported the matter to him. To the best of my recollection, the General came up to the flank of the 34th Regiment, and after a few words with the Brigadier, he rode to the quarter-guard accompanied by several officers who were present at the time. The General directed the native officer to bring his guard in front. They advanced a few paces, when the prisoner shot himself.

Question: Where was the sepoy, Mungul Pandy, during these occurrences, and what was he doing ?

Answer: He was walking up and down the parade parallel with the lines, about a hundred yards from the quarter-guard.

Question: Did you hear him say anything ?

Answer: He spoke some thing; but I could not distinguish what he said.

Question: Did you observe the sergeant-major of the regiment and the adjutant ?

Answer: No.

Question: Has there been of late anything unusual in the state of some of the sepoys of this station ?

Answer: Towards the latter end of January there was much talking amongst the sepoys, I understood, generally, of the new cartridges being made up, and in consequence they had an idea that we were going to make them Christians by force.

Question: Were any and what measures adopted by the Major-General Commanding the Division, within your knowledge, to allay this feeling ?

Answer: There was a general parade ordered on the 9th of February of the whole of the troops off duty at the station, when the General addressed them about the new cartridge paper.

Question: On the 29th March had any European troops arrived at this station?

Answer: A few were reported to be at the ghat, the Flag-staff Ghat, at this station.

Question: Were not the 19th Regiment, Native Infantry, expected to arrive about that time in this station.

Answer: Yes.

Question: Was it made known to the native troops at this station for what purpose that regiment was to be marched in ?

Answer: At the general parade, on the 18th March, the General informed the troops that the 19th Regiment, Native Infantry, would be disbanded on account of what took place at Berhampore.

The prisoner declined to cross-examine.

The Court now rose and proceeded to the bungalow of the sergeant-major, 43rd Regiment, Native Infantry, in order to take the evidence of Sergeant-Major J. T. Hewson, 34th Regiment, Native Infantry, reported not be in a fit state to attend at the Court, the prisoner and all parties being present.

2nd Witness

Sergeant-Major J. T. Hewson, *34th Regiment, Native Infantry,* is duly sworn.

BY THE PROSECUTOR

Question: What are your Christian names?

Answer: James Thornton.

Question: Will you state the occurrences of the 29th of March last ?

Answer: Between the hours of four and six on the 29th of March, the naick of the quarter-guard of the 34th Regiment, Native Infantry, Emam Khan, No. 5 Company, came to my bungalow and reported that Sepoy Mungul Pandy of No. 5 Company had armed himself with his musket loaded and was walking about in front of the quarter-guard. He said that Mungul Pandy had taken a quantity of *bhang*, an intoxicating drug. I ordered the naick to report the circumstance to the adjutant of the regiment.

I then went on the parade dressed in uniform, and with my sword. On arriving in front of the light company's bells-of-arms, a sepoy regimentally dressed but with his *dhotee* on, no pantaloons, with coat and belt, took deliberate aim and fired at me. The shot did not take effect. I then went in rear of the bells-of-arms towards the quarter-guard, and on my way there called out to the guard to fall in. On arriving at the quarter-guard, I found some of the men dressing and some dressed. I spoke to the native officer, Jemadar Issuree Pandy, in command of the quarter-guard; I asked him why he did not arrest the sepoy. He said—"What can I do; my naick is gone to the adjutant; the havildar is gone to the field officer; am I to take him myself ?"

I ordered him to fall in his guard, and load. Some of the men grumbled; and he never insisted on the men loading or falling in. I then placed a sentry on the right and the left of the quarter-guard to watch Mungul Pandy. I saw Jemadar Gunness Lalla, No. 5 Company and also Mookta Persad Pandy, color-havildar, of No. 5 Company. Jemadar Gunness Lalla spoke to Mungul Pandy, the prisoner now before me. I could not understand all he said, nor repeat it in Hindustani. What I heard Gunness Lalla, the Jemadar, say was to give up his arms.

A little after I heard the sound of horses' hoofs, and Lieutanant Baugh, the Adjutant, came riding up. The adjutant called out—"Where is he ? Where is he ?" I called out to him to look to his left, and then I said—"Sir, ride to the right for your life, the sepoy will fire at you." I then saw Mungul Pandy, the prisoner present his piece and fire. The adjutant's horse dropped. I saw him take aim. Lieutenant Baugh then dismounted and drew a pistol from his holster and fired at Mungul Pandy, the prisoner. The shot did not take effect from what I could see. The adjutant then drew his sword and rushed towards Mungul Pandy, the prisoner.

When I saw him do so, I drew my sword and followed him, at the same time calling out to the guard to load and come on. I believe we both came up at the same time in front of the prisoner. Mungul Pandy made a cut with a *tulwar* (native sword,) at me, but did not strike me. He struck the adjutant. The next cut I received myself from Mungul Pandy with his sword. At the same time I was knocked down from behind by one or two blows from a sepoy's musket. I could not recognize the features of the man who struck me; he was regimentally dressed. On rising up I advanced again towards the prisoner, and caught him by the collar of the coat with the left hand. I struck him several times with my sword, and received another cut from his *tulwar*. I was again knocked down from behind, and I remember being struck on the back and on the head when on the ground. The second time I was knocked down I was stupefied. On getting on my legs again, I saw a number of sepoys in front of the quarter-guard dressed.

I also saw Lieutenant Baugh walking slowly towards the 43rd Regiment, Native Infantry, lines. His jacket had much blood on it. I followed him. On coming near my own bungalow, I heard footsteps behind me, and on turning round I saw Jemadar Issuree Pandy of the quarter-guard. I told him he had acted in a shameful manner, and that I would put him under arrest. I tried to grasp his sword, but he stepped back. His sword was in the scabbard. I then met my wife and step-daughter, who brought me to the bungalow of the sergeant-major of the 43rd. I there saw Lieutenant Baugh, and then saw his hand much cut.

Question: Did you hear Sepoy Mungul Pandy, the prisoner, say anything when he was in front of the quarter-guard?

Answer: Yes. *"Nikul ao, pultun; nikul ao hamara sath"*—"Come out, men; come out and join me—You sent me out here, why don't you follow me."

Question: When the sepoy fired at you, did you hear the sound of a bullet passing or striking anything?

Answer: I heard the sound of a bullet close.

Question: Was any effort whatever made by the jemadar in command of, or men of, the quarter-guard to come to your aid?

Answer: I had no assistance; the men who came struck me and Lieutenant Baugh once. I saw Lieutenant Baugh struck with a musket from behind.

Question: Did you hear any shot fired after you had gone out to the front with Lieutenant-Baugh?

Answer: Yes, from the direction of the lines behind me, quite close. I think the shot passed between me and Lieutenant Baugh.

Question: At what distance did this affair occur from the quarter-guard ?

Answer: About thirty or forty yards.

Question: How many men came up to where you and Lieutenant Baugh were?

Answer: When I left the place where I was struck down, there were seven or eight men. They were regimentally dressed, and I believe they belonged to the quarter-guard.

Question: Why do you believe they belonged to the quarter-guard?

Answer: When I left the quarter-guard to assist Lieutenant Baugh, the quarter-guard was dressed, and the time was too short for other men to dress themselves and come out; and the men going on picket wear blue pantaloons: these men had white pantaloons on. There was one man I recognised,—but I could not swear to him—Heeralall Tewary of that company, who struck me. He was on the quarter-guard.

Question: Did you see any men of the regiment assembled and looking on?

Answer: Yes, there was a great number looking on from between the bells-of-arms, chiefly on the left, because three of the right wing companies have gone to Chittagong.

Question: Did any of these men come out to assist?

Answer: I did not see one. All the time I was out I kept my eye on the prisoner.

Question: Did you hear the jemadar of the quarter-guard or the men say anything when you were near them?

Answer: No, they were talking between themselves.

Question: How many sword cuts did you receive?

Answer: Two on the head.

Question: Are you now suffering from these wounds?

Answer: Yes.

(The witness is very much exhausted, and is lying on the *charpoy*.)

The prisoner declines to cross examine.

The Court now, at 3 p.m., rose and proceeded to the quarters of Lieutenant B. H. Baugh, Adjutant, 34th Regiment, Native Infantry, reported unable to leave his quarters ; the prisoner and all parties being present.

3rd Witness

Lieutenant B. H. Baugh, Adjutant, 34th Regiment, Native Infantry, is duly sworn.

BY THE PROSECUTOR

Question: You are Lieutenant Bempde Henry Baugh, and Adjutant, 34th Regiment, Native Infantry ?

Answer: Yes.

Question: Will you be so good as to state the occurrences of the 29th March last ?

Answer: On Sunday week last, at about five o'clock in the afternoon, the havildar-major of the regiment came to my quarters and reported that a sepoy of the name of Mungul Pandy, No. 5 Company, had turned out in front of the quarter-guard of the regiment and fired at the sergeant-major. I told the man to go and report the circumstance to Colonel Wheler, ordered my charger, put on my uniform, and after having put a brace of pistols in the holsters, I galloped down as hard as I could to the regimental quarter-guard.

I had scarcely pulled up at the quarter-guard when a shot was fired, and my horse fell under me. As soon as I could disentangle myself, I drew a pistol from the left holster and on seeing the prisoner in the act of re-loading I fired. He stopped loading. I immediately drew my sword and rushed in to secure him. I had proceeded about half way when the prisoner drew a *tulwar*. I looked back to see where my horse was, intending to get my other pistol, but saw that he was gone; so continued my advance and engaged the prisoner.

After a conflict of about, perhaps, five or eight minutes (during which time I received a sword cut which entirely disabled my left hand, from the prisoner, also a very deep wound in my neck, and another on my head ; the last, however, I am not certain whether it was a sword cut or proceeded from the butt end of a musket) a shot was fired close by: it came from the direction of the quarter-guard.

On finding myself gradually getting hemmed in, I commenced retreating. During this time, with the exception of Shaik Pultoo, sepoy, Grenadier Company, not a man either from the regimental quarter-guard or from the lines advanced to my assistance. Shaik Pultoo held the prisoner, and enabled me to make my retreat good. I reached the sergeant-major's bungalow of the 43rd Regiment, Native (Light) Infantry, and from there was conveyed by Captain Wiggins to Dr. Allen's, to have my wounds dressed.

Question: How far from the quarter-guard of the regiment did this take place?

Answer: My horse was shot at about, I should say, eight or nine paces from the quarter-guard of the regiment; and the conflict took place, I should say, about forty or fifty paces.

Question: Did you receive the wound in your neck also from the prisoner?

Answer: Yes.

Question: When you rode up, were many men standing in front and about the lines?

Answer: A great number.

Question: Did you observe whether any of the men who came up to you during the conflict were regimentally dressed?

Answer: I could not observe; I was so busily engaged in warding off the prisoner's blows.

Question: Did the prisoner say anything when you were fighting with him?

Answer: Not that I recollect.

Question: Was your horse wounded with a bullet?

Answer: Yes.

Question: When you attention was first directed to the prisoner, where did you see him?

Answer: He was to my left, about fifty yards from me, in front of the quarter-guard.

The prisoner declines to cross-examine.

The Court returns to their first place of assembly, the 34th Regiment Mess House, the Court, prisoner, and Prosecutor all being present.

4th Witness

Drummer John Lewis, *34th Regiment, Native Infantry,* is called into Court and duly affirmed.

BY THE PROSECUTOR

Question: Were you on duty as bugler at the quarter-guard of your regiment at Barrackpore on Sunday, the 29th March last?

Answer: I was drummer of the guard.

Question: State what you saw in the afternoon.

Answer: After four o'clock in the afternoon, the prisoner came towards the quarter-guard, crying out where is the bugler. Upon seeing me, he told me to sound the assembly. I did not obey through fear. He then pointed his musket at me. I did not then obey him; on seeing a sepoy near, he said to him, lowering his musket towards him, "Why are your not getting ready? It is for our religion." He remained there for sometime repeating the words "sound the assembly". When the sergeant-major arrived after some time, I saw from my place where I had sheltered myself that he fired his musket at the sergeant-major, who was advancing from the left wing.

I don't know where the ball struck. I heard the sound of the ball. About a quarter of an hour afterwards the adjutant also arrived from the direction of the left wing. I saw the prisoner fire his musket at the adjutant, and hit the horse. The horse dropped, and the adjutant, disengaging himself, went towards the prisoner on foot, with a pistol in his hand. The sergeant-major went also with him. The prisoner again fired his musket. I saw the prisoner also strike the sergeant-major and the adjutant with a sword.

Question: What did the jemadar of the guard do all this time?

Answer: The jemadar went towards the rear-guard.

Question: When the conflict was going on between the adjutant and sepoy, where was the jemadar of the quarter-guard?

Answer: He was present in the guard.

The witness appearing to be alarmed, is told not to be frightened.

Question: What did the jemadar of the guard do while the fight was going on?

Answer: He was standing amongst his guard. He did nothing.

Question: Did you go up with the guard to the place where the fight was going on?

Answer: I did not go.

Question: Did any of the guard go?

Answer: I did not see any one go

Question: Did sepoy Heeralall Tewary go or not?

Answer: I don't know him.

Question: Did the jemadar and men of the guard go to where the fight was going on?

Answer: No. He did not go with the guard.

The prisoner declines to cross-examine.

BY THE COURT

Question: When Mungul Pandy, sepoy, came first to the guard, how near did he come up?

Answer: About some thirteen paces.

Question: Where was the jemadar then ?

Answer: I was sewing, and did not see him.

Question: Do you know where he was?

Answer: He was inside the quarter-guard.

Question: Did any one of the quarter-guard attempt to secure the prisoner ?

Answer: No one attempted.

Question: Did the jemadar give any orders to secure the prisoner?

Answer: No, not any.

The witness withdraws.

5th Witness

Havildar Shaik Pultoo, 34th Regiment, Native Infantry, is called into court and duly affirmed.

BY THE PROSECUTOR

Question: On the 29th of March you were a sepoy in the Grenadier Company, were you not, and are now promoted to havildar.

Answer: Yes; I am now havildar.

Question: Relate what you saw on the parade on the afternoon of the 29th March last.

Answer: About half-past three I had gone out to ease myself; and on returning to the lines, I observed Mungul Pandy in his coat and hat, and accoutrements and musket in his hand. He was shouting out—"Come out, you *bhainchutes,* the Europeans are here. From biting these cartridges, we shall become infidels. Get ready, turn out all of you." He came out of his hut,—I saw him,—and ordered the bugler to sound the assembly. The two drummers hid themselves. The sergeant-major came up, and the sepoy then fired at him. The sergeant-major said to the jemadar of the quarter-guard—"See you have done nothing, and he has shot at me." Mungul Pandy was walking up and down in front of the quarter-guard, about thirty paces off.

Question: Did you see the adjutant come up?

Answer: Yes.

Question: What happened then?

Answer: The adjutant came up and looked round him, and then the sepoy, Mungul Pandy , shot the horse in the left thigh.

Question: Did he take aim?

Answer: Yes.

Question: What happened then?

Answer: The horse fell. The adjutant then took a pistol out of one holster and said to me—"Shaik Pultoo, no one is assisting me, you come with me." We then advanced, and the sergeant-major also. On reaching the sepoy, he struck the adjutant with his sword and wounded him in the hand, and afterwards the sergeant-major also on the head. The sepoy struck them again. I then came up and caught him by the waist. He wounded me in the hand. The adjutant and the sergeant-major withdrew. The sepoys in uniform struck the adjutant and sergeant- major also, who fell down, with the butts of their muskets.

Question: What sepoys were there?

Answer: Sepoys of the quarter-guard; they were in uniform.

Question: Do you know them?

Answer: No, I was twenty paces off. The adjutant was retreating when they struck him.

Question: How many sepoys were there in uniform?

Answer: I saw four.

Question: Did you hear any shot fired while the adjutant and sepoy were fighting?

Answer: Yes; from the direction of the guard. The ball passed the sergeant-major and adjutant.

Question: Did you see where it was fired from?

Answer: It came from behind me, and from the direction of the quarter guard.

Question: Was Sepoy Mungul Pandy in an excited state?

Answer: He eats *bhang;* I don't know if he had eaten any then.

Question: When the adjutant and sergeant-major retreated, what became of the sepoy, Mungul Pandy?

Answer: I had hold of him. I held him until the adjutant had gone off the ground. I called out to the jemadar of the guard, who was about thirty paces off, to send four sepoys to take charge of him.

Question: Did the jemadar send the sepoys to take charge of him?

Answer: No, not one.

Question: Did the jemadar give you any answer?

Answer: No, he was inside the quarter-guard.

Question: When did you release the sepoy?

Answer: When I could hold no longer. I was wounded.

Question: Did any sepoys interfere to make you let the man go?

Answer: Yes.

Question: Who were they?

Answer: Some of the quarter-guard.

Question: Name them?

Answer: I don't know them. There was a crowd; they called out to me from inside the guard to let him go.

The witness withdraws.

The prosecution is closed.

The prisoner being called on for his defence says—"I did not know who I wounded and who I did not; what more shall I say? I have nothing more to say".

The prisoner being asked, says—"I have no evidence".

The defence is closed.

The Court is closed.

FINDING

The Court find the prisoner Mungul Pandy, sepoy, No. 1446, 5th Company, 34th Regiment, Native Infantry, guilty of both charges preferred against him.

The Court re-opened, and the prisoner brought before it.

Captain C.C. Drury, 34th Regiment, Native Infantry, is called and sworn.

BY THE JUDGE ADVOCATE

Question: Has the prisoner been warned that his former convictions and general character will be brought in evidence against him?

Answer: There was no previous convictions; he has been warned as to his general character.

Question: What is the prisoner's general character?

Answer: Good.

Question: What is his age and length of service?

Answer: His age is twenty-six years two months and nine days. His service is seven years two months and nine days.

The prisoner declines to cross examine.

The Court is closed.

SENTENCE

The court sentences the prisoner, Mungul Pandy, sepoy, No. 1446, 5th Company, 34th Regiment, Native Infantry, to suffer death by being hanged by the neck until he be dead.

Approved and confirmed.

BARRACKPORE, (Sd.) J. B. HEARSEY, *Maj.-Genl.,*
The 7th April 1857 *Comdg. the Presy. Divn.*

The execution of Mungul Pandy, Sepoy, No. 1446, 5th Company, 34th Regiment, Native Infantry, will take place on the brigade parade to-morrow morning, the 8th instant, at half past five o'clock in presence of all troops off duty at the station.

The Court adjourned at 6.30 p.m.

From Major-General J. B. HEARSEY, C.B., *Commanding the Presidency Division, to Colonel* R. J. H. BIRCH, C.B., *Secretary to the Government of India, in the Military Department—No. 156, dated Barrackpore, 9th April 1857.*

In compliance with your instructions, I have now the honour to forward the proceedings of a Special Board of Officers which was assembled for the purpose of enquiring into the particulars of the claim of Shaik Pultoo, a supernumerary havildar of the 34th Regiment, Native Infantry, to the Order of Merit; and concurring in the opinion recorded by the Court that this soldier has behaved in a most gallant and ex-emplary manner on the occasion in question, I would respectfully beg to recommend, to the favourable consideration of the Government of India, that the third class of this honourable order may be bestowed upon him.

PROCEEDINGS of a Special Board assembled at Barrackpore, by order of Major-General J.B. HEARSEY, C.B. *Commanding the Presidency Division, on the 9th day of April 1857, for the purpose of enquiring into and recording evidence on oath or attention as to the act of personal gallantry displayed by* SHAIK PULTOO, *sepoy, Grenadier Company, 34th Regiment, Native Infantry, in defending the Life of Lieutenant and Adjutant* B.H. BAUGH, *34th Regiment, Native Infantry, on the afternoon of the 29th March 1857.*

PRESIDENT:

Lieutenant-Colonel W. ST. L. MITCHELL, *19th Regiment, Native Infantry.*

MEMBERS:

Captain R. A. SMITH, *19th Regiment, Native Infantry.*

Captain N. C. BOSWELL, *2nd Regiment, Native (Grenadier) Infantry.*

Subadar Major DURRIOW SINGH, *70th Regiment., Native Infantry.*

Subadar Major SHAIKH GOLAM MAHOMED, *2nd Regt., N. I. (Grenadiers).*

INTERPRETER:

Lieutenant GRIERSON, *70th Regiment, Native Infantry.*

The President, Members, and Interpreter all present.

The Court proceeds to the quarters of Lieutenant and Adjutant B.H. Baugh, 34th Regiment, Native Infantry, at 6 a.m., as he is, from his wounds, unable to attend at the Mess, 2nd Regiment, Native (Grenadier) Infantry.

1st Witness

Lieutenant and Adjutant B. H. Baugh, 34th Regiment, Native Infantry, is called upon by the Court to state what he knows regarding the conduct of Shaik Pultoo, sepoy, 34th Regiment, Native Infantry, on the afternoon of the 29th March 1857, who is present in Court.

Lieutenant-Adjutant B.H. Baugh, having been sworn, states as follows:- "During my conflict with the sepoy, Mungul Pandy, I was severally wounded; one of these wounds totally disabled me of the use of my left hand. Finding that other sepoys were also assisting the mutineer, I commenced retreating, and was allowed to make that retreat good solely through the means of Shaik Pultoo, who caught hold of the sepoy, Mungul Pandy, round the waist and securely held him. By this act of his I consider my life was saved."

BY THE COURT

Question: Was Shaik Pultoo armed or unarmed when he rushed to your rescue?

Answer: He was unarmed.

The Court proceeds to the quarters of Sergeant-Major J. T. Hewson, of the 34th Regiment, Native Infantry, as he is, from his wounds, unable to attend at the Mess of the 2nd Regiment Native (Grenadier) Infantry.

2nd Witness

Sergeant-Major J. T. Hewson, *34th Regiment, Native Infantry,* is sworn, and in the presence of Shaik Pultoo, late sepoy, now havildar, of the 34th Regiment, Native Infantry, states as follows:- "On the 29th March 1857,between the hours of 4 and 6 P.M., when I went out in front of the quarter-guard to try to save the life of Lieutenant and Adjutant Baugh, 34th Regiment, Native Infantry, on whom an attack was made by Mungul Pandy, sepoy, 34th Regiment, Native Infantry, I did not recognise the features of Sepoy Shaik Pultoo, I having been knocked down and severely maltreated by several sepoys of the 34th Regiment, Native Infantry, my own regiment, in uniform; and I was in that state that I could not recognise the men who attacked me. I know Shaik Pultoo very well for about the last five years; he has been a drill lance-naick, he is a man of the most excellent character."

3rd Witness

Mrs. Hewson, wife of Sergeant-Major Hewson, 34th Regiment, Native Infantry, is called into Court, and duly sworn, states as follows:- "I saw Lieutenant and Adjutant Baugh struggling with Mungul Pandy, sepoy, 34th Regiment, Native Infantry, when my husband went up to assist the adjutant. I was then standing in my verandah about sixty yards off. I was so frightened I could not distinguish any one amongst the crowd of natives. I saw a man behind Mungul Pandy holding him; he was in undress but I could not tell who he was. All this occurred about 5 or 6 p.m., on the afternoon of the 29th March 1857."

The witness withdraws.

4th Witness

Shaik Pultoo, havildar (late sepoy), 34th Regiment, Native Infantry, being in Court and having made the prescribed solemn affirmation, states as follows—

The sepoy, Mungul Pandy, about 4 p.m., was strutting backwards and forwards in front of the quarter-guard, armed with a musket and sword; he had on his red jacket and regimental cap, endeavouring to incite the men of the regiment to mutiny, saying that the guns and Europeans had arrived for the purpose of slaughtering them. Some one told the sergeant major of this, and he came towards the quarter-guard, asking the jemadar of that guard where Mungul Pandy was and why he did not confine him.

Mungul Pandy then fired at the sergeant-major, but missed him; he reloaded; the sergeant-major being alarmed ran into the quarter-guard and asked the jemadar why he did not arrest Mungul Pandy, who had re-loaded his musket, and told him to send and let the adjutant know what had occurred on the parade ground. Shortly after this the adjutant on horseback arrived at the quarter-guard, and asked the jemadar where the sepoy with the loaded musket was, and why he had not secured him. The jemadar did not tell him where the man was, but I pointed him out.

Mungul Pandy was then standing a little way in front of the quarter-guard. Just as I spoke Mungul Pandy fired at the adjutant and wounded his horse, so that he fell. I assisted the adjutant to get clear of his horse. The adjutant then pulled out a pistol from his holster, and said—"That man will kill me, he is loading again." I said—"You will not be allowed to be killed, for I am with you." The adjutant then with the pistol in his hand rushed towards Mungul Pandy, who on seeing this, did not finish loading his musket and commenced retreating.

The sergeant-major and I followed the adjutant as quickly as we could. The adjutant when within twenty paces fired at Mungul Pandy, but missed him. When the adjutant reached him Mungul Pandy drew his sword and wounded him severely. By this time the sergeant-major came up, and he also was wounded severely. I then came up and stretched out my hand to stop Mungul Pandy, who was following the adjutant, and said to him "Take care, do not strike adjutant." He aimed a blow at the adjutant's neck, which I received on my right hand. I then seized him round the waist with my left arm; the adjutant and sergeant-major then got away.

I then called out to the quarter-guard to come and make Mungul Pandy a prisoner, and told the jemadar, Issuree Pandy, of No.1 Company, who commanded the guard, to send four men and take him. Then I got hold of him and would not allow him to hurt any one. They did not come, but abused me, as also did the jemadar, and said that if I did not let Mungul Pandy go, they would shoot me. Being wounded, I was obliged to let him go. While I was holding Mungul Pandy several men of the quarter-guard followed the adjutant and sergeant-major, beating them with the butt end of their muskets. At this time a shot was fired from the direction of the quarter-guard, but I cannot say by whom.

The witness withdraws.

There being no further evidence procurable, the Court is closed to record their opinion.

From the evidence before the Court they are of opinion that Havildar (late a sepoy) Shaik Pultoo, 34th Regiment, Native Infantry, displayed most conspicuous gallantry, by which act the lives of the adjutant and sergeant-major of his regiment were saved. The Court do therefore consider him fully worthy of having conferred upon him the third class Order of Merit for his exemplary conduct on the afternoon of the 29th March 1857 on the parade ground of his regiment at Barrackpore.

The Court adjourned at 10.30 a.m.

From Major-General J. B. HEARSEY, C.B., *Commanding the Presidency Division, to Colonel* R. J. H. BIRCH, C.B., *Secretary to the Government of India, in the Military Department—dated Barrackpore, 12th April 1857.*

I have the honour to forward the Proceedings of an European Special Court of Inquiry, to investigate into the conduct of the native officers and men of the 34th Regiment, Native Infantry on duty at the quarter-guard of that corps, on the 29th March ultimo; also the evidence taken (voluntarily given) from four men who were on duty with that guard, when they were ordered to be put into fetters.

These documents I wish to be laid before Government.

From Captain RICHARDS, *Officiating major of Brigade, to Major* H. W. MATTHEWS, *43rd Regiment, Native Infantry—dated Barrackpore, 30th March 1857.*

With reference to station morning orders of this date, I have the honour, by desire of the Brigadier Commanding at Barrackpore, to inform you that the Special Court of Inquiry, of which you are President, is convened with the view of eliciting the circumstances attendant on the adjutant, the sergeant-major, and a sepoy of the 34th Regiment Native Infantry, having been wounded in the lines of that regiment, on the evening of Sunday, the 29th March 1857.

From JAMES ALLEN, Esq., F. R. C. S, *Assistant Surgeon, 34th Regiment, Native Infantry, to Colonel* S. G. WHELER, *Commanding the 34th Regiment, Native Infantry —dated Barrackpore, 30th March 1857.*

In reply to your demi-official letter of this date, I have the honour to inform you that I consider it would be hazardous at present to the health of either Lieutenant B.H. Baugh, or Sergeant-Major J. T. Hewson, for the Court of Inquiry to assemble at their quarters now for further investigation.

In the event of no unfavourable symptoms showing themselves during the next twelve or sixteen hours, the further investigation required by the Court of Inquiry may perhaps be proceeded with, and due notice of which shall be given to the officiating adjutant of the regiment for your information.

PROCEEDINGS of a special Court of Inquiry directed in station morning orders of to-day, to assemble at the Mess House of the 34th Regiment, Native infantry, at 11 a.m .to investigate circumstances which occurred yesterday evening in the lines of the 34th Regiment, native Infantry—dated Barrackpore, 30th March 1857.

PRESIDENT:

Major H. W. MATTHEWS, *43rd Regiment, Native (Light) Infantry.*

MEMBERS:

Major COOKE, *2nd Regiment, Native (Grenadier) Infantry.*

Captain GREENE, *70th Regiment, Native Infantry.*

INTERPRETER:

Lieutenant CORBETT, *43rd Regiment, Light Infantry.*

Colonel S. G. Wheler, Commanding the 34th Regiment, Native Infantry, will produce evidence.

The President, Members and Interpreter all present.

Letter dated Barrackpore, 30th March 1857, from the Officiating Major of Brigade to Major H. W. Matthews, President of the Special Court of Inquiry, is read and appended.

Colonel S. G. Wheler proceeds to call the following evidence—

1st Witness

Shaik Pultoo, 34th Regiment, Native Infantry, acting Lance Naick at the drill, is called into Court, and duly cautioned.

Question: State what occurred yesterday evening at the lines of your regiment?

Answer: At about half-past three o'clock a sepoy of the 5th Company of my regiment, of the name of Mungul Pandy, came out of the lines on to the parade-ground with a musket and *talwar*; he had his regimental coat on, and haversack, he had also his military cap on. A report of the above was made to the sergeant-major, who came out near to the quarter-guard in his uniform.

The sepoy fired at him, and missed. The sergeant-major then went into the quarter-guard and told Issuree Pandy, the jemadar of the guard, to make arrangements about seizing the sepoy. The jemadar did not obey the order he had received; he did nothing. The sergeant-major sent some one to call the adjutant of the regiment, who came riding up, after about a quarter-of-an-hour, in uniform; he came close to the quarter-guard, no one telling him that there was a sepoy on parade with his musket loaded.

While I was telling the adjutant of the sepoy being there, the sepoy fired a shot, wounding the adjutant's horse. The horse fell, the adjutant falling with it. The adjutant had a loaded pistol in his hand. The sepoy was about thirty yards off when he fired. The adjutant told the sepoys who were about him to seize the sepoy, but no one obeyed his orders; the adjutant went towards Mungul Pandy, and also the sergeant-major.

The adjutant fired his pistol at the sepoy and missed him; the sepoy then came at them with his sword, and wounded the adjutant on the face and on his left hand. The sergeant-major drew his sword. Some sepoys from behind knocked down the sergeant-major and the adjutant with the butts of their muskets; they got up and ran away.

This evidence corrects the above statement, and now says: that after Mungul Pandy had cut down the adjutant and the sergeant-major, some sepoys knocked them down with the butts of their muskets. I don't know who they were, but they had their regimentals on. I got wounded myself in the hand, trying to protect the adjutant when Mungul Pandy was cutting at him. I had got Mungul Pandy down; a great number of sepoys, in undress, were assembled round us, they abused me saying "why don't you let him go," and struck me on the back and on the head with stones and shoes. I then let him go: the adjutant had got out of the way in the meantime.

The witness having had the above read to him now states:- "I let Mungul Pandy go when the sergeant-major, as well as the adjutant, had got clear away."

BY THE COURT

Question: Where and how far from Mungul Pandy were you when you saw him go out on the parade?

Answer: I was near the kote of the Grenadier Company of the regiment. Mungul Pandy came out from the centre of the lines; he was about a hundred yards from me.

Question: What did you hear him calling out?

Answer: He called out to the whole regiment to turn out; the Europeans had arrived.

Question: Were there many men present, and within hearing, on the occasion; and how did they act?

Answer: All that were in the lines were present looking on, but were quiet. Mungul Pandy called out, "The magazine has come with the Europeans, and the Europeans are here to make us bite the new cartridges, and destroy our religion."

Question: Was there any sympathy or exhibition of feeling shown by the men who were looking on when Mungul Pandy called out to them to turn out?

Answer: No, not any whatever, except that Jemadar Gunness Lalla, of the 5th Company, remonstrated with him, and said, "Haven't you heard that you are not to bite the cartridges? Don't make a disturbance".

Question: Were all those men still spectators when the adjutant and sergeant-major were fired at by Mungul Pandy and assaulted?

Answer: Yes, they were all looking on.

Question: Did any one of them step forward to assist you in defending the adjutant and sergeant-major ?

Answer: Not one of them.

Question: How many men in uniform assaulted the adjutant and sergeant-major with the butts of their muskets?

Answer: Three or four men, but I don't know whether they belonged to the quarter guard or the pickets.

Question: How do you account for not recognizing them?

Answer: I was wounded and confused.

Question: Were there any commissioned or non-commissioned officers amongst those men you saw in uniform?

Answer: I did not see any.

Question: How were the men of the regiment engaged at the time of the occurrence, and were the bells-of-arms open?

Answer: Some were open and some shut, and some of the men were engaged in cleaning their accoutrements.

Question: Prior to yesterday's occurrence had any similar manifestation displayed itself amongst the men of the regiment?

Answer: No, not that I know of.

The witness withdraws.

2nd Witness

Gunness Lalla, jemadar, No. 5 Company, 34th Regiment, Native Infantry, is called into Court, and duly cautioned.

BY THE COURT

Question: State to the Court what occurred yesterday in your regiment?

Answer: I was sitting yesterday in my house when Goorbucus Sing, pay-havildar of the company, came and told me: "I don't know what has come over Mungul Pandy, sepoy; he is walking about on the parade with a musket and *tulwar*." I went to the front of the lines near the kote of my own company, and saw him on the parade walking about. I sent Gobin Sing, havildar, to report to the sergeant-major, the adjutant, and the commanding officer. I also sent Goorbucus Sing, orderly-havildar of the company, to report to Captain Allen in charge of the company. I heard Mungul Pandy got the musket from the kote to clean.

Question: Did you see Mungul Pandy yourself, and what was he doing?

Answer: He was walking about in front of the quarter-guard, distant about a hundred and twenty-five paces.

Question: Did he say anything at all?

Answer: He called out for a bugler to blow the assembly, and said, all who are men turn out at three o'clock.

Question: What did he do after this?

Answer: I saw him discharge his musket in the direction of No. 6 or No. 7 Company. I do not know whom he fired at. He immediately reloaded, and walked backwards and forwards in front of the lines.

Question: What occurred after this ?

Answer: The sergeant-major came up in rear of the quarter-guard, and told the jemadar of the guard, Issuree Pandy, to make his men fall in; they did so. Afterwards I saw the adjutant-coming up on horseback towards the quarter-guard. He was pretty close to it when Mungul Pandy fired at him, wounded his horse, which fell down; the men of the guard rushed up to pick up the adjutant.

Mungul Pandy was about eighty or a hundred yards off when he fired at the adjutant. The adjutant got up instantly, and went towards Mungul Pandy with a pistol in his hand, and accompanied by the sergeant-major and Shaik Pultoo, who came from the direction of the Grenadier Company; the adjutant discharged his pistol at him, and missed; he then threw the pistol at him.

The adjutant drew his sword, as also the sergeant-major; the sepoy then drew his *tulwar,* and they fought together. I spoke to some sepoys of the quarter-guard to go and assist the adjutant; when they got a short distance Mungul Pandy threw down his *tulwar*, and seized his musket by the barrel, and was striking with the butt end of it, but I could not see whom he struck. I saw Shaik Pultoo seize him by the waist. I afterwards saw Mungul Pandy loose again, but I don't know how it happened.

Question: Did you see any sepoys, either in dress or undress, strike the adjutant or sergeant-major ?

Answer: No, I did not.

Question: Did any of the sepoys assist the adjutant or the sergeant-major.

Answer: Only one man, Heeralall Ditchit, or Tewary (I don't know which), got up to them ; all the rest returned, when the adjutant made a sign to them to do so.

Question: Is it likely the adjutant, when his life was in danger, would make a sign to those who were coming to assist him to go away ?

Answer: I cannot say, but I saw him make a sign.

The witness withdraws.

The Court adjourns till to-morrow at 11 a.m. it being 4 p.m.

Barrackpore, 1st April 1857.

The Court re-assembled this day, pursuant to adjournment. President, Members, and Interpreter all present.

Letter dated Barrackpore, 30th March 1857, from Assistant-Surgeon J. Allen, 34th Regiment, Native Infantry, to Colonel S.G. Wheler, Commanding the 34th Regiment, Native Infantry, is appended; a record to this effect having been inadvertently omitted in the former day's proceedings.

In consequence of the above letter, and the Brigadier having informed the President of the Court that it was advisable not to hurry the inquiry, there has been delay of one day. Colonel S.G. Wheler proceeds to call in evidence.

3rd Witness

Mookta Persaud Pandy, *havildar, 5th Company, 34th Regiment, Native Infantry,* is called into Court, and has had explained to him para II, section 22, Military Regulations.

Question: State what occurred on the parade of the 34th Regiment, Native Infantry, on the 29th of last month.

Answer: Between four and five o'clock on the afternoon of the 29th of last month, a sepoy, Mungul Pandy, 5th Company, 34th Regiment, Native Infantry, standing near the quarter-guard of the corps, called out to the bugler of the guard to blow the "assembly". I was in my house close by and heard him. I came out and saw him standing near the quarter-guard, with his musket and a *tulwar;* he was abusing the bugler, and saying—" Why don't you sound the bugle? I will shoot you if you do not." I said to Issuree Pandy, jemadar, on duty at the quarter-guard, "Confine the man; I think his musket is loaded." The jemadar said "I cannot do so." I then said "If you don't confine him, I will report the circumstance to the captain" (meaning the captain of the jemadar's company).

At the time we were in front of the quarter-guard: we went to the rear of it, and I told him, "You have neither confined him nor reported the circumstance, which you ought to have done." I then ran to Captain Drury, and told him what had happened; he said he would come immediately, and told me to go that instant to the jemadar of the quarter-guard, and tell him to confine the sepoy on his (Captain Drury's) authority. On this I ran to the jemadar, and found him, the sergeant-major, and some sepoys, standing in rear of the quarter-guard. I gave Captain Drury's order to the jemadar. The jemadar said, "How can I confine him? His musket is loaded." I said, "It is the captain's order, he is to be confined somehow or other; you have a guard with you." He repeated what he had before said.

I then ran and reported the occurrence to Captain Allen of my company; I found he had gone to parade. I then returned, and when I had arrived opposite the lines of the Grenadier Company, I saw the adjutant on horseback; he rode up to the quarter-guard, and stopped his horse; the sepoys called out to him to come in rear of the guard. He was looking round when Mungul Pandy, sepoy, fired; the adjutant's horse fell and the adjutant fell backward; he got up and seized a pistol, and rushed towards the sepoy; the sergeant-major and Shaik Pultoo, sepoy, followed him from the right of the quarter-guard, at about eight or ten paces' interval.

The adjutant, when some ten or twelve paces from Mungul Pandy, fired his pistol at him; he missed, and threw the pistol at Mungul Pandy. By this time the sergeant-major and Shaik Pultoo had got to within two or three paces of the adjutant. The adjutant and sergeant-major drew their swords, the latter made a cut at the sepoy: he lifted up his musket to guard the cut, and the sergeant's sword broke off at the hilt.

The sepoy then took the musket in his left hand, and drew his *tulwar*, with which he made a cut at the adjutant: at this time a sepoy of the quarter-guard, Heeralall Tewary, of the Light Company, rushed forward, Shaik Pultoo having seized Mungul Pandy round the waist from the rear: he was, however, still fighting with the adjutant, who received a cut on the left hand, which fell down by his side. Mungul Pandy then broke away from Shaik Pultoo, and wounded him with a sword-cut.

It was at this time Heeralall Tewary, who had rushed from the quarter-guard, struck the sergeant major over the head with his musket; the adjutant and Shaik Pultoo had withdrawn.

Heeralall Tewary again lifted up his musket, and struck the sergeant-major, who fell, and Heeralall Tewary went back to his guard. Shortly after, the sergeant-major got up, and made towards his house; the sepoy, Mungul Pandy, made two or three cuts at him.

Mungul Pandy then went out to the parade in front of the quarter-guard, and loaded his musket; having done so, he walked backwards and forwards at about a hundred and fifty paces in front of the guard, calling out something which I did not make out, excepting once, when I heard him say, "If any one comes near me I will shoot him."

The colonel and Captain Drury then came to the quarter-guard; the colonel gave the order for two sepoys to load, afterwards for four, and then for the whole guard. The colonel told the jemadar to take his guard and seize Mungul Pandy; the jemadar took his guard about eight or ten paces to the front, halted them, and came back himself to the colonel and Captain Drury, reporting, the man's musket is loaded, and he says he will shoot anybody who goes near him. The colonel and Captain Drury said to the jemadar, "What ! are you afraid then, that you have returned?" He replied, "The sepoys say they will not advance without a European officer". The colonel said, "This is shameful; if you don't want to go, bring your guard back."

The jemadar then ordered them to the right-about, and brought them back, then ordered arms. The General afterwards came to the quarter-guard with a number of gentlemen; he asked the jemadar if his men were loaded; he said they were. He then ordered the advance, and all proceeded towards Mungul Pandy; when they had got ten or fifteen paces, he sat down and shot himself.

Question: Did you hear a musket fired by any one besides Mungul Pandy ?

Answer: No.

Question: How many musket shots did you hear fired ?

Answer: I heard one when I was reporting to Captain Drury, and a second when I saw Lieutenant and Adjutant Baugh's horse shot under him.

Question: Did you hear a third musket-shot when the struggle was going on between the adjutant, the sergeant-major, and Mungul Pandy ?

Answer: I did not.

Question: What reason did Mungul Pandy assign to the bugler when he ordered him to sound the assembly ?

Answer: I didn't hear him assign any reason.

Question: Had you a distinct view of the scuffle while it lasted ?

Answer: Yes, I had; they were about hundred or a hundred and twenty-five paces off; I was standing near a *peepul* tree, eight or ten yards to the left of the quarter-guard.

Question: What other men of the quarter-guard, besides Heeralall Tewary, did you see go forward ?

Answer: No others went forward.

Question: Did you see any men of your regiment, of any other guard, in uniform, with muskets in their hands ?

Answer: No, only those of the quarter-guard.

Question: Were many men of your regiment witnesses of the whole occurrence, and what did they do ?

Answer: Yes; I should say from a hundred to a hundred and twenty five-men were looking on.

Question: What was the jemadar commanding the quarter-guard doing all this time ?

Answer: He did nothing.

Question: How did Mungul Pandy get possession of his musket and cartridges at the same time ?

Answer: The bells-of-arms are open at two o'clock, and sepoys can take out their arms and accoutrements to clean.

BY COLONEL WHELER

Question: During the time that I was standing near the quarter-guard, did you hear any one remark to me that the man in front (meaning Mungul Pandy) is a Brahmin, and no one will fire at him ?

Answer: I did not.

The witness withdraws.

4th Witness

Bugler John Lewis, No. 8 Company, 34th Regiment, Native Infantry, is called into Court and duly cautioned.

BY THE COURT

Question: Were you at duty at the quarter-guard on the 29th of last month?

Answer: I was.

Question: Did any one call out to you from the front to blow the assembly?

Answer: Yes, the sepoy who lies wounded in the hospital (his name I don't know) ordered me to sound the assembly, and threatened to shoot me if I did not; I said I could not without proper authority.

Question: Did the sepoy assign any reason for making such an unusual request?

Answer: No, he did not to me, but I heard him say to a sepoy, by name Meher Lall, "I am doing this for my religion".

The witness withdraws.

The Court proceeds to the quarters of Lieutenant and Adjutant B. H. Baugh to take his evidence.

5th Witness

Lieutenant Bempde Henry Baugh, Adjutant, 34th Regiment, Native Infantry.

BY THE COURT

Question State to the Court what occurred on parade on the 29'h of last month.

Answer: On the afternoon of the 29th, at about half-past four or five o'clock, the havildar-major, Madhoo Tewary, came and reported to me that there was a sepoy of No. 5 Company out in front of the regimental quarter-guard, who had fired a shot at the sergeant-major. I told him to report the circumstance to Colonel Wheler; ordered my horse, put a brace of pistols in my holsters, and proceeded at full gallop to the spot. On pulling up at the quarter-guard a shot was fired by a sepoy of the name of Mungul Pandy, and my horse fell; not a sign was given me by any of the guard as to the proximity of my danger, and though I once called out to the jemadar, Issuree Pandy, in command of the quarter-guard, saying why was not some arrangement made to secure this vagabond, he stood perfectly quiet and indifferent.

On seeing Mungul Pandy, sepoy, about to reload his musket, as soon as I could disentangle myself from my horse, I took a pistol from one of my holsters, and presented at the sepoy, who was about fifty paces from me: he stopped loading and began retreating, but he again stopped, and I fired, and immediately rushed on sword in hand to secure him; I had not reached him half-way when the sepoy drew a *tulwar,* which I was not aware he had about him.

I stopped and turned round to see where my horse was, intending to get my second pistol, and seeing him gone I concluded the pistol in the holster had gone with him, so continued my advance and engaged the sepoy. I must now call the Court's attention to a remarkable fact: my syce states that on coming up to where my horse had fallen he saw Mookta Persaud Pandy, the late havildar-major, standing close by with my remaining loaded pistol in his hand; the syce asked him—"Where did you get that pistol?" He said—"I just now picked it up."

So that Mookta Persaud was positively standing by with my sole means of defence in his hand, both keeping it from me and not using it in my defence, though only a short distance from me. During my conflict with Mungul Pandy both I and the sergeant-major were jostled a good deal by men who were about us: a shot was fired by some man so close to us that I saw the sergeant-major put up his hands to his head, as though he had been hit; I received a severe cut on my left hand, and two other wounds, one on my head and one on my neck; the one on my head I believe was from the butt of a musket.

The sergeant-major complained to me when returning, that as we were retreating he was knocked down by some of the sepoys of the quarter-guard; I, myself, saw him in the act of falling, and it seemed as if he had been struck by some one behind him ; he, however, got up and joined me, and we both went to the bungalow of the sergeant-major of the 43rd Regiment, Native Infantry.

A sepoy of the name of Shaik Pultoo, Grenadier Company of my regiment, assisted me to the best of his endeavours during the whole of the fight, and received a severe sword wound in his hand. To the best of my belief my getting out of the business in the way I did was principally owing to this sepoy, as he drew off the attention of the men from us on himself, and allowed us time to retreat.

Question: At what distance from the quarter-guard did the conflict take place?

Answer: I should say at about fifty or sixty yards.

Question: Was there time for the men of the quarter-guard to have come to your assistance when your horse fell to the time of the conflict?

Answer: There was plenty of time, but none came to my assistance; My horse fell only eight or ten paces from the quarter-guard.

Question: Did you see any sepoy regimentally dressed with a musket in his hand near you during the scuffle?

Answer: Most of the men that were near me were behind me; the only men that I could see were the sergeant-major, Shaik Pultoo, and Mungul Pandy. I was so much excited that I could not take upon myself to say more than the above; my whole attention was taken up with the conflict.

Question: From what direction was the last musket short fired, and could it by any possibility have been fired by Mungul Pandy?

Answer: I believe it to have come from the direction of the quarter-guard, and not from Mungul Pandy, certainly, as he was in front of me.

Question: Did you make a sign to any men not to come to your assistance ?

Answer: Most certainly not.

The Court now proceeds to the quarters of the sergeant-major 43rd Regiment, Native Infantry, where Sergeant-Major J.T. Hewson, of the 34th Regiment, Native Infantry, lies wounded: he is duly cautioned.

6th Witness

Sergeant-Major James Thornton Hewson, 34th Regiment, Native Infantry.

BY THE COURT

Question: State to the Court what occurred on the parade of your regiment on the 29th of last month.

Answer: Between the hours of 4 and 6 p.m., the naick of the 2nd guard came to my bungalow, and reported that a sepoy of No. 5 Company had dressed himself and loaded his musket, and was standing in front of the quarter-guard. I immediately ordered the naick to acquaint the adjutant of the regiment. I then dressed myself, and went out on the parade. On reaching the left first kote, that of the Light Company, a sepoy, regimentally dressed but without his pantaloons, took deliberate aim at me with his firelock ; the shot did not take effect. I then went round in rear of the kotes towards the quarter-guard.

During the time it took me in doing so, the man loaded his piece and then returned in front of the quarter-guard. I found some of the men on duty at the quarter-guard dressed. I ordered the native officer to make them fall in. He told them to do so: they grumbled, but did not obey his order, nor did the native officer, Jemadar Issuree Pandy, No. 1 Company, draw his sword. I then spoke again to the native officer, and told him that it was his business to do his duty, and arrest the sepoy, Mungul Pandy. He answered me —"What can I do ? The havildar is gone to report the circumstance to the officer of the day, and the naick to the adjutant." I then ordered two men to be stationed, one on the right hand and the other on the left of the quarter-guard, and to keep an eye on Mungul Pandy.

Several times I went beyond the quarter-guard, and each time the sepoy presented his piece at me, at the same time saying—"Get out of the way or I will shoot you." Several of the sepoys that were standing round about in undress, called to me to get out of the way; also the native officer of the quarter-guard. I recognised the native officer of No. 5 Company, Gunness Lalla, jemadar, and the color-havildar, Mookta Persaud Pandy. Gunness Lalla advanced between the quarter-guard and No. 5 kote, and spoke to Mungul Pandy, calling on him to throw down his arms, and he refused.

A little after this time I heard the sound of horse's hoofs, and the adjutant of the regiment came riding up. He called out: "Where is the man?" and I immediately answered him—"Look to your left, and ride to the right for your life, for he will fire at you." The words were hardly out of my mouth, when the sepoy, Mungul Pandy, fired. The horse fell; the adjutant then drew a pistol, having first dismounted, fired at Mungul Pandy and missed him. The adjutant then rushed up with his sword drawn to the sepoy. I also followed him, drew my sword, at the same time calling out to the guard to come on and take the sepoy. They sepoy loaded, but had not time to put on the cap.

Before the adjutant reached him he drew a *tulwar*. He made a feint at me and cut the adjutant. I struck at the sepoy several times but was knocked down from behind. On rising up I found that the men who struck me were all dressed in regimentals and had their firelocks, but no bayonets fixed. I rushed again at the man, and caught him by the collar. I received some cuts and was again knocked down by the blows from muskets; and when down the second time I received a blow from a musket on my head. On rising up, I saw the adjutant walking away, covered with blood. I followed him. On arriving near my own bungalow, opposite the Light Company kote, I heard footsteps and on turning round I saw the jemadar of the quarter-guard following me. I told him "You have acted shamefully, and I will place you under arrest." I tried to grasp his sword, but he stepped back, and prevented my taking it. I then saw my wife a few yards off and she brought me to the sergeant-major's bungalow, of the 43rd Regiment, Native (Light) Infantry. Outside it I again saw Lieutenant Baugh. I saw then his hand was cut very badly.

Question: Did the naick of the quarter-guard, when he reported to you, mention the reason of Mungul Pandy's arming himself?

Answer: He said he had drunk *bhang* and intoxicated himself, and I myself heard Mungul Pandy, when I was near quarter-guard, calling out to the regiment to turn out.

Question: At what distance from the quarter-guard did the adjutant's horse fall?

Answer: About five or six yards to the left, and ten yards to the front.

Question: Did any of the guard advance to pick him up?

Answer: Nobody came to his assistance.

Question: Were there many men assembled near their bells-of-arms and looking on; and if so, did any of those come to his assistance?

Answer: There were a great number in undress, and none of them came to the adjutant's assistance.

Question: Did you see any one strike Lieutenant Baugh with a musket?

Answer: Yes, I saw a sepoy dressed in regimentals strike him, but I could not recognise his features.

Question: Did you hear a shot fired while you and the adjutant were engaged with Mungul Pandy?

Answer: Yes, I did from behind, close by in the direction of the line.

Question: Are you personally acquainted with Heeralall Tewary, sepoy of your regiment, and did you see him during the scuffle referred to?

Answer: I know him; he was there, along with seven or eight other men in uniform, with muskets; but though I have a strong suspicion, I am not quite certain that he struck me.

Question: Did you receive assistance from Shaik Pultoo, sepoy?

Answer: I cannot say; I did not observe him.

There being no further evidence to produce, the Court adjourned at 6 p.m., *sine die.*

Barrackpore, 6th April 1857.

The Court re-assembled this day at 6 a.m. at the Mess-House of the 34th Regiment, Native Infantry, agreeably to station orders of yesterday, for the purpose of taking further evidence, particularly as to the conduct of the native officers, non-commissioned officers, and men of the 34th Regiment, Native Infantry, on duty at the regimental quarter-guard on the 29th March 1857.

The President and Members all present.

Ensign Chamier, Interpreter, 34th Regiment, Native Infantry, is appointed Interpreter to the Court, in the place of Lieutenant Corbett, 43rd Light Infantry, on other duty.

7th Witness

Lieutenant-Colonel S. G. Wheler, Commanding the 34th Regiment, Native Infantry, is called into Court.

BY THE COURT

Question: State to the Court what happened on the evening of the 29th of last month at the quarter-guard of the 34th Regiment, Native Infantry.

Answer: Captain Drury called at my house, and informed me that there was a man parading in front of the lines, exciting the men to mutiny. I immediately proceeded with him to the lines, calling up the Brigadier, whose house was on my way, and reporting the circumstance to him. On arriving at the lines, I found all the men gathered in rear of their kotes. I at once went to the quarter-guard, and on my way there I saw the man walking up and down in front.

It was reported to me and Captain Drury that Lieutenant Baugh, the adjutant, and the sergeant major had both been wounded by the sepoy in endeavouring to secure him. On arriving at the quarter-guard I directed two or three men to load. Captain Drurry suggested it would be better to order the whole guard to load, which I did. I then directed the native officer to take his guard and secure the sepoy. He murmured, and said, "The men won't go." I repeated two or three times to the native officer, it is *("hokúm hue")* ordered. He at last ordered the guard to advance. They did so six or eight paces, and halted. The native officer returned to me, stating that none of the men would go on.

I felt it was useless going on any further in the matter. Some one, a native in undress, mentioned to me that the sepoy in front is a Brahmin, and that no one would hurt him. I considered it quite useless, and a useless sacrifice of life to order an European officer, with the guard, to seize him, as he would no doubt have picked off the European officers, without receiving any assistance from the guard itself. I then left the guard, and reported the matter to the Brigadier, who was standing in the street dividing the 34th and 43rd Regiments, Native Infantry. On this Major-General J. B. Hearsey came up, and proceeded towards the 34th Regiment, Native Infantry quarter-guard, and a number of officers were with him. He rode up to the quarter-guard, and directed them to advance. They did so for a few paces, when the sepoy in front shot himself.

Question: After you ordered the guard to advance, and they halted, did the native officer order them to halt, or did they halt of their own accord?

Answer: I cannot say, as I did not hear the order given.

Question: Did you give the order to load through the jemadar commanding the guard, or did you give it direct from yourself to the men?

Answer: I am not quite certain, but I think it was through the jemadar.

Question: Was that order readily obeyed?

Answer: Yes, I believe it was.

Question: What are the Court to understand by your last answer, inasmuch as you were a witness as to the manner of carrying out of the order?

Answer: On re-considering, the order was sluggishly obeyed.

Question: What was the conduct of the jemadar throughout; did he exert himself as he ought to have done?

Answer: Certainly not.

Question: Did the refusal of the guard to advance extend to the whole of the guard, or was there any exception?

Answer: I did not notice any exception.

Question: Had the jemadar set a proper and determined example, do you think the men would have advanced on his order?

Answer: I do not think they would, that is, to seize the prisoner, or to touch him.

Question: When Major-General J. B. Hearsey placed himself at the head of the guard, and ordered them to advance, did they obey his order at once, and did they show any hesitation during that advance?

Answer: They appeared to obey the order in starting off at once. After advancing a few paces, I noticed the rear rank began to step short, and did not lock up till directed to do so by an officer who was mounted in the rear.

Question: Were there any young sepoys in the guard who were on guard duty for the first time on that day?

Answer: I cannot say.

Question: Was there any other European officer present of your own regiment except Captain Drury, when the guard refused to advance on your order?

Answer: I did not see any.

Witness withdraws.

8th Witness

Captain Drury, 34th Regiment, Native Infantry, is called into Court.

BY THE COURT

Question: State what happened on the evening of the 29th of last month at the quarter-guard of the 34th Regiment, Native Infantry ?

Answer: I accompanied Colonel Wheler down to the lines, on reaching which we saw Mungul Pandy parading up and down at about a hundred or a hundred and twenty yards in front of the quarter-guard with a musket in one hand and a *tulwar* in the other. He kept calling out some thing; I couldn't understand what he said; he spoke in a defiant manner. Colonel Wheler first of all ordered part of the guard to load; I suggested that they should all load, that no invidious distinction should be made under existing circumstances.

The colonel gave the order and the men loaded, after which the jemadar of the guard took me aside and said he wished to say something. He said, "It's no use, the men won't go; even if you go they won't follow you; they would take the man's part." I pretended to pooh-pooh it, saying—"That was all nonsense; whatever orders the guard received they must obey." Colonel Wheler then ordered the guard to advance under the jemadar; he murmured, but led the guard on some ten paces to the front in an unwilling manner, when the guard halted, but whether by any word or sign from him, I can't say, as he being on the right of the guard, I couldn't see if he moved his hand or made any sign.

Matters seemed to be getting so serious that I suggested to Colonel Wheler that I should go and try and get a rifle somewhere and shoot the man, when I went up towards the lines of the 43rd Regiment, Native Infantry, to try and get one. At this moment Major-General J. B. Hearsey rode down, accompanied by some officers on horseback, and was joined by several others. On his arrival on parade, he rode up to the guard, who advanced with him some paces, when the man knelt down and shot himself.

Question: Had the jemedar set a proper and determined example, do you think the men would have advanced on his order ?

Answer: It is a difficult question to answer; but I think the men would have advanced, though I much doubt whether they would have fired at, or injured him in any way.

Question: Did the non-commissioned officers of the guard show the same reluctance as the other to advance when ordered?

Answer: I didn't notice any one man in particular, except the jemadar, he being the responsible person in command in the guard, but all showed equal wavering and reluctance.

Question: What reason have you for thinking that, although the guard might have advanced if properly led, they would have refused to shoot Mungul Pandy?

Answer: I judged partly from what the jemadar told me, still more so from their sulky and reluctant manner, also from their natural disinclination to kill a man of this caste, and also from the fear of the opinion of their comrades in the lines, as it is impossible to say, there being a very large proportion of Brahmins in the regiment, who were approving or otherwise of what the man was doing.

Question: Were there many men of your regiment present on the occasion?

Answer: Almost all; they were clustering about in rear of the bells-of-arms.

Question: Were any of them invited to do the duty which the quarter-guard refused to do?

Answer: No; certainly not in my hearing.

Question: From what you saw of their manner and bearing on the occasion, do you think they would have obeyed an order to shoot Mungul Pandy?

Answer: I doubt it, though individually I am certain there are numbers who were well affected; still I think the fear of consequences from their comrades would have deterred any one man from being the first to come forward on the occasion. I think that the men distrust one another, and neither dare do or say anything tending to criminate a comrade.

Question: How may Sikhs are there in your regiment?

Answer: Seventy-three by the last monthly return.

Question: Had Colonel Wheler called them out, would they have shot Mungul Pandy?

Answer: I really cannot say. I have the highest opinion of the Sikhs in every way. I don't think they are mixed up in these disturbances, but for the reasons I stated above, and their being in such a minority, I think they would have feared to come forward; I think had volunteers been called for, there would have been quite a slinking back of the men into their huts.

Question: Were they any young sepoys on duty at the quarter-guard on that day, who were on duty for the first time?

Answer: There were one or two who joined from the last squad of recruits some where in the middle of last month. I can't say whether they had been on duty before, but I think they must have been once or twice.

Question: Did you expostulate directly with any of the men of the guard at the time referred to?

Answer: No; I was on parade in a subordinate position, my commanding officer being there, and I had nothing to say to the guard.

Witness withdraws.

There being no more evidence to call the Court closes its proceedings.

The Court adjourns at 9 a.m.

From Lieuteannt-Colonel S. G. WHELER, *Commanding 34th Regiment, Native Infantry, to Captain* S. RICHARDS, *Officiating Major of Brigade—dated Barrackpore, 7th April 1857.*

I have the honor to forward the accompanying letter of this date to my address, for the information of the Brigadier commanding the station, reporting what took place at the quarter-guard of the 70th Regiment, Native Infantry, when in conversation with some of the prisoners on Sunday last.

From Ensign F. E. A. CHAMIER, *Quarter-master, 34th Regiment, Native Infantry, to Captain* C. C. DRURY, *Acting Adjutant, 34th Regiment, Native Infantry—dated Barrackpore, 7th April 1857.*

I have the honor to report, for the information of Colonel S. G. Wheler, Commanding the 34th Regiment, Native Infantry, the following circumstance:

On Sunday evening last, I accompanied Captain Drury to the quarter-guard of the 70th Regiment, Native Infantry, who was directed to make arrangements for fastening the hands of the Sikh sepoy for whom handcuffs could not be procured large enough.

In the course of putting a few questions to the prisoners, I was informed by three sepoys there confined that the jemadar commanding the guard had prevented them seizing Mungul Pandy, saying, "Do not go near the madman." These sepoys refused to state whether they were prohibited rescuing the adjutant, but two Sikhs distinctly stated that the jemadar ordered them not to go to the rescue of the adjutant. They then said that they would repeat this before a court; and added, to prove this, if the jemadar had not the courage to use his own sword why did he not give it to the sergeant-major, whose sword was broken?

Ensign Bushby, 70th Regiment, Native Infantry, was visiting the guard at the time, and, I have no doubt, will corroborate the greater portion of the above statement.

Sobha Sing, Sepoy, 6th Company, 34th Regiment, Native Infantry, a prisoner in the quarter-guard, 43rd Regiment, Native Infantry, voluntarily states as follows—

"I was on duty on Sunday, the 29th March 1857. In the afternoon, I saw the prisoner, Mungul Pandy, walking about the parade with a musket. I, and one or two others, asked the jemadar if we should load. He said—"You take your orders from me."

"The sergeant-major came up and asked for the jemadar's sword, as his own was broken. The jemadar refused to give it. The jemadar distinctly refused to let any one go to the rescue of the adjutant, and said, 'If you go at all, you must go by my orders.' Before this, the jemadar had prohibited our seizing the sepoy, who was walking up and down the parade. One of the sepoys of the guard and of the light company, I think (I should know him if I were to see him), ran forward, and, with the butt-end of the musket, struck the sergeant. The jemadar did not order the sepoy to attack the sergeant, but did not stop him. The sepoy and Shaik Pultoo both arrived about the same time. At one time, some sepoy of another regiment was passing the prisoner, who called out—'If you do not give me some water from your lotah, I will fire at you.' Havildar Mookta Persaud Pandy was standing by the bells-of-arms, but offered no assistance."

Atma Sing, sepoy, 6th Company, 34th Regiment, Native Infantry, voluntarily states as follows—

"I was on duty at the quarter-guard on the 29th March, when Sepoy Mungul Pandy came forward on the parade. The jemadar shut the front door of the quarter-guard, and assembled the guard in the rear. I, Sobha Sing, and two others, not Sikhs, offered to seize the prisoner, but the jemadar would not allow it. After the sergeant had broken his sword, he asked the jemadar for his, which the jemadar refused. We offered to go to the rescue of the adjutant, but the jemadar said , ' When you get the orders from me, then you will go.'

Taken by me, in the presence of Major H. W. Matthews, *Commanding the 43rd Regiment, Native Infantry.*

BARRACKPORE, (Sd.)F. E. A. CHAMIER, *Ensign,*
The 7th April 1857 *Qr. Mr., 34th Regt., Nat. Infy.*

From Lieutenant-Colonel S. G. WHELER, *Commanding 34th Regiment, Native Infantry, to Captain* S. RICHARDS, *Officiating Major of Brigade,—dated Barrackpore, 10th April 1857.*

> I have the honor to forward the statement of Sewbucus Tewary of the 8th Company, and Mehee Lall, of the 1st Company, 34th Regiment, Native Infantry, who were on the quarter-guard on the 29th March 1857, taken in the presence of myself, Lieutenant Bunbury, subaltern officer of the day, and Lieutenant Grierson, quartermaster of the week.
>
> The two statements differ with regard to what is said about receiving the word, "halt," after advancing by my orders. The latter one, by Mehee Lall, I beg to state, is the more correct one of the two.

Sepoys Atma Sing and Sobha Sing, having been taken to the quarter-guard of the 70th Regiment, Native Infantry, recognize the prisoners Sewbucus Tewary of the 8th Company and Mehee Lall, sepoy, 1st Company, both of the 34th Regiment, Native Infantry.

Sewbucus Tewary, sepoy, 34th Regiment, Native Infantry, on being called on, states as follows—

"On the day when Mungul Pandy fired at the adjutant and sergeant- permission to go to the rear, when I heard a disturbance, and immediately ran and fell in with the guard.

"Mungul Pandy came in front of the guard with a loaded musket and sword, and when the sergeant-major came out to the guard, he (Mungul Pandy) fired at him. I at once called out, 'Come, let us seize him'; but the jemadar called out that no man was to move without orders; that a report had been sent to the European officers, and, until orders were received from them, no man was to move.

"We were all behind the quarter-guard-house at this time with the sergeant-major, who had run there after being fired at.

"I did not see any man of the guard fire a shot during the conflict between the adjutant and Mungul Pandy which ensued, but I saw Sepoy Heeralall Tewary returning towards the quarter-guard with the cap of the sergeant-major, a sword-hilt, and a pistol. He was the only man who went to the front.

"The whole guard wished to advance to the rescue of the adjutant, but the jemadar would not allow us.

"Afterwards, when he had loaded and advanced a short distance by orders of the lieutenant-colonel, the jemadar went up to the colonel of the regiment, and said something to him (I don't know what), and then us to halt, and right-about face."

Mehee Lall, Sepoy, 34th Regiment, Native Infantry, states as follows—

"On the day in question, I was on duty at the quarter-guard of my regiment, and had obtained leave to go the rear; and on my return, seeing a disturbance was going on, I ran, and joined the guard. Both when the sergeant-major and the adjutant were fired at, I, and all the guard, wished to seize the sepoy, Mungul Pandy, but the jemadar in command ordered us not to advance until we got orders.

"I saw Heeralall Tewary returning with a pistol, a cap, and a sword-hilt in his hand from the direction in which the affray had taken place.

"His clothes were bloody, and I heard the jemadar tell him to go and change them.

"When the jemadar refused to let us advance to the rescue, I saw Sepoy Sobha Sing strike his head with the palm of his hand in grief.

"Afterwards, when we had advanced some twenty-five paces, by order of the colonel (after loading), the jemadar halted us, on Mungul Pandy aiming at us, and then went and said something to the colonel, after which he ordered us to the right-about, to take off the caps, and to pile arms."

(Sd.) W. M. GRIERSON, *Lieut.,*
70th Regiment, Native Infantry.

From Major-General J. B. HEARSEY, C.B., *Commanding Presidency Division, to Colonel* R. J. H. BIRCH, C.B., *Secretary to the Government of India, Military Department—dated Barrackpore, 17th April 1857.*

I forward the Proceedings of a Court of Inquiry conducted by Captain G. C. Hatch, Deputy Judge Advocate-General, assembled by my order, to take the evidence of Durrriow Sing, jemadar, 34th Regiment, Native

Infantry, and also Ramsahai Lalla, sepoy in that corps. In this enquiry we have a connected statement, but no evidence to prove such statement can be found.

From circumstances that have since occurred, I have but little doubt that these statements are founded in truth.

P.S. – I return the documents received from you this morning.

PROCEEDINGS of a Court of Inquiry assembled at Barrackpore on Friday, the 17th April 1857, by order of Major-General J. B. HEARSEY, C.B., *Commanding the Presidency Division, for the investigation of such matter as shall be laid before the Court by Captain* G. C. HATCH, *Deputy Judge Advocate-General of the Division.*

PRESIDENT:

Brevet-Colonel J. D. KENNEDY, *70th Regiment, Native Infantry.*

MEMBERS:

Captain R. A. SMITH, *19th Regiment, Native Infantry.*

Captain BOSWELL, *2nd Regiment, Native (Grenadier) Infantry.*

JUDGE-ADVOCATE:

Captain G. C.HATCH, *Deputy Judge Advocate-Genl., Presidency Divn.*

INTERPRETER:

Lieutenant W. M. GRIERSON, *70th Regiment, Native Infantry.*

The Court assembled this day at the quarters of the President of the Court at ten o'clock in the forenoon, according to orders. The President Members, Judge-Advocate, and Interpreter all present.

The Court met with closed doors.

The Deputy Judge Advocate-General lays before the Court the following documents—

A statement of Lieutenant and Brevet Captain A. S. Allen, 34th Regiment, Native Infantry, dated 8th February, with descriptive roll of Sepoy Ramsahai Lalla, No. 8 Company of the regiment ; the examination of Sepoy Ramsahai Lalla, dated 11th February, with transmitting letter ; a deposition of Durriow Sing, Jemadar, 34th Regiment, Native Infantry, dated 10th February, and A statement of this jemdadar taken by Lieutenant-Colonel A. Abbott at Ishapore.

BY THE JUDGE-ADVOCATE

The Major-General desired that a searching enquiry shall be made into the circumstances stated in the above documents.

Durriow Sing, Jemadar, 34th Regiment, Native Infantry, is called in and states—

On the 26th of January there was a halt of the three companies which went to Chittagong, at Calcutta, near the fort.

Subadar-Major Ram Lall of my regiment was on guard at the Lieutenant-Governor's at Alipore. On that day the guard was relieved and returned to Barrackpore. The Subadar-Major, Ram Lall, and Subadar Muddeh Khan, and Subadar Lalla Gopal, and Jemadar Lalla Gunness, sent for the munshi of the regiment, and had a letter written and sent off to Rajah Maun Sing. Ram Lall, Subadar-Major, came to my guard, which was at the treasury on the day that the guards were relieved.

He arrived about ten o'clock, and remained till twelve, talking in a treasonable manner, loud enough for all the men to hear; telling them what they were to do, and that he was going off to Barrackpore and could not remain there to conduct matters. On my guard there was a havildar, Peer Ally, who used to go to Subadar Muddeh Khan, who commanded the Mint guard, to eat with him. Peer Ally came to me, and awoke me on the night of the 26th of January, and told me an order had come that I was to get ready my guard, and to send off two men to give information to the Mint guard.

I sent two men, Sepoys Gopal Ram, Light Company, and Chunder Sookul or Tewary,Grenadier Company, round to tell all the guards to be on the alert. Muddeh Khan sent word to me to say that if there was any noise in the fort, to let him know. From that day, Subadar Muddeh Khan is in the habit of abusing me. After we arrived here, about the 10th or 11th of February, I went up to see Captain Drury, commanding the 8th Company, and on my return saw Muddeh Khan, Subadar, in the lines, crying. On the 14th February, Muddeh Khan sent Havildar Peer Ally to me, to ask if I had told anything when at the sahib's bungalow.

I found great difficulty in making my communication; Captain Drury would not listen to me; and when I went to the Colonel's, Colonel Wheler's, he would not listen to me, because I did not come from Captain Drury. Then I went on duty to Ishapore, and told the sahib there; since that I fell ill. The Subadar-Major, Mookta Persaud, havildar, formerly drill havildar, are trying to destroy me. I am afraid to leave my hut.

Question: How do you know that these persons sent from the munshi and wrote a letter to Rajah Maun Sing?

Answer: Peer Ally, havildar, was my informant.

Question: Do you know if a regular communication was carried on then with Rajah Maun Sing?

Answer: I only know it from hearing it from Peer Ally.

Question: What part was your guard to take in the arrangements on the 26th January?

Answer: We were to remain on the alert.

Question: What treasonable things did Subadar-major Ram Lall say?

Answer: He talked about the cartridges, and said he would not serve any longer, and some sepoys said the same.

Question: What arrangements did the subadar say were going on?

Answer: He did not say what arrangements were made, but that he would not bite the cartridges; and the sepoy said the same, and that arrangements would be made. I understood that he was going up to Barrackpore, and would then make arrangements, and a plan was fixed upon afterwards.

Question: Were the sepoys aware that unusual precautions were taken in the fort?

Answer: Yes; a sepoy came out and told us that precautions were made, and that Europeans were posted at the gates.

Question: Have you heard what would have been attempted if these precautions had not been taken?

Answer: Subadar-Major Ram Lall would have taken the fort. I heard afterwards on the 14th February that it was the intention on the 26th of January, if the Subadar-Major had not been relieved from the Lieutenant-Governor's guard, with the aid of the three companies that were on the way to Chittagong, and with assistance that was to have been received from the King of Oudh, to have taken the fort. Muddeh Khan, commanding the Mint guard, and the Subadar-Major, were the ringleaders of this conspiracy. I heard afterwards that all the guards were to join.

Question: How did you hear this?

Answer: Peer Ally told me that he had overheard the Subadar Major and Muddeh Khan, Gunness Tewarry, and Mookta Persaud talking about it.

Question: How were the King of Oudh's people to assist?

Answer: By all his men joining. All the four regiments here were to join, and also the Calcutta Native Militia.

Question: How were the King of Oudh's people to assist?

Answer: By all his men joining. All the four regiments here were to join, and also the Calcutta Native Militia.

Question: Did you hear how the troops were to be rewarded?

Answer: Their pay was to be increased to Rs. 10 a month. It was the common talk in the lines. I heard it mentioned too on the 6th February, and on the 5th at the meeting on the parade.

Question: Have you heard what caused the abandonment of the design of thc 26th January?

Answer: I afterwards heard that a rumour had been sent up to Barrackpore to tell them that the authorities were on the alert in the fort, and that Muddeh Khan had said I had spoilt the plan by sending my two men to warn the guards in town to be on the alert. The sepoy came from the fort, and I believe from the authorities. I don't know the name of the sepoy. The design would have been attempted if the Subadar-Major had not been relieved from the Deputy-Governor's guard.

Question: Do you know what is the cause of the recent bad feeling amongst the native troops?

Answer: It originated in the dread of the sepoys losing their caste through the cartridges. Both Mussulmans and Hindus were equally concerned.

Question: In what way did Sepoy Kassee Persaud Doobie, No. 8 Company, and Mohun Sookul, No. 7 Company, induce you to go with them to the meeting on the parade ground on the 5th February?

Answer: I had been on fort duty in December and January, and returned to Barrackpore on the 3rd February. The 4th February passed tranquilly, except that I heard a good deal of talk about the cartridges. On the evening of the 5th February these two sepoys came and said, "Mookta Persaud Pandy calls you." I said, " Where is Mookta Persaud Pandy ?" They beckoned me on and told me to come along, saying—"He is here." I went out on to the parade with them.

Question: Where is Mookta Persaud's hut?

Answer: Immediately behind the quarter-guard in the 5th Company lines. I went out by Mookta Persaud's hut on to the parade; he was not in his hut.

Question: What did you see on the parade; did you see Mookta Persaud there?

Answer: I consider that I recognized him partly from his figure, which is short and slight, and from his voice, which I have been accustomed to hear.

Question: What induced you to go out to this meeting?

Answer: I thought Mookta Persaud Pandy was in his hut. I went because he is a very high Brahmin; all the native officers are in the habit of going to his house and staying hours there.

Question: Do the men still talk about the cartridges?

Answer: No; I disabused their minds to the utmost of my power. [The witness adds] I am afraid of my life; I am accused of spoiling their plans and joining the Europeans.

Question: Did you recognise no one at that meeting?

Answer: I did not recognise any one.

The witness withdraws.

Ramsahai Lalla, Sepoy, No. 8 Company, 34th Regiment, Native Infantry, is called into Court, and, after being duly cautioned, states—

Question: Did you recognize any one at the meeting?

Answer: I did not go to it.

Question: From whom did you hear of the meeting on the 5th February?

Answer: It was the talk in the lines.

Question: Can you name any one from whom you heard what was to take place?

Answer: It was dark; every one was talking about it, and I cannot particularise any one.

Question: What is the name of the regimental munshi?

Answer: I don't know, he is called munshi; he was entertained at Lucknow.

Question: Can you state what the feeling now is in the regiment about the cartridge question?

Answer: The men are prepared to use them, but they still entertain suspicion about the paper being free from grease.

A variety of questions on different points have been put to this witness, but as the answers to all appeared to be quite useless, they have not been recorded.

The witness appears to have no further knowledge of the meeting at Barrackpore than that contained in his statement.

The Court closed proceedings at 3 p.m.

From Major-General J.B. HEARSEY, C.B., *Commanding the Presidency Division, to Colonel* R. J. H. BIRCH, C.B., *Secretary to the Government of India, Military Department—dated Barrackpore, 18th April 1857.*

In forwarding to you, for submission to Government, the Proceedings of a Special Court of Enquiry assembled at this station, by my orders to take the evidence of the European officers of the 34th Regiment, Native Infantry, with respect to the present state of feeling of the native portion of that corps, I beg to report that I quite agree with the opinion expressed by the Court, namely, that the Hindus generally are not at present trustworthy servants of the State, though to myself individually they now are, and have invariably been, most respectful and obedient.

From Major A. H. ROSS, *Assistant Adjutant-General, to Brigadier* C. GRANT C.B., *Commanding at Barrackpore—dated Barrackpore, 14th April 1857*

I have been instructed by Major-General J. B. Hearsey, Commanding the Division, to acquaint you that the Special Court of Inquiry, of which you are President, has been directed in this day's Division Orders to re-assemble to-morrow, for the purpose of receiving and recording evidence, for the information of Government, as to the present state of feeling and temper in the native portion of the 34th Regiment, Native Infantry, for which purpose the Major-General considers that it will be probably sufficient merely to examine Brevet-Colonel S. G. Wheler, and the officers commanding or in charge of the seven companies of that corps now at Barrackpore.

The Court will record their opinion as to the trustworthiness or otherwise of the 34th Regiment, Native Infantry, as soldiers of the State.

PROCEEDINGS of a Special Court of Inquiry re-assembled at Barrackpore on the 15th day of April 1857, by order of Major-General J. B. HEARSEY, C.B., *Commanding the Presidency Division, for the purpose of investigating and reporting on a matter which will be communicated to the Members by the President of the Court.*

PRESIDENT:

Brigadier C. GRANT, C.B., *Commanding at Barrackpore.*

MEMBERS:

Brevet-Colonel E. AMSINCK, *3rd Battalion, Madras Artillery.*

Brevet Lieutenant-Colonel C. S. REID, *9th Battalion, Bengal Artillery.*

Major H. W. MATTHEWS, *43rd Regiment, Native (Light) Infantry.*

Major W. A. COOKE, *2nd Regiment, Native (Grenadier) Infantry.*

CONDUCTING THE PROCEEDINGS:

Captain G. N. GREENE, *70th Regiment, Native Infantry.*

The Court re-assembled this day, at 10 a.m., at the Mess-House of the 70th Regiment, Native Infantry.

The President, Members, and Officiating Judge-Advocate all present.

Read Presidency Division Orders of yesterday's date, directing the re-assembly of the Court, and nominating Brevet Lieutenant-Colonel C. S. Reid, 9th Battalion of Artillery, a member of the Court, in room of Brevet Lieutenant-Colonel A. Huyshe, 5th Battalion of Artillery, relieved from that duty.

Read Barrackpore Station Orders of the same date fixing the hour and place of re-assembly.

Read (marked Appendix A), and appended to the proceedings, Letter of Instructions No. 163, dated the 14th April 1857, from the Assistant Adjutant-General of the Presidency Division, to the address of the President of the Court.

The Court proceed to call evidence.

1st Witness

Brevet-Colonel S. G. Wheler, *Commanding the 34th Regiment, Native Infantry,* is called into Court, and examined by the Officiating Judge-Advocate.

Question: What is your opinion as to the present state of feeling and temper in the native officers and men of the 34th Regiment, Native Infantry?

Answer: Of the temper and feeling of the three companies detached at Chittagong, I am unable to speak. Regarding the seven companies at regimental head-quarters, I am of opinion that, since the latter end of January last, the men have been more or less in an excited state on account of the new rifle cartridges, and they have shown this feeling both secretly and openly on some occasions.

The first symptom of this excitement manifested itself in the latter end of January, when it was reported to me that there was a great deal of talking going on in the lines about the Government forcing the men to become Christians. I then ordered a quiet undress parade, in the hope of allaying the excited feelings of the sepoys.

I explained to them that was quite impossible for our Government to make them Christians by force; that such a thing had never been heard of since we came into this country; that faith in our religion must come spontaneously from the heart, and not from force ; and that it was, therefore, very wrong of them to give way to such foolish reports. This apparently satisfied them, and they were afterwards quiet for a time.

In the early part of February last, Lieutenant Allen reported that a sepoy of the 5th Company (by name Ramsahai Lalla) had given information that a meeting of sepoys was to take place at a temple on the Fultah Ghat road. The circumstance was reported the same night to the Brigadier and the General by Lieutenant Allen and myself. The General suggested that an immediate roll-call should take place in the lines, which was done between 9 and 10 p.m. The sepoys with one or two exceptions were all present.

Lieutenant Allen himself rode down to the temple where the meeting was expected to be held, but did not discover any trace of it. A day or two afterwards a jemadar, by name Durriow, reported to Captain Drury that on the night previous to the one just referred to, a meeting of the men had taken place on the parade ground; that he was present at it, and that it was held for the purpose of arranging for a meeting on the following night, and that he was invited to combine with them on the latter occasion; that he refused to do so; that the object of the meeting was to plunder the station, and to destroy all the Europeans. In my opinion that meeting would have been held had it not been for the roll-call ordered by the General.

In the latter end of January, several bungalows were burnt down, amongst others the Electric Telegraph bungalow. A general parade took place on the 9th February, when the subject of the cartridge paper was explained to the men by the General. That explanation seemed to quiet the men a good deal for the time.

On the 18th March, the General again addressed the men on a public parade about the cartridge paper and the disbandment of the 19th Regiment, Native Infantry; and at a regimental parade, on the following day, it was explained to the men that they were to break, and not to bite, the cartridges.

I would remark that there must have been a smothered feeling in the regiment unknown to myself and the European officers, which, however, did not break out until the 29th March, when Sepoy Mungul Pandy went out on the parade and tried to excite the regiment into a serious mutiny. When there, he called out to the men, "It is you who have sent me here; why don't you come out and join me?"

This shows that many of the men must have been implicated with him, and such an inference is strongly supported by the fact of none of the men having gone forward to assist their officer when attacked by a mutineer, although at the time there must have been about 400 men in the lines looking on.

From all that has occurred, I am of opinion that it was the intention of the regiment to coerce and resist the Government, and that the feeling in the regiment was decidedly bad; but that now the men appear to be very much frightened.

Question: Do you consider that there now exists in the 34th Regiment, Native Infantry, a healthy feeling of loyalty towards the State?

Answer: I am of opinion that a healthy tone exists amongst the Mussulmans and Sikhs, but not so amongst the Hindus.

Question: Have the men of your regiment, of any class, in any way manifested such contrition for past misconduct as to lead you to believe that they are now trustworthy?

Answer: No; there has been no such manifestation, but it has been reported to me that the Mussulmans are very angry at what the Hindus have done.

Question: Did you at the time of any of the late occurrences in your regiment hear that the Mussulmans had stood aloof from the Hindus?

Answer: No.

Question: Suppose your regiment were now ordered on field service, would you place yourself at their head in full reliance upon their loyalty and good-conduct?

Answer: No, I would not; because I could rely only upon the Sikhs and Mussulmans.

Question: What grounds have you for placing special reliance on the Sikhs and Mussulmans?

Answer: I judge from common report, and from two recent occurrences, *viz.*, the good conduct of the Mussulman subadar who was in command of the Mint guard in Calcutta, and the gallant behaviour of Shaik Pultoo, sepoy, on the occasion of the attack upon Lieutenant Baugh and the sergeant-major. Regarding the Sikhs common report is also in their favour, and I believe they would have acted like the Mussulmans referred to, and had similar opportunities been offered them.

Question: In speaking of that portion of your regiment which you would distrust if employed on field service, did you intend to include the native officers of that class?

Answer: Certainly; because they have not done their duty of late. Had it been otherwise, recent events could not have occurred.

The witness withdraws.

2nd Witness

Captain W. W. Aubert, *34th Regiment, Native Infantry,* is called into Court, and examined by the Officiating Judge-Advocate.

Question: What is your opinion of the present state of feeling and temper in the native officers and men of the 34th Regiment, Native Infantry?

Answer: For the last six weeks I have not been in the performance of regimental duty, and therefore cannot speak as to the present state of feeling and temper; but between May last year (when I returned from furlough), and the date of my entering upon my appointment at this station, I had observed a great want of respect, on the part of the men towards their European officers. For instance, I frequently noticed, when I went to the lines on duty and in uniform, that the men did not stand up and salute me: a mark of disrespect for which I punished the men of my own company and reported those of other companies.

Again when the regiment was coming down by water, in October and November last year, we encountered a severe gale in which three boats were wrecked, but not a single sepoy came forward voluntarily to assist the European officers in getting their boats out of danger. And, likewise, when the men's boats came into collision with those of the officers, the sepoys who were seated above and looking on, never lent a hand to save their officers' boats from being damaged.

In short, from all I have observed, I do not consider that the feeling and temper of the native officers and men are what they ought to be, and I am confirmed in this opinion by what I witnessed upon the evening of the 29th March, after Lieutenant Baugh was cut down. On that occasion I saw numbers of the men of all companies collected and passively looking on, and when I taxed them with cowardice in having allowed an officer of their own regiment to be cut down in broad daylight, within fifty yards of where they were standing, not one of them attempted any explanation, but they all seemed to regard the charge as a frivolous one and some of them even laughed at it.

Question: Suppose you were now ordered to accompany your regiment on field service, would you do so in full reliance on their loyalty and good conduct?

Answer: I would not.

Question: Does that feeling of distrust embrace men of all castes?

Answer: No; it extends to the Brahmins only. I think the men of other castes are inclined to be good and true, but nearly all the native influence in the regiment is in the hands of the Brahmins, who have also a numerical superiority.

Question: Would you, in time of need, place any special reliance on the loyalty of the Mussulmans or Sikhs?

Answer: I would on both.

The witness withdraws.

3rd Witness

Ensign F.E.A. Chamier, Interpreter and Quartermaster, 34th Regiment, Native Infantry, is called into Court, and examined by the Officiating Judge-Advocate.

Question: What is your opinion of the present state of feeling and temper amongst the native officers and men of the 34th Regiment, Native Infantry?

Answer: It is bad. I have observed that the native officers and men are generally disrespectful towards their European officers. An instance of the sort happened to myself only for a fortnight ago. The subadar-major attended at my quarters for the purpose of being examined as to his knowledge of reading and writing, preparatory to being sent in command of the Government House Guard, Calcutta. I gave him a chair and treated him with all courtesy. As he sat down, he removed his turban from his head; when I desired him to replace his puggree, and pointed out to him the impropriety of his conduct, he neither attempted to excuse himself nor to apologise.

This circumstance occurred on the day on which Lieutenant Baugh was wounded. Again on the same day, when passing the quarter-guard, the jemadar commanding it saluted me but neglected to put on his cap (he being in uniform); and shortly afterwards when I repassed the guard, he repeated the salute in the same manner, although on both occasions he was standing close by his cot upon which his cap was lying.

Question: Do you consider that the bad feeling and disrespectful bearing of which you have spoken pervade men of all classes in the regiment?

Answer: No; I think that the Mussalmans and Sikhs are exceptions.

Question: Would you now accompany your regiment on field service in full reliance on the loyalty and good conduct of the men generally?

Answer: I would not do so in full reliance on the Hindus, but would decidedly trust the Sikhs and Mussalmans.

The witness withdraws.

4th Witness

Captain C. C. Drury, *34th Regiment, Native Infantry,* is called into Court, and examined by the Officiating Judge-Advocate.

Question What is your opinion as to the present state of feeling and temper amongst the native officers and men of the 34th Regiment, Native Infantry?

Answer: I believe that with the exception of a few men (whom I can't name), the general feeling of the regiment is very good indeed.

Question: How do you account for the apathy exhibited by a large body of those men in sight of where their adjutant and sergeant-major were cut down by a mutineer, aided by sepoys from the quarter-guard with the butts of their muskets?

Answer: I account for it because I think that there might have been some men who were perfectly willing to aid Lieutenant Baugh, but who did not do so from fear of after consequences. I don't think that there are a dozen men in the lines who, under the present state of things, know who are their friends and who are not. I also believe that the conduct of the jemadar commanding the quarter-guard on the 29th ultimo had a great deal to do with preventing the men from acting as they ought to have done. I know both from the regimental records and from experience (he having been for some time a native officer of my own company), that he is a most litigious, untrustworthy man.

Question: Would you now accompany your regiment on field service, in full reliance upon the loyalty and good conduct of the native officers and men of all classes and castes?

Answer: Yes.

BY THE COURT

Question: Has the behaviour of the native officers and men been of late respectful towards the European officers?

Answer: Personally I have always found it to be so; but during the last ten months I have heard officers complain of a falling off from what it used to be, and I believe it to be true.

Question: Did you on a late occasion express it as your opinion that the men were in a bad state, and that an officer's life was not safe in going to the lines?

Answer: Certainly not.

Question: How do you account for the falling off in respect towards the European officers of the regiment?

Answer: I account for it by the lax state of discipline which has been allowed, by men being permitted to commit faults, and receiving little or no punishment for the same. Also by the difficulty which officers of companies have experienced in getting adequate punishment for their men in cases when the offences were of so serious a nature as to require reference to a higher authority. In fact, to use the words of old officers of the regiment, the corps was commanded by the late havildar-major, Mookta Persaud Pandy. I wish it be understood that the foregoing reply has no reference to the period during which Colonel Wheler has been in command of the regiment.

The witness withdraws.

5th Witness

Lieutenant A. C. Bunbury, *34th Regiment, Native Infantry,* is called into Court, and examined by the Officiating Judge-Advocate.

Question What is your opinion of the present state of feeling and temper of the native officers and men of the 34th Regiment, Native Infantry ?

Answer: Good.

Question: How do you account for the indifference shown on the 29th ultimo, by the bulk of the men of the regiment in remaining passive spectators of a murderous attack on the adjutant and sergeant-major by a mutineer supported by men on duty from the quarter-guard.

Answer: I cannot account for it.

Question: Have you noticed any change in the bearing and behaviour of the men towards yourself or towards any of the European officers?

Answer: None towards myself; but I have heard other officers speak of such a change.

Question: When did you first hear of that change?

Answer: I was absent from the station on fort duty last month, and whilst there I heard of it.

Question: Would you now accompany your regiment on field service in full reliance on the loyalty and good conduct of the native officers and men of all castes?

Answer: Certainly, I would.

The witness withdraws.

There being no more officers in attendance except ensign G. R. Hennessy, who informs the Court that he returned to the station only during the current month, having been for the three preceding months on fort duty, and consequently unable to speak to recent occurrences, or even present feeling ; and also that he received charge of a company only yesterday for the first time; the Court do not think that there would be any use in examining this young officer.

OPINION

The court, from the evidence before them, are of opinion that the Sikhs and Mussulmans of the 34th Regiment, Native Infantry, are trustworthy soldiers of the State, but that the Hindus generally of that corps are not trustworthy.

The Court adjourned at 3 p.m. *sine die.*

Under instructions from the Major-General Commanding the Division, conveyed through the President, the Court is re-assembled for the purpose of taking the evidence of Lieutenant and Adjutant B. H. Baugh, 34th Regiment, Native Infantry (on the sick list), as also that of Lieutenant and Brevet-Captain A. S. Allen, and Lieutenant J. T. Liscombe, of the same regiment (on duty in Fort William), whose attendance at Barrackpore has been directed.

At 6.15 a.m., the Court proceeded to the quarters of Lieutenant and Adjutant B. H. Baugh.

The President, Members, and Officiating Judge-Advocate all present.

6th Witness

Lieutenant and Adjutant B. H. Baugh, *34th Regiment, Native Infantry,* being present in Court, is examined by the Officiating Judge-Advocate.

Question: What is your opinion of the present state of feeling and temper of the native officers and men of the 34th Regiment Native Infantry?

Answer: I do not exactly know what their present feeling may be, but their conduct hitherto has given me the greatest distrust in them. About two months ago, on the evening that the order came from Brigadier Grant for the men to be paraded in their Hindustani clothes, in order that the new cartridges might be shown to them, their conduct at that parade was most unruly and insubordinate, so much so that I took up two or three men (whom I had marked for having made use of very insubordinate expressions) to Colonel Wheler, who was on the parade ground.

The Colonel, however, advised that no further notice should be taken of them, saying that if the conduct of those men were to be noticed, he would for the same reason have to put half the regiment in confinement. Again about a month ago, the subadar-major was so extremely insolent to me on the parade ground, that I was compelled to take him to the quarters of Colonel Wheler, by whom he was then and there severely reprimanded.

Again on the evening of the 29th ultimo, after my conflict with Mungul Pandy, when I was retreating severely wounded towards the bungalow of the sergeant-major of the 43rd Regiment, Light Infantry, I looked towards the lines of my own corps, and seeing all the men collected outside, I said to those of the light company, as I passed them—"You cowardly set of rascals, you see an officer cut down before your eyes, and not a man of you advances to assist him." They made no reply, but all turned their backs on me and moved away in a slow and most sullen manner.

Indeed, the conduct of the men generally was at the time such that I do not hesitate to say that it is my firm conviction that all of them were cognisant of what was going to take place, fully prepared for what did take place, and all more or less implicated. On questioning some of the men a day or two afterwards as to where they were on the occasion referred to, I received the most futile and confused answers.

Question: Prior to the occurrence of the 29th ultimo, had you observed any change in the bearing and behaviour of the men towards their European officers?

Answer: I had observed that they were greatly wanting in respect towards the officers, and they performed their duty in such a sullen and sluggish manner that the sergeant-major one day remarked to me that he did not know what had come over the regiment.

Question: Would you now accompany your regiment on field service in full reliance upon the loyalty and good conduct of native officers and men of all castes?

Answer: Most certainly not.

Question: Would you do so as regards those of any class?

Answer: Yes; I would rely upon the Mussulmans and Sikhs, because I think that those two classes are overawed by the preponderating influence of the Brahmins.

BY THE COURT

Question: How do you account for the change in the general conduct of the native officers and men, as also for their altered manner and bearing towards their European officers?

Answer: I noticed it in December or January last about the time that the general order was received for the formation of the new rifle depots and the succeeding introduction of the new cartridges, and to that cause I attribute the change in question.

This witness's examination is closed. At 7 a.m. the Court adjourn until 11 a.m. to-day, so as to allow of the arrival from Fort William of Lieutenant and Brevet-Captain Allen and Lieutenant Liscombe.

Friday, 19th April 1857.

The Court re-assembled pursuant to adjournment. President, Members and Officiating Judge-Advocate all present.

7th Witness

Lieutenant and Brevet-Captain A.S. Allen, 34th Regiment, Native-Infantry, Is called into Court and examined by the Officiating Judge-Advocate.

Question: What was your opinion of the feeling and temper of the native officers and men of the 34th Regiment, Native Infantry, when you left this station on the 3rd instant?

Answer: With the exception of the parties who misbehaved in the quarter-guard on the 29th ultimo, I am not aware that the regiment generally has shown symptoms of disloyalty. My reasons for so thinking are–

(1) Because on the evening alluded to, the pay-havildars of both my companies came running to my quarters and informed me that Mungul Pandy, sepoy of one of those companies (No. 5), was standing with a loaded musket near the quarter-guard.

(2) Because when I proceeded towards the lines on that occasion, and as I approached, the Grenadier Company lines, I was stopped by another havildar of my company and two sepoys of other companies, who laid hold of my horse's head, and told me not to advance, otherwise I would be shot. The names of the two pay-havildars are Goorbucus Sing of No. 5, and Jewrakun Tewary of the Grenadiers.

(3) Because, about six weeks ago, a sepoy of No. 8 Company, named Ram Sahai Lalla, who reads and writes English, came to my quarters one evening and revealed to me the fact of a combination amongst the sepoys of all the regiments at Barrackpore, and the intention of their delegates to hold a meeting on that night. I reported the circumstance to Colonel Wheler and Brigadier Grant.

Question It is a notorious fact that a very large number of the men of your regiment witnessed the attack upon the adjutant and sergeant-major on the 29th ultimo; how do you account for the total apathy and indifference of those men upon that occasion?

Answer: I can only account for it on the supposition that Lieutenant Baugh was not very popular amongst the men, arising perhaps from the circumstance of the late havildar-major having been shortly before removed from his appointment by the commanding officer on the representation of the adjutant. For the attack on the sergeant-major I am wholly unable to account.

Question: Have you noticed of late any falling off from the respect which the native officers and men used to show their European officers?

Answer: I have not.

Question: Are you aware of the existence of a preponderating influence amongst the Brahmins of your regiment?

Answer: I am not.

Question: Suppose your regiment were now ordered on field service, would you have entire confidence in the loyalty and good faith of men of all castes?

Answer: I would have as much confidence in them as I would have in any native regiment.

The witness withdraws.

8th Witness

Lieutenant J. T. Liscombe, *34th Regiment, Native Infantry,* is called into Court, and examined by the Officiating Judge-Advocate.

Question: What was your opinion of the temper and feeling of the native officers and men of the 34th Regiment, Native Infantry, when you left this station on the 3rd instant?

Answer: I considered the regiment to be in a disaffected state, because when, on the evening of the 29th ultimo, I went down to the lines,

I saw what I conceived to be the whole of the men in the lines looking on at an armed mutineer, and not attempting to seize him.

Question: Are you aware of any recent change in the manner and bearing of the native officers and men towards their European officers?

Answer: No.

Question: Would you now accompany your regiment on service, in full assurance of the loyalty and good faith of men of all castes?

Answer: Having already given it as my opinion that the regiment is in a disaffected state, I would, of course, have no confidence in them in a case of emergency.

Question: Does that distrust extend equally to Sikhs, Mussulmans, and Hindus?

Answer: No; I would depend upon the Sikhs, and I understand that the Mussulmans are also good soldiers.

The witness withdraws.

The Court, upon the additional evidence before them, adhre to their former opinion, *viz.*, "that the Sikhs and Mussulmans of the 34th Regiment, Native Infantry, are trustworthy soldiers of the State, but that the Hindus generally of that corps are not trustworthy."

The proceedings are closed, and the Court adjourns at 1 p.m., sine die.

From Major-General J. B. HEARSEY, C.B., *Commanding the Presidency Division, to Colonel* R. J. H. BIRCH, C.B., *Secretary to the Government of India, in the Military Department—dated Barrackpore, 29th April 1857.*

I beg permission to forward herewith, for submission to the Government of India, the enclosed letter dated the 22nd instant, from the Officer Commanding the detachment, 34th Regiment, Native Infantry, at Chittagong, transmitting a petition from the native officers, non commissioned officers, and sepoys composing this detachment, expressive of the exceeding abhorrence with which they have viewed the disgraceful conduct of some of their comrades at regimental head-quarters, and at the same time begging to assure the Government of their own faithful and loyal feelings towards the state.

From Captain P.H.K. DEWAAL, *Commanding detachment, 34th Regiment, Native Infantry, to Major* A. H. ROSS, *Assistant Adjutant-General, Presidency Division—dated Chittagong, 22nd April 1857.*

Last Sunday, upon my commenting upon the general good behaviour and proper feeling prevailing in the detachment, 34th Regiment, Native Infantry, on duty at this station, in conversation with Mr. Steer, the Commissioner of Chittagong, that gentleman remarked that an expression of the loyal sentiments of the men, if made known, would be gratifying to the Governor-General.

On the following day I called the native officers of the detachment together at my quarters, and after describing to them the very insubordinate and violent conduct of the men at regimental head-quarters, I told them that while such acts were perpetrated in the regiment, I considered that the detachment ought not to remain in a perfectly passive attitude, but that as faithful soldiers it behoved every man to come forward and openly to express his utter abhorrence of such disgraceful behaviour, and if they wished to do so in writing, I would be happy to communicate their sentiments to Government.

Yesterday morning, Tuesday, a body of sepoys, consisting of men of almost every caste in the detachment, attended by their non-commissioned officers, waited at my quarters, and in the name of the three companies, in the most soldier-like and respectful manner, expressed the greatest sorrow and abhorrence of what occurred at regimental head-quarters, gave their approval of the well-merited punishment of the offenders, and declared their unalterable attachment to, and faith in, the Government of India.

This demonstration, which is quite in keeping with the general good conduct of the men, has given me the greatest satisfaction, and has served to confirm my former opinion, which I reported, of their steady fidelity to the State.

I beg leave to enclose the written expression of the sentiments of detachment, which was placed in my hands, and have the honor to request you will solicit the Major-General Commanding the Presidency Division to communicate the contents thereof to His Lordship the Governor-General in the usual manner.

TRANSLATION of the petition of commissioned and non-commissioned officers and sepoys of the 2nd, 3rd, and 4th Companies, 34th Regiment, Native Infantry—dated Chittagong, the 22nd April 1857.

According to orders we left Barrackpore and came to Chittagong ; we obey and have obeyed all orders; we place no belief in the reports lately circulated. It is with extreme regret we have heard of the disgraceful conduct of the sepoy and guard towards the adjutant and sergeant-major.

By a careful performance of our duties we have gained a reputation for fidelity to Government; these men have deprived us of it. We well know that the government will not interfere with our religion. We hope that the Government will consider us as faithful as ever, and we pray that this petition may be sent to the Governor-General in order that His Lordship may know the state of our feelings.

From Brigadier C. GRANT, C.B., *Commanding at Barrackpore, to Major* A. H. ROSS, *Assistant Adjutant-General, Presidency District,—dated Barrackpore, 21st April 1857.*

I have the honor to forward the accompanying numerical returns of castes of the 34th Regiment, Native Infantry, as called for by the Major-General Commanding the Division.

Detailed return showing the number of each caste present at Regimental Headquarters, 34th Regiment, Native Infantry, on the afternoon of 29th March 1857.

	Subadar-Major.	Subadars	Jemadars	Havildars	Naicks	Drummers	Sepoys	Total
At Regimental Head – Quarters.								
Off duty, and present in the lines of the regiment on 29th March 1857 -								
Brahmins ….. …..	-	2	-	7	4	-	129	142
Hindus of inferior description	-	1	4	10	10	1	145	171
Sikhs	-	-	-	-	-	-	33	33
Mussulmans	-	1	-	7	8	3	70	89
Sick in hospital and attending on sick, 29th March 1857 -								
Brahmins	-	-	-	-	1	-	8	9
Hindus of inferior description	-	-	-	1	1	-	12	14
Sikhs	-	-	-	-	-	-	2	2
Mussulmans	-	-	-	-	1	-	4	5
On regimental duty on 29th March 1857 -								
Brahmins	-	-	1	4	-	-	20	25
Hindus of inferior description	-	-	-	2	1	-	19	22
Sikhs	-	-	-	-	-	-	4	4
Mussulmans	-	-	-	-	3	1	1	5
On station duty on 29th March 1857 -								
Brahmins	1	-	-	1	-	-	18	20
Hindus of inferior description	-	-	-	-	2	-	17	19
Sikhs	-	-	-	-	-	-	12	12
Mussulmans	-	-	-	-	2	-	10	12
Total	1	4	5	32	33	5	504	584

N.B. — One sepoy, Mungul Pandy, included in the roll of Brahmins "present in the lines".

(Sd.) C.C. DRURY, *Capt.*
34th Regt., Native Infy.

BARRACKPORE,
The 20th April 1857.

(Sd.) S. G. WHELER, *Lieut.-Col.,*
Comdg. 34th Regt., Native Infy.

Numerical return of the different castes in the 34th Regiment, Native Infantry

	Subadar-Major.	Subadars	Jemadars	Havildars	Naicks	Drummers	Sepoys	Total
Brahmins...........................	1	2	4	24	10	-	294	335
Chuttrees	-	4	3	11	13	-	206	237
Hindus of inferior description ...	-	1	2	14	13	1	200	231
Christians	-	-	-	-	-	10	2	12
Mussulmans	-	2	1	12	24	8	153	200
Sikhs	-	-	-	-	-	-	74	74
Total	1	9	10	61	60	19	929	1,089

(Sd.) C. C. DRURY, *Capt.,*
Actg. Adjt., 34th Regt., Native Infy.

BARRACKPORE,
The 20th April 1857.

(Sd.) S. G. WHELER, *Lieut.-Col.,*
Comdg. the 34th Regt., Native Infantry

PROCEEDINGS in continuation of a Native General Court-martial re-assembled at Barrackpore, on Friday, the 10th April 1857, by order of Major-General J. B. HEARSEY, C.B., *Commanding the Presidency Division, for the trial of* JEMADAR ISSUREE PANDY, *34th Regiment, Native Infantry, and all such prisoners as may be duly brought before it.*

PRESIDENT:

Subadar-Major JOWAHIR LALL TEWARY, *43rd Regiment, Native Infantry.*

MEMBERS:

Subadar BHOLA OPADEAH, *17th Regiment, Native Infantry.*

Subadar HURRUCK SING, *40th Regiment, Native Infantry.*

Subadar RAM SING, *9th Battalion, Artillery,*

Subadar AMANUT KHAN, *37th Regiment, Native Infantry.*

Subadar SEWUMBUR PANDY, *34th Regiment, Native Infantry.*

Subadar DIRGA RAM, *70th Regiment, Native Infantry.*

Subadar KHOODA BUKSH, *17th Regiment, Native Infantry.*

Subadar MEERWAN SING, *70th Regiment, Native Infantry.*

Subadar SOOKHLALL MISIR, *43rd Regiment, Native Infantry.*

Subadar ADJOODHIA TEWARY, *70th Regiment, Native Infantry*

Subadar JALIM SING, *43rd Regiment, Native Infantry*

Jemadar DEWAN ALIE, *9th Battalion, Artillery*

Jemadar MOHUN SING, *65th Regiment, Native Infantry.*

Jemadar LALLA RAM BUKSH, *8th Regiment, Native Infantry.*

JUDGE - ADVOCATE:

Captain G.C. HATCH, *Depy. Judge Advocate-Genl., Presidency Divn.*

INTERPRETER:

Lieutenant J. VALLINGS, *19th Regiment, Native Infantry.*

The Court re-assembled this day at ten o'clock in the forenoon, at the Mess House, 34th Regiment, Native Infantry, the President, Members, Judge-Advocate, and Interpreter all being present, with the exception of Jemadar Dewan Alie, 9th Battalion, Artillery, reported sick. Jemadar Promode Sing, 43rd Regiment, Native Infantry, a member in waiting, takes his place in Court.

Jemadar Issuree Pandy, *No.1 Company, 34th Regiment, Native Infantry,* is brought prisoner before the Court.

Lieutenant and Brevet-Colonel S.G. Wheler, Commanding the 34th Regiment, Native Infantry, takes his place in Court as Prosecutor.

The names of the President and Members of the Court are read out in the hearing of the prisoner.

BY THE JUDGE ADVOCATE

Question: Jemadar Issuree Pandy, 34th Regiment, Native Infantry,—Do you object to being tried by the President or any of the Members of this Court-martial?

Answer: I object to none.

The Interpreter, President, Members and Judge-Advocate make the prescribed solemn affirmation.

The following charge is read and entered:-

CHARGES

Jemadar Issuree Pandy, No.1, Company, 34th Regiment, Native Infantry, placed in confinement by order of Major General J.B. Hearsey, Commanding the Presidency Division, on the following charges:-

1st— For having, at Barrackpore, on the 29th March 1857, he being then in command of the quarter-guard of his regiment, not used his utmost or any endeavours to suppress a mutiny begun by Mungul Pandy, sepoy, No.5 Company of the regiment the said sepoy having, on the afternoon of the day abovementioned, gone out in the parade ground in front of and near to the quarter-guard of the regiment armed with a sword and musket, and then and there used words to excite the men of the regiment to come forth and join him in resistance to lawful authority; and having then and there, on the parade ground and near to the quarter-guard of the regiment, discharged his loaded musket at Sergeant-Major James Thornton Hewson and Lieutenant Bempde Henry Baugh, of he 34th Regiment, Native Infantry, and then and there, with a sword, struck and severely wounded the said Lieutenant B.H. Baugh and Sergeant-Major J. T. Hewson; and he said the Jemadar not having taken any measures to arrest and confine the said sepoy throughout the aforesaid occurrences nor to assist the said Lieutenant B.H. Baugh and Sergeant-Major J. T. Hewson; and the jemadar, having moreover, then and there, discouraged and interfered to prevent any sepoys of his guard from going to their assistance.

2nd— For disobedience of the lawful command of his superior officers in not having advanced with his guard to rescue the sergeant and capture the aforesaid sepoy, Mungul Pandy, when shortly after the occurrences set forth in the first charge, he was ordered to do so by Brevet-Colonel S. G. Wheler, Commanding the 34th Regiment, Native Infantry.

BY THE JUDGE ADVOCATE

Question: Jemadar Issuree Pandy, 34th Regiment, Native Infantry,—How say you, are you guilty or not guilty of these charges?

Answer: I am not guilty.

PROSECUTION

1st Witness

Lieutenant Colonel and Brevet-Colonel S.G. Wheler, *the Prosecutor, is duly sworn.*

BY THE JUDGE ADVOCATE

Question: You are commanding, I believe, the 34th Regiment, Native Infantry, and commanded it on the 29th of last month at this station?

Answer: Yes, I did.

Question: Did you go down to the parade ground of your regiment on the 29th of last month? If so, please to state what occurred there?

Answer: I did. I received a report at my house that a man, a sepoy of the regiment, was walking up and down in front of the quarter-guard of the regiment, inciting the men to mutiny. On arriving at the lines at the quarter-guard, and observing Sepoy Mungul Pandy, of the regiment, with a musket and sword, walking up and down about a hundred yards from the quarter-guard, I ordered the quarter-guard to load, and directed the prisoner, Jemadar Issuree Pandy, who was then in command of the quarter-guard, to advance and seize the prisoner with his guard. He murmured and said to the best of my recollection—"The guard will not touch the prisoner."

I repeated the order two or three times, when he ordered the guard to advance. They did so a few paces, when they halted, and he, the jemadar, returned and said, "The guard will not advance any further, and refuse to touch the prisoner". I then went to the Brigadier, who had arrived to the left of the lines, and reported the matter to him. The General (Major-General J. B. Hearsey) Commanding the Division, came up soon after on horseback, and after speaking a few words to the Brigadier, he rode towards the quarter-guard of my regiment, accompanied by several officers, mounted and on foot. He directed the quarter-guard to advance. They did so a few paces, when the sepoy, Mungul Pandy, sat down and shot himself. The wound was not mortal, but a slight flesh wound.

Question: You ordered the jemadar, Issuree Pandy , to advance and seize the prisoner; whom do you mean by the prisoner?

Answer: The sepoy in front of the quarter guard, Mungul Pandy.

Question: Why did you repeat your order to the jemadar to advance and seize the sepoy?

Answer: Because it was not obeyed in the first instance.

Question: Did you see Lieutenant and Adjutant Baugh of the regiment and the sergeant-major of the regiment at that time?

Answer: No.

Question: Why did you order the guard to go out and seize the sepoy?

Answer: Because it had been reported to me that his musket was loaded, and that he was ready to shoot any European who exposed himself in front of the bells-of-arms.

Question: When you first ordered the jemadar to take his guard and advance, did he say anything in reply?

Answer: Yes; he said the guard would not advance or touch the sepoy.

Question: Were you near when Major-General J.B. Hearsey ordered the jemadar to advance?

Answer: Not within, I suppose, fifty yards.

Question: Did you hear what Major-General Hearsey said to the jemadar?

Answer: No.

Question: Who was with you when you gave your order to the jemadar of the quarter-guard?

Answer: Captain Drury was present.

Question: Did you hear any of the guard say they would not advance when the jemadar halted and returned to you and said they would not advance?

Answer: No.

Question: Did you perceive any reluctance in the manner of the sepoys of the guard to advance with the jemadar?

Answer: Some hesitation apparently.

Question: When the jemadar advanced a short way with his guard, where was he?

Answer: On the left flank of the front rank.

Question: In what part of the guard did you observe the hesitation you speak of?

Answer: In the rear rank chiefly. I was in rear of the guard at the time.

Question: When after you had repeated your order to advance and the jemadar did so a few paces, did he advance with alacrity and willingness or otherwise?

Answer: Yes; I saw no hesitation in the advance.

Question: Did the jemadar order the guard to halt, or did the men of the guard halt themselves?

Answer: That I did not hear, nor have ever learnt.

Question: Did you hear the jemadar say anything to encourage the men to advance?

Answer: Nothing.

Question: Did the guard load when you ordered them to do so?

Answer: Yes they were ordered through the native officer, but they loaded, I recollect, rather sluuggishly.

Question: What was the strength of the quarter-guard?

Answer: A jemadar, havildar, naick and twenty men.

Question: Had the jemadar set a proper example, do you think, from what you observed at the time, that the men of the guard would have advanced with him?

Answer: I do.

CROSS-EXAMINED BY THE PRISONER

Question How many paces in advance did I go when I left the quarter-guard?

Answer: About twelve paces.

BY THE COURT

Question: When you first saw the guard, in what state did you find it?

Answer: In front of the guard-house, at ordered arms, to the best of my recollection.

Question: Did the jemadar, either by his manner or actions, show any inclination to seize the prisoner?

Answer: No; to the contrary; otherwise he would have promptly obeyed my order in the first instance.

The Court now rose and proceeded to the quarters of the sergeant-major of the 34th Regiment, Native Infantry, reported to be unable to leave his quarters.

The Court being assembled at the quarters of the sergeant-major, 34th Regiment, Native Infantry, and the prisoner, Prosecutor, and Court being all present.

2nd Witness

Sergeant-Major James Thornton Hewson, 34th Regiment, Native Infantry, is duly sworn.

BY THE PROSECUTOR

Question: Your names are James Thornton Hewson, and you are sergeant-major of the 34th Regiment, Native Infantry?

Answer: Yes.

Question: Will you state the occurrences of the 29th of March last?

Answer: Between the hours of four and six on the afternoon of Sunday, the 29th March, I dressed myself and left my bungalow, to proceed towards the quarter-guard of my regiment. On reaching the bells-of-arms of the light company, I was fired at by Mungul Pandy, sepoy, No. 5 Company regiment. I then went in rear of the bells-of-arms, and on my way towards the quarter-guard called out for the guard to turn out. On reaching the quarter-guard I saw some of the men dressed, some dressing. I saw Issuree Pandy, jemadar, No.1 Company, 34th Regiment, Native Infantry, who was at the time in command of the quarter-guard.

I told him that I had sent to the adjutant of the regiment, and asked him why he did not arrest Mungul Pandy, sepoy, the man who fired at me. He answered me, saying—"My havildar is gone to the field officer of the day; my naick is gone to the adjutant's; am I to take him by myself?" I then told him to fall in his guard and load. He called some of the men; some of them came, and some of them did not. His manner altogether was careless whether they fall in or not, neither did he draw his own sword. He kept telling me—"The man is mad, the man is mad; don't go near him, don't go near him." During this time Mooktar Persaud Pandy, color havildar, No.5 Company, came and said that he had been at Captain Drury's quarters, and Captain Drury ordered the sepoy, Mungul Pandy, to be confined.

Question: Did Mooktar Persaud Pandy say this in the presence of the jemadar, Issuree Pandy?

Answer: Yes.

Question: Go on with your statement?

Answer: (Witness resumes) I said to Jemadar Issuree Pandy—"Do you hear?" He did not answer my question, but repeated—"The man is mad". I then lost sight of the jemadar, until after I was cut down by Mungul Pandy.

Question: State what happened to you then.

Answer: Immediately after this I heard the sound of horses' hoofs, and the adjutant of the regiment, Lieutenant Baugh, came riding up. Lieutenant Baugh called out—"Where is he! where is he!" I immediately answered—"He is on your left; look to the left, and ride towards the right." Immediately I heard a shot fired. The sepoy, Mungul Pandy, fired the shot; Lieutenant Baugh fell. Lieutenant Baugh then drew a pistol from the holster, and fired at Mungul Pandy. The adjutant then drew his sword, and rushed towards Mungul Pandy.

When I saw him go towards the sepoy I drew my sword and ran up towards him, at the same time calling out to the guard to load their pieces and come on. On coming up in a line with the Lieutenant Baugh, I found that Mungul Pandy, who had not time to complete the loading of his piece, had drawn a *tulwar,* (Native sword). Mungul Pandy made a feint at me, and struck the adjutant with his sword. The second I received from Mungul Pandy on the head. I was wounded. At the same time I was knocked down from behind by a blow from a musket in the hands of a sepoy regimentally dressed.

On rising up from the ground I ran towards Mungul Pandy again, and caught him by the collar with my left hand. I then received a second cut on the head from Mungul Pandy, and was again knocked down by repeated blows from a man dressed in regimentals, and beaten when on the ground. During the time I was facing Mungul Pandy, I heard a shot fired, which came from the direction of the lines and quite close to me.

After being knocked down the second time, on getting on my legs again, I looked round, and saw several men regimentally dressed in front of the lines. I saw Lieutenant Baugh walking slowly towards the 43rd Regiment, Native Infantry, lines, on the left of the 34th Regiment, Native Infantry, lines; I followed him. On coming near the light company's bells-of-arms of the 34th Regiment, Native Infantry, I heard footsteps behind me, and on turning round I saw Issuree Pandy, jemadar, his sword still in the scabbard.

I spoke to him. I said—"You have acted in a most shameful manner. Why did not you bring your guard to our assistance? I shall put you under arrest". I then made an effort with my right hand to grasp his sword, but he stepped back and prevented me, saying something which I did not understand; I heard him mumbling. I then went towards my house, and met my wife and step-daughter, who brought me to the sergeant-major's bungalow of the 43rd Regiment, Native (Light) Infantry.

Question: When the first shot was fired, did you see aim taken at you?

Answer: Yes; Mungul Pandy, sepoy, aimed at me.

Question: Did you hear the sound of a bullet?

Answer: Yes, close by.

Question: Where was Mungul Pandy when he fired?

Answer: When he fired at me, he was in front, between No.6 and No.7 company's bells-of-arms on the parade.

Question: How far was he from the quarter-guard?

Answer: About forty or fifty yards.

Question: When you went up to the quarter-guard, where was this sepoy?

Answer: The sepoy had loaded his piece and came up in front of the quarter-guard.

Question: How far off from it?

Answer: About forty yards to the front.

Question: Did you hear sepoy say anything?

Answer: He called out to the men to turn out—"Why don't you turn out? You have sent me out here: why don't you turn out?

Question: Did you hear the sepoy say anything about the Europeans having come?

Answer: No.

Question: What did the jemadar of the quarter-guard do while all this was going on?

Answer: He remained walking about in the rear of the quarter-guard.

Question: Did he make the men load when you told him to do so?

Answer: No, he gave no order whatever. He asked me what was the use—"The man was mad".

Question: Was there time for the jemadar of the quarter-guard to have come to the assistance of Lieutenant Baugh and yourself if he had chosen to do so?

Answer: Plenty of time; the men were all dressed.

Question: Were any other sepoys of the regiment about at the time?

Answer: A great number from each Company were between the bells-of-arms, in Hindustani clothes.

Question: Did none of these say or do anything?

Answer: Not one; a native officer came forward, Gunness Lalla, jemadar, and addressed the sepoy, Mungul Pandy. One-half what he said I could not understand, as he was at some distance from me.

Question: Did the jemadar of the quarter-guard, the prisoner now before you, address the sepoy, Mungul Pandy, or say anything to him?

Answer: No; not a word.

Question: Do you know whether the jemadar is a relation of the late sepoy, Mungul Pandy.

Answer: No; I cannot swear to that.

Question: When the sepoy, Mungul Pandy, fired at the adjutant, did you see him taking aim?

Answer: Yes, he took a deliberate aim standing.

Question: Are you still suffering from the wounds you received?

Answer: Yes; I was severely wounded in two places, and bruised about my arms with the blows from the butts of fire locks.

Question: Do you know what sepoys struck you with their firelocks?

Answer: I could not recognise them. There was one man of the light company, but I could not swear to his features.

Question: Did the sepoys of the guard (quarter-guard) show any inclination to assist you?

Answer: No; on the contrary, they beat me.

Question: How do you know they beat you?

Answer: When I left the guard to go out to assist Lieutenant Baugh the guard were dressed. Before Lieutenant Baugh came I was standing for ten minutes in rear of the quarter-guard, and had full opportunity to see whether any other portion of the regiment had put on their regimentals. I am confident they had not time to do so. Also there is a picket mounted at sundown, but those men wear blue pantaloons. The men who struck me had white pantaloons on; all the remainder of the regiment were dressed in Hindustani clothes.

Question: How far from the quarter-guard is the place where Lieutenant Baugh and yourself were engaged in fighting with Sepoy Mungul Pandy?

Answer: Sixty or seventy yards, not more.

Question: During the time you were at the quarter-guard, what was Mungul Pandy, sepoy doing?

Answer: Walking about with his firelock, sometimes at the shoulder, sometimes bringing it up to the present. Four times he presented it at me when I went beyond the rear of the quarter-guard, but he did not fire!

Question: Did he say anything during this time?

Answer: He called out to me to get out of his way, and repeated the words "Come out, men; come out, men; you have sent me out, why don't you follow me?"

The prisoner declines to cross examine. The Court now rose and proceeded to the quarters of Lieutenant and Adjutant Baugh, 34th Regiment, Native Infantry, reported to be unable to leave his quarters on account of his wounds.

The Court being re-assembled at Lieutenant Baugh's quarters and the Court, Prosecuter, prisoner and Interpreter being all present.

3rd Witness

Lieutenant Bempde Henry Baugh, *Adjutant, 34th Regiment Native Infantry,* is sworn.

BY THE PROSECUTOR

Question: You are Adjutant, 34th Regiment, Native Infantry, and were so on the 29th March last?

Answer: Yes.

Question: Will you state to the Court the occurrences on the parade of your regiment on the afternoon of that day?

Answer: On the afternoon of the 29th March, about five o'clock, it was reported to me by the havildar-major of the regiment that a sepoy of the name of Mungul Pandy was out in front of the quarter-guard of the regiment and had fired at the sergeant-major. I told the man to go and report the circumstance to Colonel Wheler, in command of the regiment, ordered my horse, and galloped down to the parade. Immediately on pulling up at the quarter-guard a shot was fired, and my horse fell. As soon as I could disentangle myself from my horse, I took a pistol from one of my holsters and presented it at Mungul Pandy, the sepoy who had fired the shot, and who was then in the act of re-loading. He stopped re-loading and I immediately fired and rushed in, sword in hand, to secure the sepoy, Mungul Pandy. I had advanced half way when he drew a *tulwar*, (Native sword) which I was not aware he had about his person. I continued my advance and engaged the sepoy, Mungul Pandy. During a conflict of eight or ten minutes, I received three wounds, one of which totally disabled my left hand.

A shot was fired close by, and I perceived myself gradually being hemmed in. As I was bleeding profusely, I commenced retreating, and was enabled to make good my retreat by the assistance rendered me by Shaik Pultoo, sepoy, since promoted to havildar, and reached the bungalow of the sergeant-major of the 43rd Regiment, Native (Light) Infantry, in the adjoining lines. During the conflict, with the exception of the havildar aforesaid, not a man from the quarter-guard or the regional lines attempted to give me the slightest assistance.

Question: Did you give any order to Jemadar Issuree Pandy, the prisoner before you, or say anything to him when you rode up?

Answer: No, not that I recollect.

Question: Who were the people who hemmed you in?

Answer: I cannot exactly say, but I believe they were men of the regiment.

Question: Were they dressed in regimentals?

Answer: I could not exactly say, for they were all in rear of me.

Question: Did you receive any blows from behind?

Answer: I got one at the back of the head, which I believe was given by the butt of a musket.

Question: While you were engaged with the sepoy, Mungul Pandy, did you hear a shot fired?

Answer: Yes, there was a shot fired close by.

Question: Did you hear the sound of a bullet?

Answer: No, I cannot say I did that; I was too much engaged.

Question: From what direction did the you hear the shot fired?

Answer: From the direction of the quarter-guard.

Question: At what distance from the quarter-guard did this occur?

Answer: About fifty or sixty paces.

Question: During this occurrence, did you hear or see anything of the jemadar commanding the quarter-guard?

Answer: No, not during the conflict.

Question: Was your horse wounded with a bullet?

Answer: Yes.

Question: During this time you were engaged with Mungul Pandy. Were you impeded in any way from using your weapon to the best effect?

Answer: No.

Question: Did Sepoy Mungul Pandy say anything when you first approached him?

Answer: Not a word.

Question: From whom did you receive the wounds you have spoken of?

Answer: The one in the throat, and the other in my hand, I received from Mungul Pandy.

Question: Did you see any one strike the sergeant-major?

Answer: No; I saw the sergeant-major tumble, as though he had been struck down by a blow from behind.

Question: When you rode up to the quarter-guard, did you see any of the guard in front of the guard-house?

Answer: Yes.

Question: Were they dressed; and how many do you think were there?

Answer: They were dressed; I cannot tell the number.

Question: Did you call upon any of the guard to assist you?

Answer: I was so anxious to prevent the sepoy Mungul Pandy, re-loading that I had not time to say much, but as far as I can recollect, when I rode up, I said—"Why are not some arrangements made to secure this man"—or something to that effect. I received no reply.

Question: Had not there been considerable excitement amongst the sepoys on account of a new kind of cartridge?

Answer: Yes.

Question: Were not the 19th Regiment, Native infantry, expected to arrive in the station?

Answer: Yes, they were.

Question: Were the sepoys of your regiment informed why the 19th Regiment, Native Infantry, was to be marched in?

Answer: I believe they were aware; a parade was held, and Major-General J.B. Hearsey informed the men that he expected he would receive orders to disband the corps.

Question: On the 29th March last, was it known that any Europeans had arrived at the station?

Answer: I believe it was.

Question: Do you know how long the prisoner now before you has served as a Native officer?

Answer: I do not ; I believe he is an old jemadar.

Question: Do you know whether there is any relationship between the jemadar and the late sepoy, Mungul Pandy?

Answer: I believe there is none.

CROSS –EXAMINED BY THE PRISONER

Question: Did he adjutant give me any order to seize the sepoy?

Answer: I gave no other order than that I mentioned.

It being near four o'clock, the Court adjourned until tomorrow, the 11th April at ten o'clock in the forenoon.

SECOND DAY'S PROCEEDINGS

Barrackpore, Saturday, 11th April 1857.

The Court re-assembled this day at 10 a.m. at the 34th Regiment, Native Infantry, Mess House; the President, Members, Judge-Advocate, Interpreter, Prosecutor, and the prisoner all being present, except Jemadar Dewan Alie, 9th Battalion, Artillery.

4th Witness

Shaik Pultoo, Mussulman, havildar, Grenadier Company, 34th Regiment, Native infantry, is called into Court, and makes the prescribed solemn affirmation.

BY THE PROSECUTOR

The witness being wounded and weak, sits down.

Question: Will you state to the Court how you got your wound?

Answer: About a quarter to four, on the afternoon of the 29th March, I went out to ease myself. On returning to the bells-of-arms of No. 3 Company, I saw Mungul Pandy, sepoy, come out of his hut and proceed in the direction of the quarter-guard, wearing his regimental coat and cap, with a musket and sword in his hand. He proceeded to the quarter-guard, and then loaded his musket and ordered the bugler to sound the assembly. He was shouting out—"The Europeans are come; you will be forced to bite cartridges contrary to your religion; come out all of you with me".

Question: Where did the sepoy, Mungul Pandy, load his musket?

Answer: On the left, about twenty paces from the quarter-guard.

Question: Where did he then go?

Answer: He stood near No. 6 Company bells-of-arms, and threatened the bugler if he did not sound the assembly.

Question: Did the sepoy remain anytime at the bells-of-arms of No. 6 Company?

Answer: A little while.

Question: Where did he then go to?

Answer: He went out on the parade between the 6th and 7th Company's bells-of-arms and marched up and down.

Question: How far was this from the quarter-guard?

Answer: About thirty paces.

Question: Was any attempt made to prevent this sepoy loading by the jemadar of the quarter-guard?

Answer: No. None was made.

Question: When the sepoy was loading his musket, where was the jemadar of the quarter-guard?

Answer: The jemadar was in front of the guard house, outside.

Question: Was the place at which the sepoy, Mungul Pandy, loaded visible from the quarter-guard?

Answer: Yes; he came out from his hut in the act of loading and had finished his loading near to No. 6 company bells-of-arms.

Question: Did the jemadar of the quarter-guard say nothing to this sepoy?

Answer: He did not say a word.

Question: What did the sepoy then do?

Answer: He walked up and and down on the road in front of the lines, about thirty paces from the quarter-guard, when the sergeant-major came from the left of the lines in front towards where the sepoy was. The sepoy, Mungul Pandy, retired a little way further on to the parade ground from the quarter-guard; when the sergeant-major came along near to the quarter-guard, the sepoy, Mungul Pandy, took a deliberate aim and fired at the sergeant-major, who was not hit, and went into the quarter-guard.

Question: Where were you when the sergeant-major went into the quarter-guard?

Answer: I was under the shelter of a *peepul* tree, about three paces from the quarter-guard.

Question: What took place between the sergeant-major and jemadar of the quarter-guard?

Answer: The sergeant-major complained that the jemadar took no steps to prevent the sepoy from firing at him.

Question: What did the jemadar say in reply?

Answer: He said nothing ; he and the sepoys were standing about.

Question: Did you hear the sergeant-major tell the jemadar to load?

Answer: He ordered the jemadar to take steps to seize the sepoy.

Question: Did the jemadar take any steps?

Answer: None whatever.

Question: What happened after this?

Answer: The sepoy took aim at him again whenever the sergeant-major showed himself.

Question: When the adjutant came up, where did the adjutant come to?

Answer: He stopped his horse near the quarter-guard, where he was.

Question: Did the adjutant say anything?

Answer: He spoke to the jemadar, and asked him why he had taken no measures to apprehend the sepoy.

Question: Did the jemadar make any reply?

Answer: The jemadar made no reply ; he was inside the quarter-guard.

Question: What happened then?

Answer: I was myself telling the adjutant to look out and take care of himself, when Mungul Pandy took aim and fired and shot the adjutant's horse on the left thigh.

Question: Did the jemadar, or any of the guard, tell the adjutant where the sepoy was?

Answer: I did not hear any one tell him.

Question: What occurred then?

Answer: The adjutant drew his pistol and went at the sepoy, and said to me—"Shaik Pultoo, come with me." I went, and the sergeant-major came out also. Mungul Pandy was rapidly re-loading his musket; the adjutant fired and missed. We advanced so quickly that the sepoy had not time to load; there was a combat between the adjutant and sergeant-major against the sepoy; the sepoy wounded both the adjutant and sergeant-major. I came up when the first blows were struck, and caught Mungul Pandy round the waist, and extended one hand to avert the blows from the adjutant, and was wounded by Mungul Pandy by a sword-cut on that hand. I retained my hold on Mungul Pandy with one hand, and told the adjutant and sergeant-major to retreat.

Question: Did any sepoy of the quarter-guard, or did the jemadar of the quarter-guard come up to assist the adjutant?

Answer: No, not one.

Question: Did any of the sepoys of the guard come up, and what did they do?

Answer: After the adjutant had retreated a little way, four sepoys came out from the quarter-guard and struck the adjutant and sergeant-major with the butts of their muskets from behind.

Question: Did you recognise any of these four men?

Answer: No; I did not. I was then holding Sepoy Mungul Pandy, lest he should again attack the adjutant.

Question: When and why did you let go?

Answer: When the adjutant and sergeant-major had got off, these men who struck the adjutant and sergeant-major with muskets threatened to fire upon me if I did not let go.

Question: When you were holding the sepoy, Mungul Pandy, did you call out to the jemadar of the quarter-guard.

Answer: Yes; I said "Send four sepoys to seize him; I have got hold of him, he can do no harm."

Question: Did the jemadar give any answer?

Answer: No.

Question: Was the distance such that assistance could have been given at the moment?

Answer: I was about thirty or forty yards ; assistance could have been given in a moment.

Question: Did you at any time see any inclination among any of the sepoys of the quarter-guard to assist?

Answer: Not when I was there.

Question: Was a shot fired during the fight?

Answer: Yes, from the quarter-guard.

Question: Did you see Mookta Pershad Pandy, the late drill-havildar?

Answer: I did not see him.

Question: Did Mungul Pandy continue to call upon the men of the regiment to turn out?

Answer: He continued to call upon them to turn out, as they would have to bite the cartridges.

The prisoner declines to cross-examine.

BY THE COURT

Question: When Sepoy Mungul Pandy came out and threatened the bugler, where was he, the bugler?

Answer: Near the guard-house.

Question: At what distance was the sepoy then?

Answer: About twenty paces.

The witness withdraws.

5th Witness

Sobha Sing, *Sikh, sepoy, 6th Company, 34th Regiment, Native Infantry,* being a prisoner, is brought into Court and duly sworn.

BY THE PROSECUTOR

Question: Were you one of the quarter-guard of the 34th Regiment, Native Infantry, at this station, on the 29th March, the day when the adjutant and sergeant-major of the regiment were cut down?

Answer: I was.

Question: State what you saw.

Answer: When the sepoy, Mungul Pandy, came out and fed at the sergeant-major I was lying on my *charpoy* undressed. I hurriedly put on my clothes. The adjutant came down afterwards on his horse, and Mungul Pandy then fired at him and wounded the horse. The adjutant then drew a pistol, fired at the sepoy, and missed him. He then drew his sword and advanced upon him. Mungul Pandy wounded him with a sword and the sergeant-major also. I was in the quarter-guard at the time. I heard the jemadar say to us "Don't go out unless I give you orders. Am I not in command of the guard?"

Question: Did any sepoy show any desire to go out to assist the adjutant?

Answer: I and another Sikh, Atma Sing, and two Hindustanis, whose names I don't know but whom I can recognise, wanted to go, especially when we saw the sergeant's sword broken. The sergeant-major asked the jemadar for his sword when his was broken.

Question: Did any sepoy of the guard go out to where the fight was going on?

Answer: Yes; Heeralall Tewary of the Light Company went out, and struck the sergeant-major with the butt of his musket.

Question: Did the jemadar of the guard try to prevent him going out?

Answer: I don't know whether he tried to stop him, but he went; whether with an order or without I don't know.

Question: When that sepoy returned to the guard, what did the jemadar of the guard do?

Answer: He told him to go and change his pantaloons, on which there was blood.

Question: Was the jemdar angry with him, or did he confine him?

Answer: He did not confine him. I did not hear the jemadar say this about changing his clothes; I have been told so by Mehee Lall, sepoy.

Question: Was a shot fired when the fight was going on?

Answer: I did not hear; there was a great row.

Question: What happened when the colonel of the regiment came up?

Answer: The colonel came and asked if we were loaded. We were not loaded then. The colonel then ordered us to shoulder arms and quick march. When we had gone twenty paces, the sepoy presented his piece, and the jemadar stepped behind the guard, and halted it, and went towards the colonel. I did not hear what was said. The guard was then faced right about, and arms were piled, and caps were taken off.

Question: Did you see Sepoy Heeralall Tewary come back to the guard after changing his clothes?

Answer: I saw the blood on his clothes. In about a quarter of an hour afterwards he was wearing clean pantaloons with the guard.

Question: As far as you can judge, are you of opinion that the guard would have continued to advance if the word "halt" had not been given by the jemadar?

Answer: We were going on when the jamadar halted us.

Question: During the whole time did the jemadar commanding the quarter-guard do anything for the assistance of the officers?

Answer: Nothing whatever.

Question: In what way did you or any other sepoys of the guard show a desire to go out and assist the officers?

Answer: Both I and others spoke to the jemadar and said—"Your officers are being murdered outside; why don't you do something;" I offered to go myself to their assistance.

Question: What did the jemadar say?

Answer: "People will be killed, and what answer shall I give? Don't you go without orders."

Question: Did the jemadar look on while the fight was going on?

Answer: He was with all the rest looking on.

Question: Did any other sepoys than those you have alluded to show any desire to go out to assist?

Answer: Not that I know; they were standing about.

Question: How many sepoys were absent from the guard at that time?

Answer: They were all there with the exception of the four sentries.

CROSS-EXAMINED BY THE PRISONER

Question: When the sergeant-major asked for a sword, where were you?

Answer: The sergeant-major was wounded, holding his hand to his head. I was outside the quarter-guard, where the sentry is.

BY THE COURT

Question: How many sepoys went out from the quarter-guard?

Answer: I only saw one, Heeralall Tewary.

Question: Did this sepoy strike the adjutant?

Answer: He struck both.

Question: When the guard was halted and ordered to the right about, who gave the order to right about?

Answer: The jemadar.

The witness withdraws.

6th Witness

Atma Sing, Sikh, sepoy, No. 6 Company, 34th Regiment, Native Infantry, being a prisoner, is brought into Court and duly sworn.

BY THE PROSECUTOR

Question: Were you on the quarter-guard of the regiment on the day when the adjutant and sergeant-major were wounded?

Answer: Yes.

Question: State what you saw.

Answer: I saw the sepoy, Mungul Pandy, fire at the sergeatnt-major. The sepoy, Mungul Pandy, called upon the men to come out for their religion. The adjutant came up, and Mungul Pandy taking aim fired and wounded the adjutant's horse. A conflict took place between the adjutant and the sepoy, Mungul Pandy. The sergeant-major was also with the adjutant. I saw the adjutant wounded, and the sergeant-major's sword broken.

Question: What did the jemadar commanding the quarter-guard do all this time?

Answer: The jemadar was at his guard, which was collected. The jemadar shut the doors of the quarter-guard looking on to the parade. Four men of the guard wanted to go out to help the adjutant, but the jemadar prevented them, saying there were no orders for them to go.

Question: How do you know these four men wanted to go out to help the adjutant?

Answer: When Shaik Pultoo called for four sepoys to seize Mungul Pandy, then the jemadar would not let any one go.

Question: Did you hear Shaik Pultoo call out for assistance?

Answer: I heard him.

Question: What did the jemadar say?

Answer: He said "If you kill that sepoy you will be hung; and if he kills you, what shall I do?"

Question: What was the jemadar of the quarter-guard doing while the fight was going on?

Answer: He remained with his guard.

Question: Did he give no orders for any one to assist?

Answer: No, he did not.

Question: Did any sepoy of the guard go out to the fight?

Answer: Heeralall Tewary, who has since absconded, went out and struck both the adjutant and sergeant-major with the butt of his musket.

Question: Where was the jemadar at this time?

Answer: He was outside the guard, looking on at the fight.

Question: What did the jemadar do when Heeralall Tewary, sepoy, returned to the guard?

Answer: I saw Heeralall Tewary change his clothes; they were bloody. The jemadar did nothing.

Question: Was the jemadar angry with that sepoy when he came back, or did he confine him, or say anything to him?

Answer: He did nothing with him.

Question: Had the sepoy changed his clothes before the colonel came to the guard?

Answer: Yes, before he came.

Question: When the colonel came up, did the guard get an order to advance?

Answer: The colonel ordered the guard to load, which was done, and afterwards to advance, which we did for about twenty paces, when Mungul Pandy aimed at the jemadar. The jemadar fell behind the guard and halted them, and returned and spoke to the colonel. I did not hear what he said. The jemadar afterwards ordered us to the right-about, which was done, and afterwards caps were removed from the nipples.

In the meantime, General Hearsey arrived, and asked if the guard was loaded ; he was told that they were, but the caps were not on. He then ordered them to be put on, and the guard to march, first at the quick, then at the double. Mungul Pandy then shot himself, having first aimed towards the guard.

Question: When the sepoy first came out in front of the guard and called to the men to come out, did the jemadar do anything?

Answer: He did nothing; he gave no order.

Question: How do you know four men wanted to go out?

Answer: They asked the jemadar to be allowed to go out. I was one of the four. Mehee Lall, sepoy, was one, Sobha Sing was another, and I myself and another man whose name I don't know.

Question: Did Colonel Wheler give the order to advance, or did he repeat the order to the jemadar?

Answer: I did not hear how many times: I was in the ranks.

Question: What did the jemadar say when you four sepoys wanted to go out?

Answer: He said "If you kill the man you will be hung." He prohibited us from going.

The prisoner declines to cross-examine.

The witness withdraws.

7th Witness

Mehee Lall, Hindoo, sepoy, No. 1 Company, 34th Regiment, Native Infantry, a prisoner, is brought into Court, and makes solemn affirmation.

BY THE PROSECUTOR

Question: Were you one of the quarter-guard of the 34th Regiment, Native Infantry, on the day when the adjutant and sergeant-major of the regiment were wounded on the parade?

Answer: Yes.

Question: Did you see the sepoy, Mungul Pandy, go out on to the parade?

Answer: I saw him on the parade when I returned from going out to ease myself.

Question: Did you hear the sepoy say anything?

Answer: He said "Come out, sepoys, come out for your religion;" and told the bugler to sound the assembly.

Question: Did the jemadar commanding the quarter-guard then do anything or say anything?

Answer: No, he did nothing.

Question: Did you see the adjutant and sergeant-major fired upon by Sepoy Mungul Pandy?

Answer: I was in the rear of the quarter-guard, and heard the sound of the firing. I did not see the musket fired.

Question: Did you afterwards see the adjutant and sergeant-major fighting with Sepoy Mungul Pandy on the parade?

Answer: I saw it from the front of the guard-house. We had all gone in front, when a sentry shouted out—"He is killing the adjutant."

Question: Where was the jemadar of the quarter-guard then when the fighing was going on?

Answser: He was with the guard in front of the quarter-guard.

Question: Did the jemadar give any orders when the fighting was going on?

Answer: He gave no orders. He stood looking on.

Question: Did any men of the guard express a desire to go out to assist their officers?

Answer: Yes, Atma Sing, Sobha Sing, Sewbuccus Tewary, and I myself asked the jemadar to let us go to the assistance of the officers.

Question: What did the jemadar say?

Answer: He prevented us from going; he said "You are not to go without orders."

Question: When the fighting was going on, was a shot fired?

Answer: I heard a shot fired ; I heard the report of three shots fired.

Question: Did any sepoys of the guard go out to where the fighting was going on?

Answer: I saw Heerall Tewary of the quarter-guard come back from the place where they were fighting, with his pantaloons bloody.

Question: Did you see Heeralall Tewary, sepoy, strike any one?

Answer: I saw him strike the sergeant-major with the butt of his musket.

Question: Did Sepoy Heerall Tewary return to the quarter-guard?

Answer: Yes.

Question: What did the jemadar commanding the quarter-guard say; did he say anything to him?

Answer: He ordered him to change his clothes.

Question: Was the jemadar angry with Sepoy Heeralall Tewary?

Answer: No, he was not.

Question: Did he order him into confinement?

Answer: No, he did not.

Question: Did you see Sepoy Heeralall go out from the quarter-guard on to the parade to where the fighting was going on?

Answer: I saw him go out.

Question: Did he say anything when he was going out?

Answer: No, he rushed out without saying anything.

Question: Did the jemadar call him back?

Answer: No.

The prisoner declines to cross-examine.

BY THE COURT

Question: Why did you want to go out from the quarter-guard?

Answer: To assist the adjutant, as it was my duty.

The witness withdraws.

8th Witness

Captain C. C. Drury, *34th Regiment, Native Infantry,* is called into Court and duly sworn.

BY THE PROSECUTOR

Question: Are you now Acting Adjutant of the 34th Regiment, Native Infantry?

Answer: Yes.

Question: Did you go with Colonel Wheler, Commanding the 34th Regiment, Native Infantry, to the quarter-guard of the regiment on the afternoon of the 29th March last?

Answer: Yes.

Question: Will you state what then took place?

Answer: On arriving at the guard, the sepoy, Mungul Pandy, was pointed out to us parading in front of the guard, about a hundred and twenty yards off, calling out something. I could not hear what he said. Colonel Wheler ordered part of the guard to load, and afterwards the whole guard, and gave the order to Issuree Pandy, jemadar, who was commanding the guard, to advance and capture the sepoy, Mungul Pandy. The jemadar took me aside, behind the quarter-guard, and said—"It is of no use, they will not advance, they will take the man's part, they are with the man."—or words to that effect.

I said—"Nonsense, you must go where you are ordered; fall in with your guard, and obey the orders you have received." The jemadar fell in with his guard in a reluctant kind of manner, and advanced them some eight or ten paces, when the guard halted. The jemadar fell to the rear. This state of things lasted for two or three minutes. I went in the direction of the 43rd Regiment, Native Infantry, to try if I could get a rifle. As I went along to the left of our lines Major General Hearsey, Commanding the Division, rode up to the guard, and the guard advanced with him, and some twelve or more mounted officers, when the man, Mungul Pandy, sepoy, knelt down and shot himself.

Question: Did Colonel Wheler have to repeat the order to the jemadar to advance?

Answer: I think more than once; I can't be positive. To the best of my belief the order was given more than once.

Question: When the guard advanced with the jemadar a little way and then halted, who halted it?

Answer: I did not hear any order given to halt; whether it was done by any mutual understanding between the jemadar and the guard I cannot say. The jemadar was on the left rear. From where I was, I could not see the jemadar.

It being near four o'clock, the Court adjourned until 11 a.m., on Monday, the 13th April.

THIRD DAY'S PROCEEDINGS

Barrackpore , 13th April 1857.

The Court re-assembled this day at their former place of meeting. The President, Members (except Jemadar Dewan Alie, Artillery), Judge-Advocate, Interpreter, Prosecutor and prisoner being all present, the examination of Captain Drury is continued.

BY THE PROSECUTER

Question: When yourself and Colonel Wheler arrived at the quarter-guard, did Jemadar Issuree Pandy make any report of any sepoy of his guard having gone out and taken part in the conflict?

Answer: He made no report of that nature.

Question: Is Heeralall Tewary, sepoy of the Light Company, now present with the regiment?

Answer: No; he deserted the second day after the affair occurred, namely, the evening of the 31st March.

Question: When you went up with Colonel Wheler, did you see many men of the regiment collected about the bells-of-arms of the different companies?

Answer: Yes, a great many.

Question: About how many men were in the lines off duty on that afternoon?

Answer: About 400, including commissioned and non-commissioned officers, from the reports I have received.

Question: After the jemadar had told you that the men of his guard would not touch the sepoy, did he again get an order from Colonel Wheler to advance with his guard?

Answer: Yes.

Question: Did he then obey?

Answer: He obeyed so far as to advance some ten paces in a hesitating manner.

Question: Had the jemadar done his duty with alacrity and without hesitation, are you of opinion, from all you then observed, that the men would have continued their advance?

Answer: I think they would.

Question: Did you see General Hearsey march off the guard?

Answer: Yes.

Question: Did the guard continue to advance with General Hearsey until the sepoy, Mungul Pandy, shot himself?

Answer: Yes.

CROSS-EXAMINED BY THE PRISONER

Question: Did I not tell Captain Drury …….(two lines totally damaged)

Answer: I cannot recollect whether he did; numbers of men told me to do so; amongst them a member of this Court, Sewumber Pandy, subadar, 34th Regiment, Native Infantry.

Judge-Advocate to Court—It appears that this subadar has a knowledge of the whole of this case, and yet he sat as a member. This was altogether unknown to me, and ought to have been stated to me by the subadar when the charges were read out.

The Court is closed.

The Court re-opened.

Question: Did the Colonel give me an order to fire upon the sepoy, Mungul Pandy, or to seize him?

Answer: He got orders to seize him. His guard was loaded. It was of course at his option either to shoot him or to bayonet him, to secure him in whatever way he chose.

BY THE PROSECUTOR

Question: Is the jemadar an officer of long standing, or recently promoted?

Answer: I think he is an officer of 1850 or 1851.

The witness withdraws.

9th Witness

Lieutenant J. Hearsey, *38th Regiment, Native Infantry,* is called into Court and sworn.

BY THE PROSECUTOR

Question: You are Aide-de-Camp to General Hearsey, Commanding the Presidency Division?

Answer: Yes.

Question: On the afternoon of the 29th March, did you go down with General Hearsey to the quarter-guard of the 34th Regiment, native Infantry? If so, please state what took place there?

Answer: The Major-General came up; he asked the jemadar commanding the quarter-guard why he did not seize the man. He replied—"what does it matter-kyapurwa,—he will only shoot some of us." The General then asked if the muskets were loaded. The jemadar replied that they were not capped. The General then told the men to cap and follow him, which they did. On the guard nearing Sepoy Mungul Pandy about fifty or sixty yards, he knelt down and shot himself.

Question: Did the General have to repeat any order to the jemadar now before the Court?

Answer: No.

Question: Was there any hesitation, as far as you could see in the guard obeying the orders of the General?

Answer: At first there was a little. The men did not seem to assemble quickly.

Question: Did the jemadar appear to obey willingly the orders of the Major General or otherwise?

Answer: He showed a little hesitation at first.

Question: Did you observe any one speak to the rear rank as they were advancing?

Answer: No.

Question: Did you hear the jemadar say anything more than the words you have stated?

Answer: Nothing more than what I have said.

Question: Had the Major-General a revolver pistol in his hand?

Answer: Yes.

Question: Did the Major-General show the guard that he had it?

Answer: He had it in his hand. He had no holsters, I think.

The prisoner declined to cross-examine.

The witness withdraws.

The prosecution is closed.

The prisoner is put on his defence, and states as follows:-

DEFENCE

When the sepoy (whose name I don't know, but who has since been hanged) came out on to the parade, I was informed of the same by the havildar of the guard, who said that the man was in front of the guard with a sword and a loaded musket. I sent immediately to inform the regimental officer of the day, and also the sergeant-major by the naick of the guard, Emam Khan, and also to the adjutant.

I then called out to Mungul Pandy, "Have you heard the orders General Hearsey gave on parade; are you going to obey them?" I then ordered some sepoys of the guard to seize the prisoner. The sepoy threatened me if I do not sound the assembly, when I screened myself behind the *peepul* tree; I also ordered the door of the bells-of-arms to be shut, and said "Don't allow any blockhead to approach." I also told the bugler not to sound the assembly, or he would be blown away from a gun.

The sergeant-major then arrived. I then left the shelter of the *peepul* tree, and told the sergeant to take care of himself. I then heard a shot fired from the parade ground I don't know if it was fired at the segeant-major or myself. I then sent four sepoys to seize the sepoy and said whoever seizes him will be a brave man". The sepoys whom I told to go were from different companies. I said to Shaik Pultoo, who has since been promoted. "The other sepoys are in regimentals, you are in undress; you will be able to get behind him". I said to the sergeant-major "Keep in shelter yourself, or you will be killed".

The adjutant then came up. Then Mungul Pandy fired and hit the adjutant's horse on the thigh. I said to the adjutant "Your horse is wounded; do you stay here, and let me go and seize the sepoy". I said to the sepoys, "what are you doing?" The adjutant then fired his pistol. The sergeant-major said something to the adjutant. I said to the sepoys, "What are you looking at? Do not you see the adjutant's horse has been struck? Go forward." I then saw the sepoy strike the adjutant and sergeant, and also that the sergeant-major's sword was broken.

Shaik Pultoo then ran up towards the sepoy and the sergeant-major. Another sepoy was also with him of the light company. He was not of the guard. Mungul Pandy then loaded his musket and aimed at me. I then retreated, as I thought my sword was of the same kind as the sergeant-major's which had broken. A Sikh sepoy then went towards the sergeant-major. I said to him "Take care where you are going to; why are you going towards the sergeant-major?" This Sikh sepoy was on the guard, a stout man; I don't know his name. The sergeant-major and the adjutant were both wounded. I sheathed my sword first, and said "Who has wounded you; was it Mungul or another sepoy?"

The sergeant-major then told me to give up my sword; I did not give it; I retreated. I then said to the men of my guard, "You have allowed four men to be wounded; why have you done so? You could have prevented this, if you had liked; you have connived at it." I then determined to report this to all the authorities. I proceeded to the house of the officer of the day, and related to him all that happened. I asked him if I should go and report it to the General myself, or whether he would go. The officer of the day told me to go and take care of my quarter-guard.

I told the men of the guard to seize the sepoy in any way they could; four or five sepoys got ready. I asked if they were loaded. I said "if any European officer should come, I will go in front, you come behind." After this the colonel and Captain Drury came. I then told the colonel and Captain Drury to keep in shelter. The Colonel then ordered me to load the guard. I loaded the guard, and called Captain Drury aside, and said "I doubt about two or four of the men of the guard". Captain Drury said "Never mind". I then again told him to keep in shelter, and the colonel also. The colonel asked if we were ready, and ordered us to shoulder arms.

We advanced about twenty or twenty-five paces, when three sepoys spoke and said—"what ! are not the colonel and Captain Drury coming?" I then halted the guard, and ran towards the colonel, and said the guard are disobedient. The colonel then ordered me to bring back the guard. The General, General Hearsey, *Saheb Bahadoor*, then arrived, and asked if we were loaded. I said, "we are, but the caps are not on." The General then ordered me to shoulder arms, which I did, and to quick march, which I ordered the men to do; then afterwards to double.

General Hearsey had a loaded pistol in his hand. As we advanced, the sepoy first presented his musket at us, and then shot himself. The General then gave orders about funeral ceremonies for the man. The General then told us to unload our muskets. This is all. Some of the sepoy on the guard were young, and there were no non-commissioned officers at the moment with me.

The prisoner being asked, says "I have no witness to call."

The defence is closed. The Court is closed.

FINDING

The Court find the prisoner, Jemadar Issuree Pandy, No.1 company, 34th Regiment, Native Infantry, guilty of both charges preferred against him.

SENTENCE

The Court sentence the prisoner, Jemadar Issuree Pandy, No.1 Company, 34th Regiment, Native Infantry, to suffer death by being hanged by the neck until he be dead.

(sd.) JOWAHIR LALL TEWARY, *Subdr.-Maj. 43rd Regiment, Native Light Infantry, President of the Court.*

(sd.) G. C. HATCH, *Capt., Deputy Judge Advocate-General,*

(sd.) JAMES VALLINGS, Lieut., *Interpreter to the Court,*

BARRACKPORE,
The 13th April 1857.

Approved and confirmed.

(sd.) G. ANSON, *Genl, Comdr.-in-Chief, East India*

HEADQUARTERS,
SIMLA,
The 20th April 1857.

REMARKS

The Court closed proceedings on this trial at 3.30 p.m. and adjourned until further orders.

(sd.) G. C. HATCH, *Capt.,*
Deputy Judge Advocate-General,

It is unnecessary for General Anson to observe that it is a most painful duty to order the execution of the sentence of death upon any officer or soldier of the army he has the honour to command, but there is not, in the whole of the evidence on which Jemadar Issuree Pandy has been convicted, one single extenuating circumstance upon which he could rest a claim for mercy.

The extreme punishment of military law has been justly awarded and General Anson trusts that the enormity of the crime will be regarded with horror by every native officer, non-commissioned officer and soldier of his army. Should, however, there be any still undetected, who have looked on with apathy or passive encouragement at the act of mutiny of which the jemadar has been found guilty, his ignominious end, and that of Sepoy Mungul Pandy, will be a warning to them of the fate which awaits all mutineers, and which General Anson would fain hope will have a beneficial influence upon their future conduct.

The 20th April 1857.

(Sd.) G. ANSON, *Genl.,*
Comdr.-in-Chief, East India.

Telegram from Colonel R. J. H. BIRCH, C.B., *Secretary to the Government of India, in the Military Department, Calcutta, to the Commander-in-Chief, Simla—No. 382-164, dated 14th April 1857.*

With reference to trials now going on at Barrackpore, Government considers it expedient that Major-General J. B. Hearsey should have power, under Article 73, to confirm all sentences on native commissioned officers. Will you be pleased to issue a special warrant to Major-General J. B. Hearsey accordingly, and to intimate to me by telegraph that you have done so.

From Colonel R. J. H. BIRCH, C.B., *Secretary to the Government of India, in the Military Department, to Colonel* C. CHESTER, *Adjutant-General of the Army—No. 382-A, dated 14th April 1857.*

I am instructed to acquaint you, for the information of the Commander-in-Chief, that a telegram to the following effect has this day been transmitted to His Excellency: -

"With reference to trials now going on at Barrackpore, Government consider it expedient that Major-General J. B. Hearsey should have power, under Article 73, to confirm all sentences on native commissioned officers. Will you be pleased to issue a special warrant to Major-General J. B. Hearsey accordingly, and to intimate to me by telegraph that you have done so."

2. I am desired, with reference to the above, to explain for the information of His Excellency that as it seems probable that the native officer of the 34th Regiment, Native Infantry, now undergoing trial for his conduct while in command of the quarter-guard of that regiment on the 29th ultimo, during the attack upon Lieutenant and Adjutant B. H. Baugh and Sergeant-Major J. T. Hewson, will be sentenced to death, Government consider it very desirable, not only for the sake of discipline but on account of the troops who are assembled under canvas at Barrackpore awaiting the result of the trial, that no delay that can be avoided should take place in carrying out any sentence that may be passed by the Court.

From Colonel R. J. H. BIRCH, C.B., *Secretary to the Government of India, in the Military Department, to the Officiating Military Auditor-General—No. 430, dated Fort William, 16th April 1857.*

I am instructed to inform you that the Right Hon'ble the Governor-General of India in Council has been pleased to confirm the Presidency Division Order of the 5th April 1857, promoting Shaik Pultoo, sepoy of the Grenadier company, 34th Regiment, Native Infantry, to the rank of havildar, and directing that he be borne on the rolls as a supernumerary from the 29th March 1857.

Telegram from General ANSON, *Simla, viâ Umballa, to Colonel* R. J. H. BIRCH, C.B., *Secretary to the Government of India, Military Department—No. 98, dated 16th April 1857.*

With reference to Act, seventh Victoria, Chapter 18, warrant to the Commander-in-Chief, which is in the following terms—"Provided that nothing in this warrant shall be deemed or taken to empower you to authorize any officer to confirm any sentence of death, transportation or cashiering on any commissioned officer employed on our staff, or serving in any of our regular regiments, or on any commissioned officer of the East India Company's service."

Telegram from Colonel R. J. H. BIRCH, C.B., *Secretary to the Government of India, in the Military Department, Calcutta, to Major-General* J. B. HEARSEY, C.B., *Commanding the Presidency Division, Barrackpore—No. 457-175, dated 17th April 1857.*

The Commander-in-Chief refuses to empower you to confirm sentences of courts-martial on commissioned officers.

Telegram from Colonel R. J. H. BIRCH, C.B., *Secretary to the Government of India, in the Military Department, Calcutta, to the Commander-in-Chief, Simla—No. 541-A-176, dated 18th April 1857.*

Message of 16th instant received. Seventh Victoria, Chapter 18, does not affect the Commander-in-Chief's power to issue warrant under 73, Articles of War for native troops,—see Section 6 of 7th Victoria, Chapter 18. Be pleased to grant warrant to General Hearsey to confirm sentence on native commissioned officers. If not, if sentence passed on Issuree Pandy, jemadar, be confirmed by you, please intimate by telegraph that sentence is confirmed and may be carried into effect. The jemadar's trial was sent to you by express on Tuesday last, the 14th instant.

From Colonel R. J. H. BIRCH, C.B., *Secretary to the Government of India, in the Military Department, to Colonel* C. CHESTER, *Adjutant-General of the Army—No. 541-B, dated Fort William, 18th April 1857.*

I have the honor to acquaint you, for the information of the Commander-in-Chief, that a telegram to the following effect has this day been despatched to His Excellency—

"Message of 16th instant received. Seventh Victoria, Chapter 18, does not affect the Commander-in-Chief's power to issue warrant under 73, Articles of War for native troops,—see Section 6 of 7th Victoria, Chapter 18. Be pleased to grant warrant to General Hearsey to confirm sentence on native commissioned officers. If not, if sentence passed on Issuree Pandy, jemadar, be confirmed by you, please intimate by telegraph that sentence is confirmed and may be carried into effect. The jemadar's trial was sent to you by express on Tuesday last, the 14th instant."

With reference to the above telegram, I am directed to explain that part of the warrant from Her majesty to which the Commander-in-Chief's message refers is understood to be based upon Section V of the Act, 7 Victoria, Chapter 18, and it appears to Government that the term "a commissioned officer of the East India Company's service," used in the Act and in the Warrant, relates to European commissioned officers only.

Should it, however, be considered that the words cited relate to native commissioned officers also, still it is observed by Government that while the Statute and the Queen's Warrant expressly refrain from empowering any officer inferior to a Commander-in-Chief to confirm sentences of death, transportation or cashiering on commissioned officers, yet neither the Act nor the Warrant contains any prohibitions to the delegation of authority to confirm such sentences, provided the power to delegate be otherwise committed to the Commander-in-Chief by competent authority.

The Government of India is such competent authority, and in the Articles of War for the native troops passed by the Government of India, Article 73 empowers the Commander-in-Chief to appoint general or their courts-martial, and to issue his warrant to any general or other officer having the command of a body of troops to appoint general or other courts-martial for the trial of native officers and others, and to confirm and otherwise dispose of all sentences passed by such courts.

Further, I am instructed to remark that the 6th section of the Act, 7 Victoria, Chapter 18, expressly provides that excepting in some of its provisions which do not relate to the present topic, this Act shall not alter or affect any Article of War for the East India Company's forces, whether natives or not of the East Indies.

Telegram from General ANSON, *Simla, via Umballa, to Colonel* R. J. H. BIRCH, C.B., *Secretary to the Government of India, in the Military Department Calcutta—No. 113, dated 20th April 1857.*

The sentence passed upon Issuree Pandy, Jemadar, 34th Regiment, Native Infantry has been approved and confirmed by General Anson, and instructions have been sent to General Hearsey to carry the sentence into execution without unnecessary delay. The warrant to confirm sentence on native commissioned officers has, as requested, been sent to General Hearsey by this day's post.

Telegram from Colonel R. J. H. BIRCH, C.B., *Secretary to the Government of India, in the Military Department, Calcutta, to Major-General* J. B. HEARSEY, C.B., *Commanding the Presidency Division, Barrackpore—No. 623-182, dated 21st April 1857.*

The Commander-in-Chief has confirmed the sentence on Jemadar Issuree Pandy, and he is to be executed without delay. If you require the four howitzers, they can be sent to you this evening, and can be manned by the golundauz. Pray reply immediately by telegraph on this point.

Telegram from Major-General J. B. HEARSEY, C.B., *Commanding the Presidency Division, Barrackpore, to Colonel* R. J. H. BIRCH, C.B., *Secretary to the Government of India, in the Military Department, Calcutta—No. 114, dated 21st April, 1857.*

The execution takes place this afternoon at 6 p.m. A telegraph message will be sent as soon as it is over. It is too late to send for howitzers.

From Major-General J. B. HEARSEY, C.B., *Commanding the Presidency Division, to Colonel* R. J. H. BIRCH, C.B., *secretary to the Government of India, in the Military Department—dated Barrackpore, 21st April 1857.*

I have the honor to report, for the information of the Right Hon'ble the Governor-General of India in Council, that, conformably with instructions which I received to day at 11 a.m. from Army Headquarters by a telegraph message, Jemadar Issuree Pandy, 34th Regiment, Native Infantry, was duly hanged by the neck this afternoon at six o'clock, in presence of all the troops at the station. The crimes, finding and sentence of the general court-martial before which he was arraigned, approved and confirmed by His Excellency the Commander-in-Chief, having been first carefully explained to all the native corps.

It may perhaps be satisfactory for the Government to learn that when on the scaffold the jemadar made a voluntary confession of his guilt, and admitted the justice of the sentence which had been passed on him, at the same time imploring all his fellow-soldiers who were present to take warning by his untimely fate.

The prisoner's bearing and behaviour upon the scaffold were manly and becoming the solemn position of one about to be launched into eternity.

MINUTE by Governor-General of India in Council, concurred in by MR. DORIN, *dated 30th April 1857.*

The disposition and temper of the 34th Regiment, Native Infantry, has for many weeks occupied the serious attention of the Government of India.

The share which that regiment appeared to have in the disturbances that took place at Barrackpore in January, the fact that the presence at Berhampore of two detachments from their corps was followed by the outbreak of the 19th Regiment, Native Infantry, at that station; the murderous attack by Mungul Pandy, a sepoy of the 34th Regiment, Native Infantry, upon his officers on the 29th of March, and his language at the time, which showed that his comrades had instigated him to it; and, above all, the conduct of the native officers and men of the regiment present on that occasion, whether on duty or only as spectators, coupled with other rumoured indications of a bad spirit in the corps, led the Governor-General of India in Council to determine that evidence as to its state of feeling and temper should be taken by a Special Court of Inquiry composed of field officers.

The result of this investigation is now before the Government, as are also the proceedings taken in the cases of the sepoy, Mungul Pandy, and of the Jemadar, Issuree Pandy, which led to the conviction and execution of both.

Enquiry has also been made into the conduct of the quarter-guard of the 34th Regiment, Native Infantry, which was under the command of Issuree Pandy; and the depositions of Durriow Sing and Ramsahai Lalla, who have tendered evidence bearing upon the general question, have been received and recorded.

The Special Court of Inquiry above-mentioned have declared their opinion that the Sikhs and Mussulmans of the 34th Regiment, Native Infantry, are trustworthy soldiers of the State, but that the Hindus generally of the corps are not trustworthy.

Of eight officers of the regiment summoned as witnesses, five, amongst whom are the colonel and the adjutant, express their opinion to the same effect, and state that if the regiment were ordered on field service they should not accompany it with full reliance on its loyalty and good conduct.

Studie disrespect towards their officers, and the use of insubordinate language on parade, are clearly established against the regiment; and I see no reason to doubt that the opinion expressed by the Court, as to the Hindu portion of it, is correct.

When such a verdict as has been given by the Court of Inquiry can with truth be passed upon a regiment, and when a large part of the corps has furnished such indisputable proof of disaffection and sympathy with mutiny as was exhibited by the 34th Regiment, Native Infantry, on the 29th of March, it becomes necessary that the punishment and remedy should be sharp and effectual.

I should, indeed, have been glad if some punishment, short of the disbandment of the seven companies of the 34th Regiment, Native Infantry, now stationed at Barrackpore, could have been considered thoroughly adequate for the occasion ; but upon a careful examination and comparison of the proceedings which are before the Government, I am satisfied that no penalty less general than this would meet the exigencies of the case, or be effectual as an example.

The disbandment may be, and ought to be, so far tempered as that those of all ranks who were manifestly absent from the lines on the 29th of

March shall be exempted from it, as also those who upon that or any other recent occasion have shown attachment and fidelity to their officers and to the State.* But I see no possibility of drawing a line of separation between creeds, in the spirit of the decision given by the Special Court of Inquiry, and which should have the effect of relieving the Sikhs and Mussulmans who were present from the punishment to be inflicted upon the Hindus. It would be impolitic and dangerous to attempt it.

All must suffer together; and indeed, as regards the conduct of the corps on the day of the mutinous exhibition by Mungul Pandy, all were equally culpable. The proportion of Hindus to Mussulmans and Sikhs amongst those who may be assumed to have been present, appears to be about eight to three.

The reports of the conduct and temper of the three companies of the 34th Regiment, Native Infantry, who were stationed at Chittagong are very favourable. There is no good evidence of their having been implicated in the misdoings, or of their sharing the spirit, of their comrades at Barrackpore. I annex a draft of a G.O. which I would propose to issue directing the disbandment.

(Sd.) CANNING.

I assent entirely to the measures proposed by the Governor-General of India in Council.

In my opinion it is impossible that a regiment can be in the state of insubordination disclosed in these proceedings, without grave fault on the part of the commanding officer, and much of Lieutenant-Colonel Wheler's conduct appears to me open to serious question.

I forbear, however, from discussing this subject at present, as I know it is the intention of the Governor-General to consider it separately.

1st May 1857. (Sd.) J. DORIN.

MINUTE by Major-General Low, *dated 2nd May 1857.*

The disloyal feelings and the insubordinate and disrespectful conduct which have of late been, in various ways, evinced by the native officers and the

* Those who deserve exemption on this account are : - Subadar Sewumber Pandy who warned Captain C. C. Drury of his danger on the 29th of March, and did his duty as a member of the court-martial on Issuree Pandy ; Subadar Muddeh Khan in command of the Mint guard on a recent occasion; Jemadar Durriow, Sing, who has given evidence to Government which, whatever its value may be, appears to be honestly given; Havildar Shaik Pultoo, distinguished by his fidelity on the 29th March; havildar Goorbucus Sing and Havildar Jewrakun Tewary, - these two brought notice of the disturbance on the 29th of March to Captain A.S. Allen (see his evidence before the Special Court of Inquiry); Sepoy Ramsahai Lalla, who gave useful information to Captain A. S. Allen on the 6th of February; Sepoys Sobha Sing, Atma Sing, Mehee Lall, and Sewbuccus Tewary, all of the quarter-guard of the 34th Regiment, Native Infantry, on the 29th of March, but who may be believed to have been anxious to do their duty had not the jemadar restrained them.

men of the 34th Regiment, Native Infantry, have formed the subject of many full and anxious discussions at the Council Board since February last, and we have read so many public and demi-official letters and papers connected with the present condition and conduct of that corps, including the voluminous records of proceedings now circulated, that it is clearly unnecessary to delay any longer to punish the offenders in the most public way possible, and thereby give a wholesome warning to the Native Army generally.

2. The narrative of what has taken place connected with the misconduct of the 34th Regiment, Native Infantry, the measure proposed as the requisite punishment, and the reasons for inflicting the punishment, to the specified extent and in the particular manner described, are all so clearly detailed in His Lordship's minute of the 30th ultimo, that it is needless for me now to say more than that I fully concur with His Lordship in all the sentiments therein recorded.

I greatly regret to think that in all probability there are some good soldiers, especially Sikhs and Mahomedans, in the 34th Regiment, Native Infantry, who, by the measure proposed, will be punished along with the real delinquents ; but under the peculiar circumstances of the case, the risk of this must be incurred, for it is in the highest degree important to avoid any act which could be supposed by the Indian community to indicate that Government is more indulgent towards certain classes of men among its native soldiers than it is to any other class on the score of their religion. We should endeavour in all our measures to show that our grand object is to have a faithful and trustworthy army of natives of India, and that we have no desire nor intention to meddle in any way with the religion of the soldiers composing that army, or to show by our treatment of them the least preference of one religious creed over another. We should try to impress upon the minds of all our native soldiers that they will be protected and rewarded, and punished, solely according to their own conduct as soldiers.

In conclusion, I have only to state I entirely agree in regard to all parts of the4 measure now proposed by the Governor-General and in the reasoning on which that measure in founded.

(Sd.) J. LOW.

MINUTE by J. P. GRANT, *Esq., dated 2nd May 1857.*

I have read all these papers carefully, and I have come to this conclusion that no measure short of that proposed by the Governor-General of

India in Council is adequate for the occasion. I agree entirely with all that has been above recorded on this subject.

That an extremely disloyal and mutinous feeling has existed in the seven companies of this regiment now at head-quarters for some months past; that the feeling was general, and its prevalence known to every native officer and man of these companies; and that this feeling has taken outwards shape in including the 19th Regiment, Native Infantry, to commit the offence for which they have been justly disbanded, and in the disgraceful affair of the 29th March in which the mass of the 34th Regiment, Native Infantry, itself, in the light of day, were actively or passively participators, are facts admitting of no doubt. It is probable that some sections of the regiment were not affected with a spirit of active mutiny, but here there has been, besides the offence of the active encouragement of disloyalty, concealment of the fact, and failure to denounce the workers of the mischief in order to enable the authorities to repress it, which is an offence but one degree removed from active mutiny. And although some sections of the regiment may be free from any deep participation in the former crime (a supposition, however, which is not proved) all certainly are equally implicated in the latter.

The punishment which is to be imposed is after all but a deprivation of the advantages of further military service. It appears to me that this necessary punishment is leniently inflicted when it is restricted to those only who presumably were present, and at least passive spectators of the outrage of the 29th of March. Soldiers who in a large body, whether on or off duty, armed or unarmed stand quietly by, when other soldiers are in open mutiny attempting to murder their officers before their eyes, deserve a very much heavier punishment than the mere loss of a service which they have disgraced; and it cannot be right to retain in the service men each one of whom may be fairly presumed to have acted in the manner.

(sd.) J. P. GRANT

MINUTE by B. PEACOCK, *Esq., dated 3rd May 1857.*

I am of opinion that nothing short of the punishment proposed by the Governor-General of India in Council would be sufficient for the late mutinous proceedings which have brought dishonour and disgrace upon all, with only few exceptions, of the native officers and sepoys of the seven companies of the 34th Regiment, Native Infantry, who were at Barackpore on the 29th of March last, and no less punishment would, in my judgment, operate as a sufficient warning and example to others.

In my opinion the subadar, Muddeh khan, and the sepoys, Sobha Sing, Atma Sing, and Mehee Lall, ought not to be exempted from the punishment. If the evidence of Durriow Sing is to be trusted, I think that there can be little doubt that Muddeh Khan was one of the principal ringleaders. Major General J. B. Hearsey reports that he has but little doubt that the statement is founded on truth, and Durriow Sing is to be exempted from punishment for having given it. If there were any reason for supposing that he gave false evidence as regards Muddeh Khan, he ought to be punished rather than excused. I think it will be very inexpedient to declare that recent events have satisfied the Governor General of India in Council of the fidelity of Muddeh Khan to the Government, when most probably it must be known to himself, as well as to many of those who are to be punished, and of those who are to escape punishment, that he was actually engaged in promoting mutiny and disaffection. I do not mean to say that there is legal evidence to criminate him, but if he was in the lines at Barrackpore on the 29th I do not think the fact of his having given the two men into custody at the Mint, which took place some time before the 29th, ought to operate to exempt him from the general punishment awarded for what took place on that day, when upwards of 400 men, according to the evidence of Colonial Wheler, must have been in the lines looking on, while a murderous attack was made on two of their officers, without attempting to render them the slightest assistance, or to bring the actual perpetrators of the crime to justice. For this act those who were present are to be punished, and I see no sufficient ground, on the face of the evidence of Durriow Sing to make Muddeh Khan an exception.

If he was one of those who were absent from the lines on the 29th, he will fall within the general exception; if he was present, I would punish him in the same manner as the others.

Each of the three sepoys admits that he saw Heeralall Tewary strike the sergeant-major with the butt of his musket; that he saw him come back with his pantaloons bloody, and that he went and changed them. Yet this man was allowed to remain until the 31st, when he absconded, without being arrested, as he would have been if those witnesses of his guilt had acted as they ought to have done, and informed any of their European officers of what they had seen.

With that evidence of actual dereliction of duty on record, I think there is no sufficient ground to exempt them from the general punishment, which will probably fall on many less deserving of it than they. I think a mere offer to go to the assistance of those officers, even if it is believed that they did offer, is not, under the circumstances, sufficient to excuse them from the general punishment.

The very fact of their having come to the knowledge of Heeralall Tewary's mutinous act, without immediately giving information thereof to their commanding officers, was a grave offence for which, in strictness, they were liable, by the Articles of War, to a much more severe punishment than that of dismissal.

I also doubt whether there is sufficient ground to exempt Sewbuccus Tewary, who was one of the quarter-guard, from the general punishment. In all probability many of the quarter-guard, if they had been examined, would have sworn that they were willing to go to the assistance of the officers. The fact would still remain that they did not go.

(sd) B. PEACOCK

MINUTE by the Governor-General of India in Council, dated 4th May 1857.

I have read with attention the observations of my honourable colleague Mr. Peacock upon the exceptions it is to be proposed to make in the disbandment of a certain portion of the 34th Regiment, Native Infantry.

I am still of opinion that the subadar, Muddeh Khan, should not be included in the disbandment.

However reliable the evidence given by Durriow Sing, as to the meetings held at Barrackpore in the early part of the year, may be (and on this point it has been confirmed from other sources), and however truly he may believe all that he has said respecting the designs upon the fort at the end of January, it is to be observed that his testimony against Muddeh Khan individually is not direct, except, so far as regards Muddeh Khan's abuse of him; in other respects it rests entirely upon messages brought to Durriow sing by another person professing to come from Muddeh Khan.

On the other hand, we have the incontestable facts that Muddeh Khan did, on a subsequent occasion, seize and give upto justice the traitors who attempted to seduce his guard from its post at the Mint; and that a year ago Muddeh Khan was recommended for the second class of the Order of British India on the ground of long and honourable service.

It is by no means impossible that Muddeh Khan may have been at one time an honest and well conducted soldier, at another time on the verge of treason and mutiny, and that circumstances may have brought him back again to better courses; but I do not think that Durriow Sing's evidence can be held to establish conclusively the intermediate condition of evil-mindedness against Muddeh Khan and if good and faithful conduct exhibited since disaffection has been rife in the regiment is to entitle to exemption at all, I still recommend that Muddeh khan should be one of the exempted.

There is no doubt a seeming inconsistency in rewarding Muddeh Khan for fidelity, whilst Durriow Sing, who is rewarded as an informant, charges him with being a traitor. But Durriow Sing gave some information of the truth and importance of which there is no question; and I think it not unreasonable or impolitic to assume that he was mistaken in respect of Muddeh Khan, in favour of whom facts speak, but that his evidence, which in many other points was correct was given conscientiously throughout.

With respect to the sepoys of the quarter-guard whom it is proposed to exempt, it is true that they witnessed Heeralall Tewary's attack upon the officers; but they were on duty at the time, with their jemadar at their side forbidding them to move; the jemadar saw what passed as well as they. As soon as the colonel of the regiment came upon the ground, he addressed himself to the jemadar; the jemadar appeared to have the full confidence and approval of the Lieutenant-Colonel, who sanctioned the return of the guard after they had marched a few paces towards the mutineer, and the piling of their arms.

I am not surprised, and I do not think it inexcusable, that in these circumstances the men of the guard did not step forward to tell the lieutenant-colonel of Heeralall Tewary's assault upon the officers.

It is true that the evidence of the good disposition of these men comes from themselves; but it is given with an appearance of sincerity; they confirm each other's testimony on all principal points without any sign of concert, and I think that the perusal of the evidence leaves a conviction that they did not offer to go to the assistance of their officers, and to seize the mutineer, and were prevented from doing so only by the prohibition of the superior under whose orders they were at the time.

Whether this be a sufficient ground for exemption is another question. My own opinion is that it is so; and that although a more sweeping measure than that which has been proposed would be perfectly defensible in military justice, it will be sound policy to make the punishment a discriminating one wherever this can be done with fair show of reason.

(sd.) CANNING

MINUTE by Mr. DORIN *and Major-General Low, dated 4th May 1857.*

I cannot say I am satisfied that any of the native officers and men of this regiment have been altogether untainted with mutiny; but I think it good policy to make the punishment as discriminating as possible, and would uphold the exemptions proposed by the Governor General.

I specially question the character and loyalty of the subadar, Muddeh Khan, but consider, nevertheless that whatever his real motives and intentions may have been, his action at a somewhat critical juncture entitles him to the liberal consideration of the Government.

(sd.) J. DORIN

I also entirely concur in the sentiments recorded by the Governor-General in his minute No. 2 of this date on this sad subject.

(sd.) J. LOW

MINUTE by J. P. GRANT, ESQ., *and* B. PEACOCK, *dated 4th May 1857.*

I quite agree with the Governor-General in the propriety of adhering to the exception from the general disbandment of the four individuals whose cases are now specially in question.

As to the subadar, Muddeh Khan, whatever may be our conjectures, what we certainly know of him, and the only thing we certainly know of him, is that, very lately, he seized, denounced, and brought to justice, two secret mutineers connected in some way with the disaffection that has placed out in his own regiment. We do not know that he was present on the 29th of March, and the actively loyal officer-like conduct which we do know him to have displayed lately, in connection with the same general matter, is in my judgment more than a counterpoise in his individual case, to that fair presumption on which the general measure of punishment is founded. Moreover, his act of loyalty, which is a certain fact, is all that the army at large will ever hear of this subadar's conduct; and I think it would have a bad effect if the next thing they are to hear of him were to be dismissal from the service without trial or charge.

As to the three sepoys of the quarter-guard, although it is quite true, as His Lordship admits, that the evidence of their good disposition comes from themselves, yet this is not all the evidence they gave. It was upon their evidence, spontaneously proffered, that their disloyal jemadar was tried, convicted, and hanged. Surely it would be neither just nor politic to reward this good service with dismissal. They did not act, and they do not pretend to have acted, with unimpeachable propriety throughout; but they were in a very trying position, and they have, by their later conduct, not without personal risk, separated themselves by a wide interval from the mass of their misconducted comrades. As to their own good disposition, I must say for myself that I place as full credit upon that part of their evidence as I do upon that which proved the treachery of the jemadar. For why was it that, of the whole guard, all of whom had the same opportunity, when arrested, of professing their own good disposition, and of denouncing their officer, these three men alone availed themselves of the moment?

(Sd.) J . P. GRANT.

I very much regret that the expression of my opinion should have caused any delay from the necessity of re-circulating the papers. It is not my wish to re-argue the question, but I feel bound to state that I still retain the opinion before expressed. I have no doubt that I have taken an erroneous view of the case, seeing that I stand alone in the opinion which I have formed.

(Sd.) B. PEACOCK.

From Colonel R. J. H. BIRCH, C.B., *Secretary to the Government of India, in the Military Department, to Major-General* J. B. HEARSEY, C.B., *Commanding the Presidency Division—dated Fort William, 4th May 1857.*

I am directed to transmit to you the accompanying G.O. by the Governor-General of India in Council, directing the dismissal of the seven companies of the 34th Regiment, Native Infantry, at Barrackpore.

His Lordship in Council requests that you will carry out this order as speedily as possible.

To save time the necessary instructions have been issued from this department to the Pay Department to forward to Barrackpore sufficient money to pay up the seven companies; to the body-guard to proceed escorting the treasure, so as to reach Barrackpore by to-morrow evening ; and to the musketry depot and native artillery details at DumDum, to march to-morrow morning early, and arrive at Barrackpore by to-morrow evening.

The steamer and flat have been directed to proceed to Chinsurah, so as to bring the 84th Foot down to Barrackpore by to-morrow evening. You are requested to send tents sufficient to shelter the dismissed men, to Ghyretty Ghat, whither they are to be made to proceed after dismissal. The European officers should not accompany the men to Ghyretty; but the Governor-General of India in Council leaves it to your discretion to keep the dismissed men under proper surveillance during the day of their dismissal, to enable them to settle their accounts with the bunneahs, and to get together their property for the conveyance of which, across the river to Ghyretty, carriage will be provided by the Government; and should you so arrange, the men themselves may be marched over under proper escort to their camp on the other side of the river in the evening. The Governor-General of India in Council directs me to request that you will have a good translation of the G.O. made at once, and that a copy of that translation may be forwarded to me; it being the intention of His Lordship in Council to cause the same translation to be read to all the regiments in the army.

GENERAL ORDER by the Right Hon'ble the Governor-General of India in Council, dated Fort William, 4th May 1857.

No. 645 of 1857.—On the 29th of March, a sepoy of the 34th Regiment, Native Infantry, stationed at Barrackpore, armed himself with a loaded musket and sword, advanced upon the parade ground in front of his lines, and, after conducting himself in a violent and mutinous manner, and calling upon the men of the regiment to come forth and to join him in resisting lawful authority, attacked and wounded the adjutant and sergeant-major of his regiment, who approached to restrain him.

This man has been tried, condemned, and hanged.

On the same occasion, the native officer, a jemadar, in command of the quarter-guard of the 34th Regiment, Native Infantry, refused to obey his superior, by whom he was ordered to seize the above-mentioned sepoy.

After being tried by a Court of native commissioned officers, this man, himself a commissioned officer, has paid the penalty of his mutiny by the same ignominious death.

But these men were not the sole offenders upon that occasion.

The Governor-General of India in Council laments to say that the conduct of the native commissioned and non-commissioned officers and men of the 34th Regiment, Native Infantry, who were then present has been shown to be such as to destroy his confidence in them as soldiers of the State, and to call for severe and exemplary punishment.

The mutinous sepoy was permitted to parade himself insolently before his assembled comrades, using menaces and threatening gestures against his officers, without an attempt on the part of any to control him.

No such attempt was made even when he had deliberately fired at the sergeant-major of the regiment.

None was made when, upon the appearance of the adjutant, Lieutenant Baugh, and after having re-loaded the musket unmolested, the mutineer discharged it at that officer and shot his horse.

When the horse fell, not a sign of assistance to Lieutenant Baugh was given either by the quarter-guard or by the sepoys not on duty, although this took place within ten paces of the guard.

During the hand-to-hand conflict which followed between the mutineer and Lieutenant Baugh, supported by Sergeant-Major Hewson, the men collected at the lines in undress looked on passively; others in uniform and on duty joined in the struggle, but it was to take part against their officers, whom they attacked with the butts of their muskets, striking down the sergeant-major from behind, and repeating the blows as he lay on the ground.

The Governor-General of India in Council deeply regrets that of the ruffians who perpetrated this cowardly act, the only one who was identified has escaped his punishment by desertion.

There was, however, one amongst those who stood by who set an honorable example to his comrades; Shaik Pultoo, sepoy (now havildar), of the Grenadier Company, obeyed the call of his officer for assistance unhesitatingly. He was wounded in the endeavour to protect Lieutenant Baugh from the mutineer, and did all that an unarmed man could do to seize the criminal. His conduct was that of a faithful and brave soldier.

When the adjutant, maimed and bleeding, was retiring from the conflict, he passed the lines of his regiment and reproached the men assembled there with having allowed their officer to be cut down before their eyes without offering to assist him. They made no reply, but turned their backs and moved sullenly away.

For the failure of the quarter-guard to do its duty, the jemadar who commanded it has already paid the last penalty of death. In this guard, consisting of twenty sepoys, there were four who desired to act against the mutineer, but their jemadar restrained them ; and when eventually the order to advance upon the criminal was given by superior authority, the majority yielded obedience reluctantly.

Upon a review of these facts, and of all the circumstances connected with them, it is but too clear to the Governor-General in Council that a spirit of disloyalty prevails in those companies of the 34th Regiment, Native

Infantry, which are stationed at the headquarters of the Presidency Division. Silent spectators of a long continued act of insolent mutiny, they have made no endeavour to suppress it, and have thereby become liable themselves to the punishment of mutineers. The Governor-General of India in Council can no longer put trust in them, and he rejects their services from this time forward.

Therefore, it is the order of the Governor of India in Council that the native commissioned and non-commissioned officers and men of the seven companies of the 34th Regiment, Native Infantry, now quartered at Barrackpore be disbanded and dismissed from the Army of Bengal, with the following exceptions in favour of those who in the course of recent events have given the Governor-General in Council good reason to believe in their fidelity to their officers and to the Government—

Subadar Sewumber Pandy.
" Muddeh Khan.
Jemadar Durriow Sing.
Havildar Shaik Pultoo.
" Goorbuccus Sing

Havildar Jewrakun Tewary.
Sepoy Ramsahai Lalla.
" Sobha Sing.
" Atma Sing.
" Mehee Lall.

Sepoy Sewbuccus Tewary.

All those non-commissioned officers and sepoys will be excepted whose absence from the lines on the 29th of March, whether as having been on duty, in hospital, or from other cause, can be established.

But this exemption will not apply to the native commissioned officers, all of whom, with the exception of the three above named, are dismissed from the Army.

The Army of India is well aware that it is to the native officers that the Government looks for maintenance of order and fidelity in their respective corps. This was solemnly proclaimed in the General Order of the 23rd January 1856, No. 132; and each regiment may rest assured that it is a principle which will be rigorously and invariably enforced.

The disbandment will be carried out at the headquarters of the Presidency Division, in the presence of all available regiments stationed within two days' march of the spot.

The regiment will be paraded for the purpose, and every dismissed man, after giving up his arms and receiving the pay due to him, will be deprived of his uniform and be required to leave the cantonment.

The foregoing part of this order does not apply to the three companies of the 34th Regiment, Native Infantry, which are stationed at Chittagong, and against which there is no reproach. There remains one point which the Governor-General of India in Council desires to notice.

The sepoy who was the chief actor in the disgraceful scene of the 29th March called upon his comrades to come to this support for the reason that their religion was in danger, and that they were about to be compelled to use cartridges, the use of which would do injury to their caste; and from the words in which he addressed the sepoys, it is to be inferred that many of them shared this opinion with him.

The Governor-General of India in Council has recently had occasion to remind the Army of Bengal that the Government of India has never interfered to constrain its soldiers in matters affecting their religious faith. He has declared that the Government of India never will do so ; and he has a right to expect that this declaration shall give confidence to all who have been deceived and led astray.

But whatever may be the deceptions or evil counsels to which others have been exposed, the native officers and men of the 34th Regiment, Native Infantry, have no excuse for misapprehension on this subject. Not many weeks previously to the 29th of March it had been explained to that regiment, - first by their own commanding officer, and subsequently by the Major-General Commanding the Division, - that their fears for their religion were groundless. It was carefully and clearly shown to them that the cartridges which they would be called upon to use contained nothing which could do violence to their religious scruples. If, after receiving these assurances, the sepoys of the 34th Regiment, Native Infantry, or of any other regiment, still refuse to place trust in their officers and in the Government, and still allow suspicions to take root in their minds, and to grow into disaffection, insubordination, and mutiny, the fault is their own, and their punishment will be upon their own heads. That it will be a sharp and certain punishment the Governor-General of India in Council warns them.

This order is to be read at the head of every regiment, troop, and company in the service, at a parade ordered for that purpose.

Telegram from Major-General J. B. HEARSEY, C.B., *Commanding the Presidency Division, to Colonel* R. J. H. BIRCH, C.B., *Secretary to the Government of India, in the Military Department—dated Barrackpore, 6th May 1857.*

The 34th Regiment, Native Infantry, has been disbanded. All quiet: time on parade.

From Major-General J. B. HEARSEY, C.B., *Commanding the Presidency Division, to Colonel* R. J. H. BIRCH, C.B., *Sectretary to the Government of India, in the Military Department—dated Barrackpore, 6th May 1857.*

I have the honor to report, for the information of Government, that a portion of the 34th Regiment, Native Infantry, as per margin, was disbanded this morning between the hours of five and seven in presence of all the troops within two marches of this station.

The disbanded portion of the regiment, after being stripped of their coats on parade, as well as disarmed, were sent under escort of two companies of Her Majesty's 84th Foot and troop of the body-guard to Fultah Ghat. One of the steamers on board of which the private baggage of these men was loaded was sent under charge of a guard of native sepoys to Chinsurah, where it will be delivered over to them on their arrival there.

From Major-General J. B. HEARSEY, C.B., *Commanding the Presidency Division, to Colonel* R. J. H. BIRCH, C.B., *Secretary to the Government of India, in the Military Department—dated Barrackpore, the 7th May 1857.*

I have the honor to report for the information of Government, that being now able to dispense with the services at Barrackpore of the undermentioned troops, I directed them to return this morning to their respective cantonments at Chinsurah, Dum Dum, and Ballygunge—

Governor-General's Body-Guard.

3rd Company, 5th Battalion Artillery, with No. 20 Light Field Battery.

412 men of all ranks.

A wing of Her Majesty's 53rd Regiment.

Her Majesty's 84th Regiment.

Rifle Musketry Depot.

2. The 84th returned to their barracks at Chinsurah yesterday in the steamers.

3. It is not probable that I shall again require the presence of any of these troops at this station.

4. I have also permitted the commanders of both the Government steamers and their accommodation flats to return to Calcutta.

EPILOGUE

The trial and execution of a dying Mangal Pandey and the disbanding of his regiment failed to terrorize the sepoys into abject submission and May 1857 saw Meerut protest the bullet of abomination. Draconian punishment followed and the offenders were humiliated by having handcuffs and fetters welded on their limbs in the presence of fellow soldiers and imprisonment with common criminals. This sparked a mass revolt. The sepoys killed British officers, released their comrades and stormed into the capital 'Shahjahanabad Dillee' to proclaim the Emperor Bahadur Shah 'Zafar'—a surprised, 82-year-old man (even his father had never seen battle)—as leader.

The city withstood siege by the British for four months. Leaderless sepoys repeatedly sallied forth bravely to attack and be repulsed from entrenched and professionally manned British positions. But British agents infiltrated into the Emperor's Council of War. The information smuggled out caused the city to be penetrated and lost in September.

The Emperor retreated into the Humayun's Tomb. He had before himself the only option of going east, to join forces with Begum Hazarat Mahal of Awadh, with the surviving troops.

Beguiled by the offer of a peace with honour, the tired and bewildered old man surrendered in good faith. But deceit and shock awaited him. As his two imprisoned sons and a grandson were nearing the city, they were, without warning, shot dead in full public view.

'Haay! Dughaa' (Alas! We are betrayed!) is all they had time to cry out before dying! Brutal vengeance was wreaked on the fallen city. Men were dragged out of their houses to be cut down by sword, shot or hanged. Women flung themselves into wells to avoid dishonour.

Boat loads of loot arrived in London and mule and donkey loads of gold and silver in the Punjab. The battle scene moved to Lucknow, Jhansi and Arrah and similar atrocity, loot, arson and massacre were repeated.

The Emperor was tried for treason, found guilty and exiled by a trading company operating under a license, granted by his ancestor. The last flicker of the lamp of India was extinguished. Delhi lost its central status. India was no longer ruled by the Mughals, but a British queen staying in a far-off land.

A resource of learning was being built up slowly through generations, which in addition to original Sanskrit and vernacular sources had absored Arabic, Persian and Turkish science, literary styles, etc. This rich and open tradition suffered a sudden and brutal onslaught with western sciences denying all that was eastern as inferior and unscientific.

Art, architecture, painting, calligraphy, book binding, jewellery designing, weaving and dyeing textiles of cotton, silk, wool and exquisite gold and silver thread, music and dance, Islamic, Vedanta and Sufi studies—all these aspects of knowledge and expertise interwoven with the life and culture which had taken millennia to come of age and mature, suffered sudden loss of patronage and slow death.

Transfer of wealth was institutionalized and made permanent by raising land revenue to unprecedented levels. With no surplus left to the peasant, even a single year's failure of rain spelt famine. Peasants were forced to grow indigo and sell it at lower prices without making any profit.

Famine, an infrequent and localized occurrence in the pre-British period became endemic, covering larger and larger areas. Millions died of hunger—many times that number, especially children, remained malnourished in the growth stage. On the other hand, the British were paid inordinately high salaries—high enough to form a massive drain on India's resources.

The Industrial Revolution began to take shape after the wealth of Bengal went to Britain in 1757 to provide the capital input. After 1857, there was no accountability or check on the drain of resources.

Abolition of slavery was made possible in Britain by the plentiful supply of bonded Indian labour under the title 'indentured'. With Indian troops to win territory and Indian wage-earning slaves to develop new areas, the British had the world at their feet.

Playing God was natural to the British and the alien rulers assumed a paternalistic *(maaee-baap)* role and Indians were forced to believe that whatever was done by the British was a favour. Any doubt or disagreement was tantamount to treachery. Whenever Indians showed the temerity to disagree, question or complain, the British felt justified in accusing them of ingratitude and to exact submission at the point of gun or by the policy of divide and rule.

The British Magistrate, trying Lokmanya Bal Gangadhar Tilak after his arrest in 1906 for sedition, ruled that 'lack of attention' was disaffection or sedition and as such culpable to sentence Tilak to exile for eight years. After the trial Tilak was sentenced to six years of imprisonment in Mandalay or Burma.

The father of independent India, Mohandas Karamchand Gandhi was repeatedly imprisoned by the British rulers as he churned up time and again mass movements like the satyagraha, the non-cooperation and civil disobedience.

Indian studies became unfashionable after 1857 with the *babu* culture created by English-educated Indians. But, western education gave Indians new ideas as people came to know of the French Revolution, the Italian and Irish nationalists. The failure of the uprising of 1857 saw the unification of the country under the Crown rule. Thus, the seeds of nationalism sown by the soldiers of the mutiny began to grow and mature throughout the country.

It is hoped that this book would keep alive the memory and sacrifice of those who fought for our freedom

New Delhi, March 2007 **Akhilesh Mithal**